The Book of Revelation

The Book of Revelation

What the Spirit Says to the Churches in America

SCOTT STORBAKKEN

WIPF & STOCK · Eugene, Oregon

THE BOOK OF REVELATION
What the Spirit Says to the Churches in America

Copyright © 2021 Scott Storbakken. All rights reserved. Except for brief quotations in critical publications or reviews, no part of this book may be reproduced in any manner without prior written permission from the publisher. Write: Permissions, Wipf and Stock Publishers, 199 W. 8th Ave., Suite 3, Eugene, OR 97401.

Wipf & Stock
An Imprint of Wipf and Stock Publishers
199 W. 8th Ave., Suite 3
Eugene, OR 97401

www.wipfandstock.com

PAPERBACK ISBN: 978-1-6667-0727-4
HARDCOVER ISBN: 978-1-6667-0728-1
EBOOK ISBN: 978-1-6667-0729-8

08/05/21

To the members of the adult Sunday School class I taught at Calvary Evangelical Free Church in Rugby, North Dakota from 2013 to 2014.

Contents

Introduction: How to Read This Book   ix
Abbreviations   xv

Chapter 1	How to Read the Book of Revelation (Rev 1–3)	1
Chapter 2	Worship in the Heavenly Realm (Rev 4–5)	31
Chapter 3	The Seven Seals (Rev 6:1—8:5)	103
Chapter 4	The Seven Trumpets (Rev 8:6—11:19)	138
Chapter 5	The Seven Bowls: Judgment from Jesus's First Coming to His Second Coming (Rev 12–19)	157
Chapter 6	Jesus's Second Coming (Rev 20–22)	184
Appendix 1	*Biases vs. Lies*	237
Appendix 2	*Submission to Authority*	240
Appendix 3	*Simplistic Responses to Complex Problems*	242
Appendix 4	*Dictators, Cult Leaders, and American Politics*	244
Glossary		247
Bibliography		251

Introduction

How to Read This Book

1. HOW THIS BOOK CAME TO BE

In 2014, I planned to write a handbook for pastors on how to preach through the book of Revelation. I recognized the need for accurate interpretation and appropriate application of Revelation in the church. It appeared that most pastors in the United States either overlooked the book (with the occasional exception of Rev 2–3) or overemphasized it and used it abusively. As time passed, however, I realized that the need extends beyond what a handbook for pastors could address. Whether overenthusiastic about Revelation or terrified of it, the average Christian is interested in the book but void of the tools to understand it as it was originally intended.

2. INTENDED AUDIENCE FOR THE BOOK

I view myself as a pastoral scholar. I do not pastor a church and do not foresee doing so in the future. Nevertheless, I want to present scholarship that does not stay in the academic realm as is usually the case. My main purpose for writing this book is to make the fruits of my research in the book of Revelation accessible to the average Christian. Because I am a scholar, though, I present the sources I used in footnotes throughout the book. I hope that those theological resources will also make the book beneficial to scholarly individuals, though I do not consider such people to be in my primary audience. For those of you who are not biblical scholars, I encourage you to ignore the notes on technical biblical studies matters. At the end of each chapter, I include a "further reading" section that you can use for deeper investigation into topics that you find particularly interesting. If you want to check my sources on content regarding the American culture that I connect to the congregations of Asia Minor, you can do so by using the short citation at the bottom of the page to locate the source in the bibliography at the back. Likewise, the body of the book includes multiple technical terms, with which I do not expect you to be familiar. Whenever I use such a word or phrase, I highlight it in *italics*, so you can look it up in the glossary at the back. The other instances for which you will see *italics* in the body of the book are titles or foreign words and phrases, so context will clarify which of the three options is applicable each time.

3. FEATURES OF THIS BOOK

3.1 English Translations

At the beginning of each chapter, I provide my own English translation of the Greek text that the chapter covers. The purpose of that translation is to alert readers of nuances in language that modern English translations do not render well. Therefore, many portions of my translation are admittedly and purposefully awkward. I recommend you use whichever translation of the Bible you are most comfortable with in tandem with my translation. In the body of each chapter, I periodically translate relevant short portions of Scripture from outside of Revelation. I used the same literalistic approach for every translation, so you should want to compare these translations to your favorite translation as well. Most often for passages outside Revelation, however, I give only a book/chapter/verse citation. For these reasons, I recommend keeping an English translation of the whole Bible handy as you read any portion of this book.

3.2 Critical Thinking Exercises

In the United States, we have become increasingly accustomed to consuming everything quickly, and we have become comfortable with various sources telling us what to think. When these tendencies exist in education, the results are manipulative and harmful, robbing people of the ability to think and learn for themselves. Therefore, one of my goals for this book is to teach critical thinking skills. As an educator, my purpose is always to instruct students how to think, not what to think. Throughout the book, I have included a few critical thinking exercises regarding topics that are important but not central to our discussion. In these exercises, I limit my own comments and encourage you to process the data I present so as to reach your own conclusions based on the data, not on what others tell you to think.

3.3 Liturgical Sections

Whenever we move beyond interpretation of the text into present-day application, if you have never considered Revelation in the ways we discuss, it will require a paradigm shift. I apply Revelation's predominant question to us. That question is, "Who do you worship: God or the empire?" Though we must reword that question and address it differently since we do not live in an empire, my challenge is the same as John's. John wanted his audiences to assess the object(s) of their worship and to answer the question of whether or not God should be pleased with their worship. This self-assessment requires a great deal of introspection and meditation. When we reach the most challenging parts, I am often confrontational, attempting to echo John's confrontations of the seven congregations. Naturally, that will be uncomfortable for some readers. In order to handle these confrontations as lovingly as possible, I occasionally put liturgies in between major sections. John did the same thing as he confronted his audiences.

In some cases, I have written out prayers for you to recite, Scripture passages for you to study, or a small portion of established church liturgy for you to declare. For most liturgical sections, I name at least one hymn or worship song. For copyright purposes, my best option was merely to name the songs and provide their pertinent information. That limitation means it will be up to you to locate the lyrics and a recording of each.

4. ABOUT THE BOOK'S SUBTITLE

I chose the subtitle, "What the Spirit Says to the Churches in America" based on John's language in Revelation 2–3. Revelation speaks directly to the churches' situations. Similarly, I desire to speak pastorally and prophetically to the churches (and individual believers) in my context in the twenty-first-century United States. I intend to do so through a reasonable application of John's words to our culture. Recognizing what the Holy Spirit first said to the seven congregations of Asia Minor leads us toward this application.

Comparing a modern culture to an ancient one is tricky business. No perfect parallels exist. The use of the whole Bible and other ancient documents, however, help to make these comparisons fruitful. I wrote the entirety of this book between November 2016 and October 2020, applying Revelation to the events in the United States at that time. The specifics will be old news to you, but many will have lasting impact on our nation and world. When I compare the United States of that time to the Greco-Roman environment in which Revelation was written, I also tie the comparisons to the founding of our country. Through an examination of the spiritual aspects of our nation's foundation, I hope to keep the material relevant even when the events I discuss are not. Although the "current events" may not be current any longer, I invite you to read this book as a conversation with me. Through my blog, "For God or Country?" (forgodorcountry.com), we can continue the conversation. As you learn to process this material for yourself, I do not expect you to agree with all my conclusions. We can use the blog, then, to have actual conversations to discuss the ways the messages of Revelation relate to events impacting the church, culture, and world at the time of our communication.

Like John, I address a specific group of people in a particular location. I also follow John's pastoral goal as I constantly ask the question "Who do you worship?" This confrontational question is not limited to a modern American audience any more than it was limited to the congregations of Asia Minor in the first century. Just as I took precautions to make certain that this book can remain relevant long after the events I discuss, so the emphasis on worship helps make the material relevant for people who are not of the culture I specifically address. Although my title might sound like I am addressing believers in the whole country, I must admit that my own experience in the American church is denominationally diverse but generally white in culture. The question of worship, nevertheless, ensures that you can heed the call of the Holy Spirit within your own cultural framework no matter how different it might be from the one I approach. Further, the same emphasis can also assist believers and congregations outside the United States to apply John's words to the cultures of other nations.

5. STRUCTURE OF THE BOOK

The most significant problem that I hope to remedy through this book is the tendency of a lopsided approach to interpreting Revelation. In our fast-paced culture, we are prone to jump toward applying the words to our own context before we understand what they actually mean. All of the Bible says what it says because human authors inspired by God wrote for particular audiences in ancient cultures that are very distinct from ours. English translations do not always reflect the original languages well. Many passages appear clear in English though they derive from intentionally vague texts, and others appear vague when the original text is exceedingly clear. Also, ancient writers used genres that do not often align with ways we are accustomed to reading. Revelation is full of language and images that we should find unsettling. If we think we know what it says without taking the original language, cultural background, and literary context into account, we are gravely mistaken. When we assume too much about the book, we risk treating it as if it was written about us, but it was not.

Revelation's first three chapters provide the key for understanding the whole book. I have structured this book in a similar way. In chapter 1, I work with Revelation 1–3 to provide a roadmap of where we will go in the chapters that follow. We will discuss how to read Revelation and understand it as the seven congregations would have. Then, the subsequent chapters deal with interpreting and applying the body of the Apocalypse (Rev 4:1—22:5). Once we know what the Holy Spirit communicated to the congregations in Asia Minor, then we can begin discerning what he might be saying to us through the same words. I affirm that the Bible is a reliable witness; it is the inspired word of God. As such, it transcends the time and setting in which it was written so as to maintain its impact until Jesus returns. If we leap to application, however, we bypass what the words actually mean, and our application (especially for Revelation) becomes prone to harm people.

Once we have established how to interpret what the Spirit of God communicated to the seven congregations in Asia Minor, then we learn how the text demanded them to respond. As we discuss their application, then we can see how the transcendent divine words of Revelation speak to us within our current settings. For that reason, I used many of John's writing techniques to compose my own book. Using his forms of writing, encouraging, and confronting, I hope to help us discover together "what the Spirit says to the churches in America."

As you begin reading this book, the most important advice I can give you is to encourage you to read it slowly. I have organized the book with the desire to teach you how to think about the words of Revelation as its earliest audiences would have. As such, I want to lead you through a crosscultural experience. You should expect to feel culture shock and to become uncomfortable at portions of your reading.

Because this book requires you to learn new ways of thinking about the Bible, about worship, and about life in general, I also warn you to be patient with yourself. If you struggle to understand a concept, the reason is probably either unfamiliarity with it or reading too fast. Therefore, I recommend slowly rereading any section that confuses you. If you are still confused after doing that, then move forward, and the context should help you make sense out of what you struggled with initially. Using this book as a tool for a group Bible study can also enhance your crosscultural learning experience; I organized the book to be adaptable for either an individual or group context.

Abbreviations

1 Cor/2 Cor: 1 Corinthians/2 Corinthians

1 En.: *1 Enoch*

1 Kgs/2 Kgs: 1 Kings/2 Kings

1 Pet/2 Pet: 1 Peter/2 Peter

1 Thess/2 Thess: 1 Thessalonians/2 Thessalonians

1 Tim/2 Tim: 1 Timothy/2 Timothy

Ann.: *Annals* by Tacitus

Antichr: *Treatise on Christ and Antichrist* by Hippolytus of Rome

BCE/CE: Before Common Era/Common Era. Church fathers developed the calendar system we use in the West. They based their BC ("before Christ") and AD (*anno Domini*) labels on the best historical information they had available to them. Later historians, however, have demonstrated that Jesus was born earlier than what the church fathers thought. As such, if we maintain the traditional abbreviations, we are at best nonsensically claiming that the Christ was born before the Christ was born. At worst, we could be construed as saying that Jesus is not the Christ (Messiah) if we maintain that he was born in the era "before Christ." Therefore, I use the modern abbreviations for "before common era" and "common era." These labels allow us to use the same calendar system with which we are familiar but avoid the problem that the older labels cause in light of recent knowledge.

C.f.: Compare with

Col: Colossians

Comm. Apoc.: *Commentary on the Apocalypse* by Dionysius of Alexandria

Cor.: *De corona* by Tertullian

Dan: Daniel

Deut: Deuteronomy

Did: *Didache*

e.g.: *exempli gratia*, "for example"

Eph: Ephesians

Exod: Exodus

Ezek: Ezekiel

Gen: Genesis

Heb: Hebrews

i.e.: *id est*, "that is"

Isa: Isaiah

JW: *Jewish Wars* by Josephus

Jer: Jeremiah

John: John's Gospel

Jub: *Jubilees*

Jud: Judges

Lam: Lamentations

Lev: Leviticus

Luke: Luke's Gospel

Matt: Matthew's Gospel

Mic: Micah

Mark: Mark's Gospel

Nat. d.: *De natura deorum* by Cicero

Num: Numbers

NT: New Testament

OT: Old Testament

Phil: Philippians

Prov: Proverbs

Ps: Psalms

Rev: Revelation

Rom: Romans

Test. Abr.: *Testament of Abraham*

Zech: Zechariah

Chapter 1

How to Read the Book of Revelation (Rev 1–3)

1 ¹ The revelation of Jesus the Messiah, which God gave to him in order to show his slaves what must take place in a short time, and he made it known by sending his angel to his slave John, ² who bore witness to all that he saw: the word of God, namely the testimony of Jesus the Messiah. ³ Blessed are the reader and the hearers of the words of the prophesy; especially blessed are the ones who keep what is written in it, since the time is near. ⁴ John, to the seven congregations that are in Asia: Grace to you and peace from the one who is, who was, and who is coming, from the seven spirits that are before his throne, ⁵ and from Jesus the Messiah, the faithful witness, the firstborn from among the dead people, and the ruler of the kings of the earth. To him who loves us and freed us from our sins by his blood ⁶ and made us a kingdom, priests to his God and father, to him be glory and dominion forever and ever, Amen.

⁷ Behold, he is coming with the clouds, and every eye will see him, even the ones who pierced him, and all the tribes of the earth will weep on account of him. ⁸ "I am the alpha and the omega," says the Lord God, "who is, who was, and who is coming, the Almighty."

⁹ I John—your brother and co-sharer in oppression, in the kingdom, and in endurance in Jesus—was on the island that is called Patmos for the sake of the word of God, namely the testimony of Jesus. ¹⁰ I was in the Spirit on the Lord's day, and I heard a loud voice like a trumpet behind me, ¹¹ saying, "Write what you see in a scroll and send it to the seven congregations: to Ephesus, Smyrna, Pergamum, Thyatira, Sardis, Philadelphia, and Laodicea." ¹² Then I turned in order to see the voice that spoke with me, and upon turning I saw seven golden lampstands, ¹³ and in the midst of the lampstands I saw one like the son of a human, dressed in a long robe and girded around the loins with a golden sash. ¹⁴ Now his head and his hair were white, like white wool, like snow, and his eyes were like a flame of fire; ¹⁵ his feet were like bronze when it has been refined in a furnace, and his voice was like the sound of many waters. ¹⁶ He also held in his right hand seven stars, and out of his mouth proceeded a sharp, two-edged sword, and his face was like the sun when it shines at its fullest capacity. ¹⁷ So when I saw him, I fell at his feet like a dead man, but he put his right hand on me and said, "Do not be afraid. I am the first, the last, ¹⁸ and the living one; indeed, I was dead, but behold I am alive forever and ever, and I possess the keys for death and Hades. ¹⁹ Therefore, write what you see, specifically, what is and what is about to be after these things. ²⁰ This is the mystery of the seven stars that you saw in my right hand and the seven golden lampstands: The seven stars are the messengers of the seven congregations, and the seven lampstands are the seven congregations."

2 ¹ To the messenger of the congregation in Ephesus, write: "Thus says the one who holds the seven stars in his right hand, who walks in the midst of the seven golden lampstands. ² 'I know your works, trouble, and endurance; I also know that you are unable to tolerate evil deeds, since you tested those who call themselves apostles but are not, as you found them to be false. ³ Indeed, you possess endurance, and you hold fast because of my name and have not lost heart. ⁴ Nevertheless, I have this against you: You have disowned your first love. ⁵ Therefore, remember from where you have fallen, repent, and do the former works, but if you do not, I am coming to you, and I will remove your lampstand from its place if you do not repent. ⁶ On the other hand, you have this: You hate the works of the Nicolaitans, which I also hate. ⁷ Let the one who has a pair of ears hear what the Spirit says to the congregations. To the one who prevails, I will give to eat from the tree of life, which is in the paradise of God.'"

⁸ Then to the messenger of the congregation in Smyrna, write, "Thus says the first and the last, who was dead but came to life: ⁹ 'I know your affliction and poverty although you are rich, and I know the slander from those who claim themselves to be Jews though they are not; rather, they are a synagogue of Satan. ¹⁰ Fear nothing that you are about to suffer. Behold, the devil is about to throw some of you into prison in order that you be tested, and you will have affliction for ten days. Be faithful unto death, and I will give you the crown of life. ¹¹ Let the one who has a pair of ears hear what the Spirit says to the congregations. The one who prevails will never be hurt by the second death.'"

¹² Then to the messenger of the congregation that is in Pergamum, write, "Thus says the one who has the sharp two-edged sword: ¹³ 'I know where you live: you live where Satan's throne is, and you hold fast to my name and have not denied my faithfulness, even in the days of Antipas my faithful witness who was killed among you where Satan dwells. ¹⁴ Nevertheless, I have a few things against you: You have in that place people who hold fast to the teaching of Balaam, who was teaching Balak to place a stumbling block before the children of Israel with the result that they ate foods sacrificed to idols and committed sexual immorality. ¹⁵ Thus, you also have people who likewise hold fast to the teaching of the Nicolaitans. ¹⁶ Therefore repent, but if you do not, I am coming to you quickly, and I will wage war against you by the sword from my mouth. ¹⁷ Let the one who has a pair of ears hear what the Spirit says to the congregations. To the one who prevails, I will give of the hidden manna, and I will give him a white stone and a new name engraved on the stone that no one has known except the one who receives it.'"

¹⁸ Then to the messenger of the congregation in Thyatira, write, "Thus says the Son of God, who possesses eyes like a flame of fire and feet like bronze: ¹⁹ 'I know your works, love, faithfulness, service, and your endurance. Your later deeds even exceed your former ones. ²⁰ Nevertheless, I have this against you: You tolerate the woman Jezebel, who claims herself to be a prophet, and she teaches and leads astray my slaves with the result that they commit sexual immorality and eat foods sacrificed to idols. ²¹ Now, I gave her time in order to repent, but she did not want to repent from her sexual immorality. ²² Behold I throw her into a sickbed along with those who commit adultery with her into great affliction if they do not repent from their deeds; ²³ then her children will kill her with something deadly. ²⁴ But I say to the rest of you who are in Thyatira (as many as there are who do not hold to this teaching, who have not known the depths of Satan

as they say): I will not cast on you another burden, [25] but hold fast to what you have until the time when I come. [26] Then as for the one who prevails and who keeps my works until the end, I will give him authority over the nations, [27] and he will rule them with an iron rod like when clay jars are shattered. [28] As I also have received from my Father, so I will give him [the one who prevails] the morning star. [29] Let the one who has a pair of ears hear what the Spirit says to the congregations."

3 [1] Then to the messenger of the congregation in Sardis, write, "Thus says the one who has the seven spirits of God and the seven stars: 'I know your works: You have a reputation that claims you are alive, yet you are dead. [2] Be alert and strengthen the remainder that was about to die, because I have not found your works completed in the sight of my God. [3] Therefore, remember how you once received, heard, and observed; then repent. [4] Nevertheless, you have a few people in Sardis who have not soiled their garments, so they will walk with me in white, because they are worthy. [5] The one who prevails will thus be clothed in white garments, and I will never remove his name from the book of life, but I will declare his name in the presence of my Father and in the presence of his angels. [6] Let the one who has a pair of ears hear what the Spirit says to the seven congregations.'"

[7] Then to the messenger of the congregation in Philadelphia, write, "Thus says the holy one, the true one, the one who possesses the key of David, the one who opens so no one will shut, and the one who shuts so no one will open: [8] I know your works. Behold, I placed before you an open door that no one is able to close. Because you have little strength but have kept my word and have not denied my name, [9] behold, I will cause people from the synagogue of Satan—who claim themselves to be Jews though they are not, for they lie—to come and bow down before your feet, and they will know that I love you. [10] Because you kept my enduring word, I also will keep you from the hour of trial that is about to come on the whole world to test all who dwell on the earth. [11] I am coming soon; hold fast to what you have so that no one can take your crown. [12] As for the one who prevails, I will make him a pillar in the temple of my God, so he never needs to go out of it again, and I will write on him the name of my God and the name of the city of my God—the new Jerusalem that comes down from heaven from my God—and my new name. [13] Let the one who has a pair of ears hear what the Spirit says to the congregations."

[14] Finally to the messenger of the congregation in Laodicea, write, "Thus says the Amen, the faithful and true witness, the beginning of God's creation: [15] 'I know your works. You are neither cold nor hot. How I wish that you were either cold or hot. [16] For this reason, because you are lukewarm and are neither cold nor hot, I am about to vomit you out of my mouth. [17] Because you say 'I am rich, have abounded and have no need' yet you do not know that you are wretched, miserable, poor, blind, and naked, [18] I counsel you to buy from me gold refined by fire in order that you may become rich, white garments in order that you may be clothed and that the shame of your nakedness may not be revealed, and salve to anoint your eyes in order that you may see. [19] I love whomever I rebuke and discipline; therefore, be zealous and repent. [20] Behold, I stand at the door and knock; if anyone listens to my voice and opens the door, then I will come to him and dine with him and he with me. [21] As for the one who prevails, I will grant him the right to sit down with me at my throne, just as I have prevailed and sit with my Father at his throne. [22] Let the one who has a pair of ears hear what the Spirit says to the congregations.'"

1. WHAT IS A REVELATION? (REV 1:1)

1.1 Defining the Word "Revelation"

The first word in the Greek text of the book we call Revelation is *apokalypsis*. Most translations render this word as "the revelation," although there is a long tradition of referring to the book in its entirety as John's Apocalypse. Both are equally true to the Greek word, and I will use the words "revelation" and "apocalypse" interchangeably. The word "apocalypse," however, has taken on some unfortunate meanings in our culture. Among these are: 1) the end of the world, 2) any sudden catastrophic event, 3) and in some current literature and film, it can even refer to zombie attacks!

In our vernacular, "apocalypse" is always something to be feared. The meaning of the word at the time John either wrote it or dictated it to a scribe could not be any further from these ways we use it now. Because the words "apocalypse" and "revelation" are synonymous, an apocalypse appearing in the Bible must be a revelation of something divine, something glorious, something full of mercy and compassion, something providing hope for those who receive what is revealed.

The two most common misconceptions about John's Apocalypse are that it is frightening and mysterious. However, if it is in fact a divine revelation, then it must be something that gives God's people a clearer picture of who God is. Since it stands as one of the latest books of the NT written, all those who first experienced the words of John's Revelation had already heard the saving knowledge of Jesus the Messiah. They already knew from the letters of Paul that God is love, that Jesus is the perfect reflection of God's love, and that perfect love casts out fear. With this knowledge base firmly in their minds and hearts, the original audience members would have been joyfully excited to hear the word *apokalypsis* immediately, because it would indicate to them that they were about to get to know more of this God who is love. With such a mindset, no room remains for fear when believers receive an apocalypse of divine origin.

The first audiences also would have been excited because this word would have told them that they were about to gain knowledge into some deep mystery that they had long desired to know. Scripture is loaded with miniature apocalypses in which mysteries once unfathomable are revealed. Pittsburg Theological Seminary professor Edith Humphrey refers to the incarnation—the birth, life, ministry, death, resurrection, and ascension of Jesus—as the central apocalypse of the Bible.[1] The first audiences would have already received this "greatest apocalypse" before hearing the words of Revelation. Therefore, they would expect this document to help them learn and to grow, not to confuse them. They anticipated mysteries to be revealed, not concealed. Many modern audiences inappropriately assume that the book of Revelation is so esoteric that it cannot be understood. Its actual intention, as carried in the connotation of its first word, however, is to make known things that were once unknowable.

This revelatory function of the book, therefore, must mean that the original audiences had no trouble understanding the symbolic language, the complex structure, or any of the meanings that the author wanted to convey like we do (or that if they did have any lingering questions after hearing, they had access to a fuller understanding).[2] In fact, the Greek word John uses that translates as "to show" in Revelation 1:1 carries an underlying connotation that explains how he will communicate his apocalyptic message. Several Greek verbs can be rendered as "to show" or "to demonstrate," but the one John uses first implies that he will make the revelation known by the symbols he uses.[3] Why, then, is the book so unclear to us in such a

---

1. Humphrey, *And I Turned*, 15.
2. Bauckham, *Theology*, 7.
3. Beale, *Revelation*, 52.

technologically advanced age? Very simply, we do not live in the same time and culture as John's audiences. We see the world through different lenses than they did. The worldviews that shape our thinking conflict with theirs. Just because we do not live in the same time and culture as them, however, does not mean we have no access to the unveiling of formerly mysterious things. It merely means that things that were not mysterious to them are mysterious to us, but it is possible to clear up those questions.

We have access to many historical and linguistic tools that have helped scholars uncover many such mysteries. Biblical scholars have learned a great deal about the NT churches and about how people in the first century would have understood and applied the words of Scripture. As we learn to enter their culture, we should expect to experience culture shock, realizing that we cannot understand this document appropriately through a twenty-first century American mindset. The same is true for the whole Bible. Once we enter their ancient world, we begin to learn what these words actually mean. As we uncover the true meaning of what God revealed, then and only then, we can begin to apply that revelation to our present situations.

Most people reading this book probably agree with me that the Bible is the inspired word of God. Because it was written in a particular time, by particular people, and for particular people far removed from our own cultures, however, we must accept that in one sense none of the Bible was written for us. When we accept this fact and learn about the worldviews of the people it was written by and for, then we can receive it as something that in another sense is indeed written for us, since it is the timeless, universal word of God.

The most important tools we have at our disposal with regards to receiving the hope and the wisdom that Revelation has to offer are the Holy Spirit and the church. All of us who have placed our trust in God the Father and Jesus the Messiah, who belong to him and have given our lives to him as his servants have received the indwelling of the Holy Spirit. The Spirit is the one who leads all believers into truth. This means that as we consume the living word of God as given to us in the Bible, we have access to God at work within us to help us understand it. I must be abundantly clear, though, that the Holy Spirit never bypasses our minds or our communities. The same Holy Spirit in us works through the people who use tools such as linguistics and history. When local churches are united as they are supposed to be, those who have studied using all the various academic tools the Holy Spirit has made available to them should then teach these truths to the congregation. Since the whole church is empowered by the same Spirit, each member's gifts work together to receive the truth the Holy Spirit makes available for the whole body of Christ. This unity helps the church grow in how it reads Scripture under a Spirit-led *hermeneutic* that makes use of all the truth we have available from all types of sources. Then, we can come to the fullest understanding possible of what these sacred words actually mean. That goal is my primary purpose in writing this book. Even more than educating specifically about Revelation, I hope to equip Christians to think more accurately and more powerfully about the Bible, about theology, and about life in general as God has designed it.

Thus far, we have worked toward definitions for the synonymous terms "revelation" and "apocalypse." Though much of our culture views the book of Revelation as something that is scary and/or unfathomable, the very word that begins the document expresses the exact opposite of those two presuppositions. Now, because it is the first word of the Greek book, the word also suggests that it has something to do with the genre of the work. It gives expectations that the first hearers would have used as a road map for what they would hear throughout the reading of John's Apocalypse, so we will now turn to what it means to say that the book of Revelation fits within the ancient genre of the apocalypse.

1.2 Defining the Literary Genre of Apocalypse

Ancient literature often opens with words, phrases, or descriptions that give the intended audience a glimpse into what is coming in the rest of the document, providing a picture of its purpose. When an ancient document does this, it helps those of us reading it many centuries later to discern its genre. Just as today, we would not read a blog in the same way that we read a history textbook, ancient writers wrote for different purposes, and those reasons for writing help us to categorize them.

Revelation includes several genre indications in its first chapter. This fact tells us that the book weaves together multiple genres. The first word suggests a type of literature that was produced commonly in *Second Temple Judaism*. Many apocalypses were written before Jesus's advent and were messianic in nature. As such, they point us toward what certain groups of Jews expected about the Messiah's soon arrival. Because no developed understanding existed yet that the Messiah would come twice, Jewish apocalypses also provide help in learning what these Jewish communities understood about *eschatology*. The coming of the Messiah, for them, was the ushering in of a new age that would establish the kingdom of God on earth. Of course, this description is true of Jesus's first coming, but only in part. Nobody prior to Jesus's resurrection, except Jesus himself, perceived that the Messiah would come more than once to fully establish God's kingdom on earth.

Apocalypses written before Revelation reflect accurate expectations of what Jesus's coming would accomplish. They merely conflate the two comings (and all that each entails) into one *eschatological* event. The only examples of apocalypses that exist in the *canon* of Scripture are Daniel and Revelation. This does not mean, however, that other apocalypses are without spiritual, historical, and literary value. For various good reasons, they do not appear in the Bible as we have it, but they can still help us understand the world in which the Bible was written. The following list of common features is not exhaustive. It will combine some elements into concise categories. You will also notice—even if you have never read an apocalypse other than Revelation and Daniel—that not all of these characteristics apply to every apocalypse. You will recognize these inconsistencies, because they do not apply to both Revelation and Daniel.[4]

- Constant use of symbolic language that is not factual but metaphorical.
- Reports of *ecstatic* visions that include prophetic material.
- Transcendent in its view of reality, both temporally and spatially (thoroughly grounded in the present time in which it was written and in the location of its audience, but presenting a view of reality that surpasses the known realities of time and space).
- Angelic guide that leads a *seer* through the vision and sometimes interprets the symbols that the *seer* sees.
- Presentations of judgment, justice, and resurrection.
- A dual *eschatology* that involves both the heavenly and earthly realms.
- Pseudepigraphic (assuming the name of a well-known Jewish leader or prophet to seek credibility for the vision) such as *1 Enoch*, *4 Ezra*, *Apocalypse of Moses*, and *Apocalypse of Elijah*, each written long after the death of the respective figure for whom it is named.
- Centers around a call to resist the ways of empire.

1.2.1 Symbolic Language That Is Not Factual but Metaphorical

To say that apocalyptic language is not factual is not the same as calling it untrue. Rather, it suggests that such language communicates truth through figures of speech and are thus not intended to be taken literally. In a seminar

---

4. Aune, "Problem of Genre," 67–87; Barr, "Beyond Genre," 85; Craffert, "Altered States," 127; Hemer, *Seven Churches*, 12; Koester, *Revelation*, 107; Rowland, *Open Heaven*, 49; Smalley, *Thunder and Love*, 23–29.

at Asbury Theological Seminary, my professor Craig Keener illustrated this comically by suggesting that if we take Revelation 17:5 literally, then we should immediately locate a prostitute and tell her, "I just read about your mother." By that joke, Keener points out that the language refers not to a literal prostitute but to someone or something the original audiences would have understood, just as we know today not to expect a new large pet to cuddle when someone says, "hold your horses."

Many apocalypses include interpretations of its symbols. The dreams recounted in Daniel are prime examples of this interpretation. The dreams are vivid, dark, and mysterious. They are also apocalyptic (revelatory), however. After describing the vision in detail, therefore, the author refuses to leave them mysterious, always providing explanations. Revelation, on the other hand, does not often explain its symbols. The people receiving the revelation, then, must have had access to understanding its symbols.

The symbolic language of Revelation is a composite of many sources. Some of the images are very similar to those in Daniel (e.g., Rev 17:8–14/ Dan 7:1–8). Some are parallel to other portions of the OT (e.g., Rev 4:6–8/ Isa 6:1–3). Some reflect the images of *non-canonical* apocalypses (e.g., Rev 22:3/1 *En.* 69:29). Others are grounded in the world of the Roman Empire (e.g., the number 666 almost certainly refers to Nero) and more specifically to the cultures of the seven cities addressed in Asia Minor.

The seven congregations of Revelation would have varied in their degrees of familiarity with each of these sources, but the combination thereof ensures that all hearers could understand the symbols. The cultural diversity present in the audiences and the mode of delivery (which we will discuss when we get to Rev 1:3) ensured that everyone had the capability to understand. The symbols point to realities, beliefs, or mythologies that the audience would have recognized. As audience members recognized the referents for the images, they could then determine the truth communicated through the symbolic language. The same is true for us. As we learn what the metaphorical language refers to, we can then understand the truth conveyed to the audience. Once we comprehend that truth, then we are empowered to seek out how it applies to our own twenty-first-century world. The subtitle I chose for this book may appear as if I am presenting a new prophetic word for the churches in the United States founded on the words of Revelation. Such, however, is not my intention. Although I fully believe in the gift of prophecy as something active in the church today, my desire is to show how the ancient prophecies in Revelation communicate to us today.

1.2.2 Ecstatic Visions and Prophecy

During the *Second Temple* period, the prophecy that was common in the OT era appears to have been in decline. Daniel and other apocalyptic works written at the same time (*4 Ezra* and parts of *1 Enoch*) help to demonstrate how the conventions of prophecy continued even when they were not practiced in the same ways as they had been in an earlier era. The *ecstatic* visions reported in Daniel sent a message to the people of their own time. Daniel's kingly figures most likely point to Antiochus Epiphanes, king of the Seleucid Empire from 175 to 164 BCE (see "Abbreviations" in the front for the historical, practical, and spiritual reasons why I choose BCE/CE instead of BC/AD) and those ruling at the same time. This form of connection between God and his people is similar to OT prophecy. The mode of the message, however, is far more dramatic than what was usual among OT prophets. Apocalyptic visions could point to present realities, future realities, or even past realities (which is known as prophecy *ex eventu*).[5]

1.2.3 Transcendent Space and Time

Many apocalypses include events called *ascensions*, in which the *seer* reports being transported out of the natural realm and into a heavenly realm. Revelation reflects this tendency of earlier apocalypses every time the heavenly throne room is in view. It transcends earthly realities of space and time. In explaining his vision, John must use temporal phrases like "and then I saw," to recount the contents of his vision in an order that hearers could follow. The realities that his vision points to, however, are often not bound by time in the same way that John was as an author.

We often want to know whether something in John's Apocalypse refers to the past, the present, or the future. More often than not, however, the answer is "all of the above." Yes, it was written in a way that the first audiences could have thoroughly understood, alluding to their past and their present. In that respect, it was written for them, not us. Many of the symbols, nevertheless, are so pregnant with meaning that they transcend what the original audiences could have understood. The messages were for the seven congregations addressed, and those audiences reaped the benefits of the words. These messages, however, are also universal in a way that means they speak to the past, present, and future all at the same time.

---

5. Russell, *Method and Message*, 73–103, 178–95.

1.2.4 Angelic Guides

The book of Revelation follows a long tradition of earlier apocalyptic literature as well as some prophetic literature (e.g., the last portion of the book of Ezekiel), in which an angel guides the *seer* through a vision. This tendency is especially common when offering *eschatological* material. For example, an angel appears multiple times in Revelation, usually to show John something about the full establishment of God's kingdom.

1.2.5 The Coming of the Messiah: Justice, Judgment, and Resurrection

The concept of divine justice expanded broadly in Judaism during the *Second Temple* period. Along with this growth, many divergent ideas developed amongst the various parties and sects (e.g., Pharisees and Sadducees). Since these thoughts flowed out of the OT, however, some sort of expectation for judgment against the wicked and blessing for the righteous remained consistent. For some Jewish groups, this vindication was understood as an *eschatological* hope, while for others it was understood as a present reality at work within the same world in which they lived. Others combined the two thoughts, seeing the justice of *YHWH* as both a present reality and something that would occur in the future.[6]

The concept of resurrection matured as a theological thought within the Judaism of the period. Apocalypses including Daniel provided reasons for people to expect a connection between the coming of the Messiah and resurrection long before Jesus died and rose again. The portions of the OT written earlier refer often to a place or state called *Scheol*, which involves nothing more than a vague recognition that an individual's existence continues in some way or another after death. Most OT authors depict existence in *Scheol* as gloomy, empty, and lifeless even for God's chosen people (see David's Psalms in particular). The early apocalypses, however, depict the place as one of consciousness and justice. In *Scheol*, Abel obtains justice after his brother murdered him (*1 En.* 22:7). The Jewish patriarchs actively worship God, constantly remembering the acts of divine justice recounted in the *Pentateuch* (*1 En.* 61:12). Abraham fights on behalf of those who die prematurely as a result of social injustice (*Test. Abr.* 20). So, the apocalyptic worldview dramatically changed how people viewed death. The most dramatic aspect of this shift was the belief that death and *Scheol* are not final. Through these developments, *Scheol* became understood primarily as an

---

6. Russell, *Method and Message*, 23–28, 285–303.

intermediate state in which people await resurrection. Daniel 12 provides the most vivid portrayal of a future, general resurrection written prior to Jesus's resurrection.[7]

Revelation includes all these same motifs. Very simply, the reason it diverges from earlier apocalyptic messianic thought is because its writer believed that the Messiah had already come. The Lamb throughout Revelation is very similar to the "one like the son of a human" in Daniel and the "chosen one" in *1 Enoch*. The difference is Daniel and *1 Enoch* consider the ways the world will be changed once the messianic figure has come. Revelation assumes that Jesus is the Messiah, that he has come once, and that he will return to the earth. Thus, Revelation declares the Messiah worthy not because of what he will do in the future (as earlier apocalypses depict), but because of what he has already accomplished.

1.2.6 Dual Eschatology

Revelation reflects the dualistic language of earlier apocalypses with its *eschatology* that involves both the heavenly and earthly realms. Revelation's cosmic disturbances ("thunders, lightnings, and rumblings") all show the convergence of these realms throughout the book. Revelation 3:12 refers for the first of many times to a "new Jerusalem." Chapters 21–22, by expanding on the "new Jerusalem," point to the fullness of that convergence. The idea behind this newness is that the earth itself will experience God's redemption and salvation. John's Apocalypse takes seriously God's promise to Noah after the flood to never again destroy the earth. Even though Revelation is full of destroyers, their destruction does not have the final say. God's redemption has the final say, even over the earth. Thus, our hope for the future is not found in going to heaven when we die, but rather in the anticipated resurrection that ushers in the fullness of human life in a restored earth free from sin, death, and decay.[8]

In addition to this cosmic dual *eschatology*, Revelation has another dualistic trait which apocalypses before it did not have access to. They were written before the coming of the Messiah and the general expectation tended towards a single messianic appearance in which all Jewish hopes would be fulfilled. Such was not always the case, yet no evidence points

---

7. Russell, *Method and Message*, 353–90.

8. Wright, *Surprised*. Wright's book concerns itself with addressing misconceptions of heaven and the need to replace most of our convictions about heaven with expectations for resurrection.

toward multiple advents in mainstream Jewish thought.[9] Jesus's ascension into heaven and his post-resurrection conversations with his disciples, nevertheless, demonstrated that he would return and at that time fulfill all promises that had not yet been satisfied.

The kingdom of God was a common *Second Temple Jewish* emphasis. This kingdom was established on earth at Jesus's coming, but the kingdom of God has yet to be fully established on earth. That fullness will occur at his second coming. This dualism has created what is known as *eschatological tension*, the idea that the results of the Messiah's initial coming are both "now" and "not yet." This tension is one of the most crucial insights toward an appropriate understanding of John's Apocalypse.

1.2.7 Pseudepigraphy and Revelation's Author

Each book in the collection of apocalypses called *1 Enoch* was written long after the OT figure named Enoch ceased to exist on earth. The corpus named after him, however, purports to be the visionary experience of that same biblical figure. *Pseude* means false; *pigrapha* means attribution of a literary work. The authors of *1 Enoch* used the name of a highly regarded historical figure to gain authority with their audiences. They attributed their own works to Enoch. Most ancient apocalypses are works of pseudepigraphy like *1 Enoch*.

Many conservative scholars believe that the book of Daniel is a collection of legendary material. Legend means that the material was passed down orally and was an important part of storytelling in *Second Temple Judaism*. Calling an ancient book legendary does not mean it must be fictional. The stories collected are from different times with different leaders. Though no historian has discovered significant empirical evidence towards the existence of the biblical character Daniel, the legendary evidence suggests that he (or at least the stories about him) were extremely highly regarded during the period. The collection would use his name, therefore, to gain credibility and to tell the story of the book. The book of Daniel, however, includes no attribution to its author—only to its *seer*—anywhere in the text. Since it does not claim its author(s), it cannot technically be called pseudepigraphic, but it follows similar conventions.

Revelation, on the other hand, explicitly names its author as John. The name was just as common among first-century Jews as it is in many cultures today.[10] As such, Revelation's author was not seeking the type of authority

---

9. Collins, *Apocalyptic Imagination*, 11–14.
10. Bauckham, *Eyewitnesses*, 74–78.

that earlier apocalyptic writers sought. If he had, he might have attributed his work to John the Apostle or John the Elder, who were prominent figures in the author's recent past.[11] Apocalyptic authors, nevertheless, tended to attribute their works to saints who were already deceased. If Revelation's author wanted to follow that convention of pseudepigrapha, then, he most likely would have attributed the work to John the Baptist. That particular John called for holiness and preparation for the Messiah, much like Revelation's John. By naming himself merely as John, however, Revelation's author claims that the attribution of the work is not particularly important. He wants the vision and the experience to be known as his, but he expects the material to speak for itself because of its divine source. He apparently did not sense any need to claim any further authority. For that reason, it does not seem likely that either John the Apostle or John the Elder wrote the book. It appears more probable that a prophetic minister known well to the seven congregations but not named elsewhere in Scripture had the experience he claimed to have on Patmos and either wrote or dictated that vision himself. If this attribution is correct, then we know nothing about the author of Revelation other than what he recorded about himself in the book.[12]

1.2.8 Resistance Literature

Some apocalyptic literature taught recipients ways in which to resist, while others merely presented the need for resistance. Daniel's first audiences "resisted by remaining faithful to the law of Moses, circumcising their children, reading the scrolls, and refusing to eat pork or sacrifice to other gods. They resisted by preaching and teaching, fasting, and dying."[13] The apocalypse became a significant literary movement at the same time as the dawn of the political system that eventually evolved into the Roman Empire.[14] John wrote Revelation after that evolution had fully occurred. His audiences would have understood clearly that he was warning them to stand against the ways of empire. Many of the book's symbols (and obviously the seven messages of Rev 2–3) offer directions toward that resistance. In a wide variety of ways, the book constantly confronts its audiences to make sure it avoids compromising with the idolatrous and loveless ways of the Roman Empire.

---

11. Witherington, *Revelation*, 3.
12. Koester, *Revelation*, 68–69.
13. Portier-Young, *Apocalypse against Empire*, xxi.
14. Murphy, *Apocalypticism*, 3.

1.3 An Apocalypse unlike Any Other

So far, we have looked at 1) what it means for the author to begin the book with the word *apokalypsis*, 2) how the original audience would have understood that word as opposed to the limited and inaccurate definitions of it that abound in our culture, and 3) what makes an ancient literary work an apocalypse by genre. The next two words in the Greek translate to "of Jesus the Messiah" in English. This shows us that the apocalypse we are about to read is unlike any that came before it.

Earlier apocalypses indeed intended to reveal something about the Messiah and his coming, but they could not claim to directly reveal the person of the Messiah. Only *seers* after the Messiah's advent could accomplish that goal. For that reason, Revelation's author used these two Greek words to explain the theological focus of his revelation: the Messiah named Jesus who has come and is coming again. The translation of these two words is tricky, because it carries a vague prepositional idea that could be rendered, "of Jesus the Messiah," "from Jesus the Messiah," or "about Jesus the Messiah." Each one of these ideas carries a different connotation regarding what audiences should expect from this apocalypse.

Because the next clause tells us that God gave it (the revelation) to him (Jesus), the passage discounts the possibility of the book being a "revelation from Jesus." God the Father has something to reveal to his people through Jesus, his Messiah. The content of the apocalypse involves "the things which must take place in a short time." That phrase implies that it is insufficient to say that the book is a revelation about Jesus; it is about Jesus, but it is about other things too.

Since God gave the revelation to Jesus, it is Jesus's apocalypse. It belongs to him, and it reveals him. Therefore, using the preposition "of" in its possessive sense appears to be the best way to understand the nature of the relationship between Jesus and this revelatory message. The seven individualized messages of Revelation 2–3 clarify this matter. Jesus speaks directly to the seven congregations of Asia Minor. He conveys the messages that God the Father has given to him for the congregations. Throughout the rest of Revelation, Jesus gives the words, the visions, the prophecies, the promises, and the warnings that the Father has appointed him to give to the same seven congregations collectively. He does so through two mediators between himself and the congregations: the angel that John encounters, and John himself.

1.4 A Revelation for God's Slaves

When we see the word "slave" in the twenty-first century, we tend to think of the atrocities of the Atlantic slave trade that existed between the seventeenth and nineteenth centuries. The United States became a nation within that time frame and was formed by that wickedness. The forms of slavery discussed in Scripture, however, are drastically different from the unquestionable evil of the Atlantic slave trade. Most English translations of Scripture use forms of "servant" instead of "slave." The Greek word, however, carries no distinction between these two concepts. We should understand them as synonymous in the biblical worldviews. Servants or slaves were owned by their masters. That ownership in the ancient Mediterranean world looked nothing like the abusive and murderous ownership of slaveowners in the latter half of the last millennium. Since our culture distinguishes between the two words, I chose forms of "slave" for my translation, because the word conveys the concept of ownership better for us than "servant" does. The Bible teaches that all people are owned by another spiritually. We either belong to God, or we belong to Satan. To be God's slave implies a life of worship. The main theme of Revelation is whether or not its audiences give sole worship to God. Therefore, I believe that the English word "slave" gives us a better picture of what John had in mind when he wrote these words.

1.5 A Revelation of Things Which Must Take Place in a Short Time

The Greek word that translates to "in a short time" means imminent. Many like to apply the scriptural concept that for God "a day is like a thousand years and a thousand years like a day" to this passage. There are certainly temporal realities that Revelation discusses in which it is appropriate to apply that concept, but this phrase is not one of them. The word carries a connotation too immediate. These things that the Lord is about to reveal to the seven congregations are things they would experience in their lifetime and in some cases were already experiencing by the time they received John's communication. Most scholars agree that John wrote the book sometime in the 90s CE when Domitian was emperor in Rome.

This simple word introduces the book in a way that requires what for many of us in the United States is another major paradigm shift. John's Apocalypse is about things that were either already happening or forthcoming in the culture's time. To say that the book is about such things does not discount the possibility that some material may point to a potentially distant future as well. Indeed, Revelation discusses future *eschatology*. The apocalyptic purpose of the document, however, is to reveal things that relate directly to the audiences, not to people who will live centuries later.

For us, Revelation is not really about the future. It certainly includes expectations we should have about the future, but the book is about the message God had for the seven congregations of Asia Minor. The "things" it revealed to them all center around their devotion (or lack thereof) to worshiping God the Father and Jesus the Messiah. The book demands their faithfulness to God within an environment that was not always friendly to such devotion. As such, the real purpose and message of Revelation is easily applicable to any time period and culture, since every phrase asks the question, "Who do you worship?"

The concept of biblical worship can be difficult to trace throughout the NT. OT worship is much easier, in part because of the Ten Commandments (Ex 20), the *Shema* (Deut 6:4), and the OT's only apocalypse—Daniel. The commandments begin by defining Israel's responsibilities in its vertical relationship with *YHWH*. The rest of the commandments are about horizontal relationships; the way in which a person treats others reflects his/her devotion to God or lack thereof. The *Shema* is often translated very vaguely: "Hear O Israel, *YHWH* your God is one." One what? The way in which "one" appears in the Hebrew, however, is not ambiguous. It best translates to "the one and only." Thus, we can translate it (as NRSV and other very literal translations do), "Hear O Israel, *YHWH* your God is God alone." The implication of the *Shema* is very lucid: Only *YHWH* is worthy of humanity's worship. The apocalyptic imagery in Daniel portrays a vivid picture of faithfulness in the midst of opposition to monotheistic worship. Governing authorities created and enforced laws that demanded the worship of kings and local gods. The message is clear that such idols are folly. Thus, God shows his power and sole worth of humanity's worship throughout the OT.

The NT, on the other hand, is more difficult to assess for matters of worship, because we can translate the Greek verb *proskuneo* as "to worship," "to bow down," or "to prostrate oneself." As such, context must determine whether the word refers to worship that must be reserved for God alone or to a physical expression of reverence. We find an example of this difficulty in Luke's birth narrative; the verb is ascribed to the wise men that present their gifts before the baby Jesus. They recognized that the baby was thought of as a king, so to present gifts to a king would certainly have involved bowing or prostration. The words in the Greek text, however, do not necessarily mean that they turned from their Egyptian gods and began worshiping *YHWH* when they encountered the Messiah. No historical evidence can demonstrate any likelihood for spiritual convictions motivating their action.[15] Many translations, nevertheless, wrongly state that the wise men "worshiped" Jesus. This linguistic problem makes NT worship a knotty interpretive issue. One use of the word must be reserved for God alone, while the other can be appropriately expressed in a secular manner to any worthy person.

Revelation is the only NT book that does not force interpreters to ask the question, "Is *proskeno* something one is only supposed to do for God?" Even though the verb appears in both contexts in Revelation, the context is always exceedingly clear. For example, when John attempts to bow before and/or worship an angel, that angel rebukes him for starting to give him what rightfully belongs to God alone. It must, therefore, refer to worship. The "things that must soon take place," then, are not so much promises or warnings about the future as they are the means of clarifying that only God is worthy of worship. They are the very events depicted throughout John's Apocalypse.

2. WHAT DID JOHN SEE? (REV 1:2)

The construction of the Greek phrase in Revelation 1:2 is quite difficult to render in English. It continues the sentence that began in the first verse, and everything in the phrase applies to John. Most literally, it translates to, "who bore witness concerning the word of God, namely the testimony of Jesus, all that he saw." So, what did John actually see according to this verse? All three of the items to which John bore witness ("all that he saw," "the word of God," and "the testimony of Jesus") are appositional to one another. In other words, they all refer to the same thing. All three items in this list describe the content of John's vision. In my translation at the beginning of this chapter, I ordered them differently from how they appear in the Greek. I did so, because this type of apposition places more importance on clarification than word order. By clarification, I mean that each item says something to clarify another; when we do this in English, we begin with the vaguest and clarify from there, as reflected in my translation. The vaguest is "all that he saw," and the clearest is "the testimony of Jesus."

Because the apocalypse proper has not begun yet, we do not yet know any details about what John saw. The phrase "the word of God" tells us that he saw something prophetic, something that came directly from God that provided wisdom. We tend to use the phrase "Word of God" to mean the entirety of Scripture, but that is not the way it is intended here (nor many other times when the Bible uses it). John's visual experience also involves hearing

15. Jobes, "Distinguishing," 201–11.

a very specific message with divine origins. So, the first thing we learn from this phrase is that John experienced something with a verbal, prophetic message in addition to a visionary element. The third item according to the ordering that English prefers is "the testimony of Jesus." Revelation 1:1 tells us that God gave Jesus this revelation, and that John is the liaison between Jesus's reception of the revelation and the audiences' receptions. For John, then, to see "the testimony of Jesus" means he experienced the same "word of God"—the same prophetic revelation—that God had already given Jesus.

So, what did John see? He saw a revelation of God through Jesus. He saw a series of visions that indicated the way in which God had chosen to reveal himself through Jesus to the people for whom this document was initially written. He saw visions of events that were already happening amongst the congregations about to be addressed. He saw visions of events very soon to take place for those same people. He also saw the ultimate realities of judgment, rewards, and new creation that would give eternal significance to these events and how the people receiving this revelation should respond to them.

3. THE BLESSING (REV 1:3)

3.1 The Form of a Beatitude

Revelation 1:3 is a *beatitude*. Both the OT and NT are full of *beatitudes*. Those in the OT tend to be prophetic in nature and individual in address, especially common at someone's death. The dying person makes specific pronouncements about each individual he blesses. In the NT, the most common beatitudes are for groups of people. OT blessings tend to emphasize the characteristics of an individual. NT blessings point more toward how the actions of a community should reflect the nature of Jesus.

Revelation's beatitude is threefold, and it is unique in that it addresses both an individual ("the reader") and two groups ("the rest of the hearers" and "those who obey"). There is no specific content describing what the blessing for each addressee entails, but there is a degree of blessing implied. Those who experience this revelation in the first place ("the reader" and "the rest of the hearers") indeed are blessed simply because they have experienced a divine message delivered to them. The greater blessing, however, is reserved for those who not only receive the words of that message but also put them into practice.

3.2 The Reader and Greco-Roman Rhetoric

3.2.1 Introduction to Rhetoric

The first-century Mediterranean world was not a culture of silent reading. Literacy and education were for the elite. The written word was respected universally, especially if it was of a religious nature. Often, pagans even held reverence for the Jewish Scriptures because of their presumed divine origin. Pagans certainly would not have agreed that it came from the one and only God, but they nevertheless understood the written word of the Hebrew Scriptures as having some degree of authority. The written word, however, was not valued as much for its content as it was for the mere fact that the words had been written down. The act of writing meant the words were deemed worthy to be communicated beyond a single occasion. For all instances of interpersonal communication, nevertheless, orality was always preferred to the written word.[16]

The first-century Mediterranean world was a culture of hearing, discussing, and debating. Followers of Jesus throughout the first century were no different from the rest of the culture in this respect. They were surrounded by Greco-Roman rhetoricians whose speeches and debates were the predominant form of entertainment for the common people in the first century Roman Empire. The earliest leaders of the Jesus-following movement were in many ways rhetoricians themselves. All the letters of Paul are full of rhetorical conventions, and they were written to be read aloud to the audiences Paul addressed. Before ever explaining clearly that the book of Revelation is a letter (that happens in 1:4), John refers to it as an oral document; that designation makes it like Paul's letters. The phrase "oral document" might sound like an oxymoron in the twenty-first century, but it is the most common kind of document that existed in the first century. Things were written down in order to be read aloud, so that the audience could hear and experience the communication from the writer as if the writer was present. It served as a replacement for oral communication in situations when face-to-face communication was impossible.[17]

To relate the author's words, a person like a rhetorician, known as a reader, would be hired to deliver and read the letter to the group. Most books of the NT were first received in this way. The book of Romans is obviously addressed to Romans, to converts from paganism to Christianity. The names throughout that book are all Roman names until we get to the last chapter; then, Paul greets Jews who have recently returned to Rome

---

16. Witherington, *Rhetoric*, 1–5.
17. Witherington, *Rhetoric*, 4.

following an exile. The way in which he writes this portion of the book suggests that he most likely intended it as a cover letter for the people who would be involved with delivering the letter to the Romans. It suggests that Phoebe was Paul's reader. She would not merely read the words Paul had written to the Roman audience, but she would also enact the rhetorical devices Paul used. Her responsibilities involved explaining the theological implications that the audience might not understand (especially the Jewish origins of their faith, with which they had not been familiar, since Jews had been exiled from Rome until very shortly before Paul wrote the letter to the Romans). She filled the role of a pastor and evangelist to reach the people Paul could not at that point in time.[18]

Phrases like "let the reader understand" that appear in our English translations of Scripture tend to confuse modern readers, because we usually read silently. Even if we are not reading the words silently, we are still not reading them in the same cultural situations in which they were written. "Let the reader understand" is a command for the appointed reader to be intimately familiar with the background behind the writer's statement. Matthew 24:15 includes one of these statements. Matthew commands his reader to understand Daniel's prophecy about the abomination that leads to desolation, because he makes mention of it without giving a clear explanation. He therefore demanded that his reader be familiar with the Danielic background of the passage so that he or she could act in a pastoral capacity to teach and preach the message Matthew intended.

In Revelation, John pronounces a blessing on his reader. Unlike the book of Romans, we know nothing about the reader for Revelation. Perhaps each of the seven congregations had its own reader. It is equally likely, however, that the same reader traveled in a circular fashion, since the geography of the seven cities lends itself to that manner of travel.[19] We know nothing about the type of blessing the reader expected to receive. All we know from Revelation is that its reader is blessed in some way or another. On the other hand, we do know from the culture of rhetoric and from the way in which the early church embraced that aspect of the culture, that the reader must have acted as a representative for John and as a minister to the congregations. God had first given a message to Jesus; then Jesus conveyed it to John. Finally, the reader would be responsible for conveying what John saw to the seven congregations that Revelation 1:4 addresses.

---

18. Witherington and Hyatt, *Romans*, 4–5.
19. Koester, *Revelation*, 110.

3.2.2 How Rhetoric Informs Interpretation of Revelation

The main goal of all Greco-Roman rhetoric was to persuade audiences. Rhetoricians used a speech as an attempt to convince the audience 1) to accept a new way of thinking, 2) to adapt a new lifestyle or habit, 3) to shun a lifestyle or habit, 4) to commend a person's life, behaviors, and choices, as in a funerary eulogy, 5) to condemn a person's life, behaviors, and choices, 6) or to argue the guilt or innocence of an individual in a legal setting. The NT authors were surrounded by all these types of rhetoric as parts of their daily lives, and if you look back at this list of possible motives for a Greco-Roman speech, you should be able to think of NT sections that fit each of them.[20]

Revelation addresses seven congregations located in Asia Minor, each in a city subject to the rule of the Roman Empire. Each city played a different role in the overall function of the empire. Similarly, each city possessed a different type of relationship with the whole of the empire. As such, each of the seven congregations that John addressed had different levels of compromise to the ways of the empire and thus different levels of devotion to God. The seven messages of Revelation 2–3 begin to show the rhetorical force of Revelation. John shows, through these messages, that God knows (as John also knows) their situations, their needs, and their failings. The rest of the book constantly points back to that knowledge, with all of its symbols, images, and prophetic words attempting to persuade believers in at least one of the ways listed above.[21]

When we understand that John determined to speak persuasively to his seven distinct audiences through his reader or readers, we get a better grasp on his symbolic language. We can begin to recognize parallels he made between his symbolic language and the culture in which his audiences lived. The more we learn about the historical situation of the seven congregations, the more we understand Revelation's primary purpose. It functions as a call for all who profess Jesus to shun the ways of empire and to come fully in line with the ways of the kingdom of God, to worship God and not the emperor or his gods.

3.2.3 How Rhetoric Informs the Modern Application of Revelation

The development of Greco-Roman rhetoric as it was known around the time of Revelation derives from the various philosophical movements from the last centuries BCE through the first century CE. Earlier, I described the culture as

---

20. Witherington, *Rhetoric*, 7.
21. Hemer, *Seven Churches*, 1–4.

a listening, discussing, and debating society. As such, it was a thinking culture. Rhetoric was the most significant aspect of all levels of Greco-Roman education. At the center of that rhetorical education is what we now call critical thinking. Evidence was assessed, questions were posed, hypotheses were made, and civil arguments were conducted, debating how to understand that evidence and what that evidence might prove or disprove. Ancient rhetoric is partially foundational for the scientific method and for all aspects of modern liberal arts education. People in such educational institutions tend to refer to this era as pre-critical, and this designation is appropriate. We must understand, nevertheless, that it is foundational both for what is critical and for how the NT authors embraced and fostered this type of thinking.[22]

In many parts of the West in the twenty-first century, we tend to avoid debates and confrontations. We get comfortable with our ignorance and do not want our ideas challenged. We may deceive ourselves into believing that such behavior is polite, lightly throwing around the phrase "agree to disagree," when in reality we resist learning. Such resistance prevents intellectual, moral, and spiritual growth. We may avoid reading or listening to anyone with whom we are likely to disagree. This attempt to escape keeps us from seeing other viewpoints and from entering other worldviews. It not only prevents us from learning, but it also prevents us from loving others who see the world differently than we do. Therefore, it may even thwart us from fulfilling the Great Commission.

Those of us who have succumbed to this resistance against learning have given into a type of anti-intellectualism that is quite rampant in much of the United States. When I say "anti-intellectualism," I am not commenting on anybody's intelligence. Rather, I am saying that we have chosen not to think for ourselves. Nevertheless, most have come to this decision almost unwittingly through behaviors that we have learned from others and from what I will call "cultural brainwashing." All cultures brainwash people toward ingrained patterns of thought and lifestyle. We are all products of culture. The reality of that brainwashing is inherently neither good nor evil. However, when our culture tells us that our way is the right way, the best way, or the only way to do things that have little to no morality attached to them, we accept lies of ethnocentrism. We get so stuck in what we are comfortable with, that we assume anybody who acts or thinks differently must either be wrong or weird.

Secular journalist Annalisa Quinn wrote a fascinating article on how people are easily influenced. She provides an accurate historical and linguistic *etymology* of the word "influence." She never tries to sidestep the long

---

22. Witherington, *Rhetoric*, 4.

history that this word has in the early church. She makes the point that today's societies are more susceptible to being manipulated by others because of social media and the extreme deluge of information (and misinformation) coming from every direction. Her *etymology* of the word provides the answer to the problem she poses, though she does not say whether or not she believes that she has offered a solution. In the third century CE, church fathers commonly used the Latin word *influo* (meaning "to flow into") to depict the power that the Holy Spirit has over people who will allow him to flow in every part of their lives.[23] The United States contains many sources of manipulation that want to *influo*[24] us. Advertisers convince us how to spend our money. The entertainment industry tries to control the ways we understand matters of sex. Hostile foreign misinformation campaigns use social media to manipulate how we think about our political system and likely how we vote. The problem may seem to have us at an impasse, but God has given us a solution by the Holy Spirit, by the Bible, and through the church. When we are influenced predominantly by God's voice (available in numerous ways, but most often through the three sources I just mentioned), we can reject the voices that try to manipulate our thoughts and feelings. This battle over *influo* is one of John's predominant goals for the seven churches. In Revelation 22:9, John alludes to the circle of prophets to which he belonged. As a prophet, he wanted true prophetic words originating from the Scriptures and from the Holy Spirit to *influo* the seven congregations, not the ways of the empire. In other words, he wanted them (and later readers, indirectly) to recognize the difference between truth and lies, so that all people can worship God "in spirit and in truth" (John 4:23).[25]

Because anti-intellectualism is widespread in the United States, our churches are not immune. In fact, it seems to flourish the most in some well-meaning congregations, even though we have a solution available to us. This problem is monumental for American congregations who want to be representatives of the global church, and thereby representatives of Jesus himself. If we do not think for ourselves in a way influenced foremost by God's voice, we allow our culture (both believing and unbelieving aspects of our culture) to inform how we understand the Bible and the world. Instead, we must allow the Bible to speak for itself, from within its own cultural setting.

---

23. Quinn, "Influence," para. 5.

24. I use the form of the Latin verb outside of Latin grammatical conventions solely for the purpose of clarity and consistency for a popular level audience.

25. Koester, *Revelation*, 91.

Because we are far removed culturally and temporally from the time in which Revelation was written, it is no wonder that we struggle to understand what John meant. As we discover what John's words meant to those who first heard it, however, we can begin interpreting it as accurately as possible, while we also try to find its application for today. We have evidence to weigh, process, think about, wrestle with through meditation, and debate about with people who disagree with us. This process empowers us to gain a better grasp on what the Bible actually says. It also challenges how we view the world around us, so we are no longer bound to an anti-intellectual shunning of growth, responsibility, and love. Then, we can truly allow the Holy Spirit to lead us.

All of the Bible forces us into an intercultural experience. We must begin removing the culture-tinted lenses through which we look at Scripture, so we can see the world in which those words were written. As we do so, we will experience culture shock. We will be confronted with ideas and customs we are not familiar with. The texts force us to make the decision to either enter into the ancient culture and learn what the Bible actually conveys or to stay comfortable with our American religious worldview that might contradict what the Bible truly teaches. Our thoughts and our ways of life will be confronted. Some of our most deeply cherished convictions might even be at stake. If our faith is not based in historical reality, then our faith is vain and blind. Our pursuit to understand Scripture must be founded on what it actually says in its historical background. Scholar N. T. Wright expresses this best: "History is very good at clearing away the smoke screens behind which unfaith often hides. History and faith are, respectively, the left and right feet of Christianity."[26]

In an attempt to ease us into that process with Revelation, I will use a method of teaching critical thinking at various junctures in this book. Revelation discusses many topics that are controversial and do not have easy answers, but they are not central to the aims of this book. For such topics, I will not offer my own conclusions, but I will present opposing views that have merit, so you can weigh through options and evidence and learn to be persuaded by presentations and interpretations of facts rather than by the sway of culture. As we learn to think critically, we must expect some uncomfortable growing pains. Evaluating facts helps us expose our biases as well as understand the difference between bias and untruth. Everyone views the world with biases; there is no way around that, so we must learn to recognize the difference between a disagreement and a lie. In Appendix 1, I illustrate these differences through a discussion about how to relate to the

---

26. Wright, "Historical Jesus," 27.

world around us through our relationship with news media to mark the difference between fake news and biased news. Biased news presents facts and critically interprets them; we may or may not agree with the interpretations, but that does not make them lies. At this stage in our discussion, that illustration might seem irrelevant to our interpretation of Revelation, but I hope to show later how connected these two expressions of critical thinking are.

3.3 The Time Is Near

What time is near? The Messiah's second coming? A time of *eschatological* suffering? A time of *eschatological* blessing? A time of persecution that the original audience would likely experience? A time of blessing that the original audience would likely experience? All of the above?

All of the possible answers to the question posed are important themes of John's Apocalypse. The book's introduction, nevertheless, establishes an intimate connection between the author and his immediate audiences. Thus, anything outside of the scope of what those audiences could directly experience does not seem likely for this particular "time" that John refers to. This temporal language is the same type of speech we discussed above in sections 1.3 and 1.5 dealing with "what must take place in a short time" (Rev 1:1).

Therefore, all of Revelation's introduction shows modern readers that we live in a very different world than that of those who first heard John's Apocalypse. The things that were temporally near for them occurred many centuries ago. As we continue to dig into the specifics of what was imminent for them, however, we can discern the larger, more universal themes of Revelation that do apply to the present time. We can also learn to discern the differences between which parts of Revelation are entirely grounded in the past and which are discussing the potentially distant future.

4. EPISTOLARY, THEOLOGICAL, AND LITURGICAL INTRODUCTION (REV 1:4-8)

4.1 Revelation as a Letter

Revelation's first word introduces the book as belonging to the genre of apocalypse, and Revelation 1:3 places it within the realm of prophetic literature. Now, Revelation 1:4-6 points out that the book is also an *epistle*. John introduces himself as the letter writer, and he introduces seven congregations in Asia Minor as his recipients. He follows this introduction with a greeting that structurally follows the letters of Paul.[27] Although he includes much more theological content in his *epistolary* introduction than Paul ever does, John indicates his knowledge of his audiences through this genre. He shows that he believes he knows the congregations and their situations well enough to speak to them pastorally. This purpose unites all NT letters. It is important to emphasize here that John's indication of the book as a letter is the first way in which he suggests that the entire book is a letter. We have grown accustomed to understanding Revelation 2–3 as the "letters to the seven churches." Some translations even use headings in these chapters that identify each of the messages as such. When we discuss those two chapters, however, I will attempt to prove that they are not letters at all, but prophetic *oracles*. These *oracles*, then, are merely one constituent of a single letter.

4.2 John's Theological Introduction

John greets the seven churches with a "grace and peace" formula we are familiar with from other biblical *epistles*. He communicates differently, however, with regards to the sources of that blessing. John's three sources are "the one who is, who was, and who is coming," "the seven spirits," and "Jesus the Messiah, the faithful witness, the firstborn from among the dead people, and the ruler of the kings of the earth." All three theological sources of blessing appear many times in Revelation. In chapter 2, upon another reference to the "seven spirits," we will discuss whether or not this is a trinitarian greeting, in which the first listed source of blessing represents the Father, the second the Holy Spirit, and the third the Son of God.

4.3 John's Liturgical Introduction

Immediately after his complex theological greeting, John continues to theologize, giving more information about Jesus. He offers a brief prayer of thanksgiving that is possibly also a song. This praise highlights the primary attributes of Jesus that John will focus on throughout his Apocalypse: love, sacrificial death that liberates people, kingship, and spiritual authority that calls God's people into participation in God's reign. This is the first of many occurrences in John's Apocalypse of spontaneous liturgy. Some of them are unquestionably hymns; all of them encourage people to worship Jesus the Messiah. Because Revelation is a liturgical book, I will include liturgy at

---

27. Klauck, *Ancient Letters*, 299.

various junctures in this book that help us apply the messages of Revelation to our own relationships with God.

5. THE SEVEN MESSAGES TO THE SEVEN CONGREGATIONS (REV 1:9—3:22)

I mentioned earlier that I do not believe the traditional designation of "seven letters" appropriately indicates the nature of these messages. Along with the *epistolary* opening we discussed in section 4.1, the book's closing features a second *benediction* (Rev 22:21), like the blessings common in letters. These two factors are not enough to determine that the whole of Revelation is a letter. Many works of ancient literature included these two features without otherwise conforming to the genre of a letter. The context in between these two *epistolary* features, however, indeed fits well within the same literary world of the other NT *epistles*.[28] Revelation 2–3 provides individualized messages for each of the congregations addressed in the book's introduction. Revelation 4:1—22:5 continues the apocalyptic imagery to tell a story that often revisits the images of the seven messages. Repetition of such images suggests that John has something to say directly to the church that received the individualized message consisting of that imagery.[29] The contents of Revelation 4:1—22:5, nevertheless, are generally broader than those of Revelation 2–3. The story does not consist of individualized messages like the prophecies; rather, it aims at sending a transcendent message applicable to all congregations in all areas at that time and even in the future. When John pinpoints parts of the story that he wants a single audience to pay special attention to, he clarifies that this story, transcendent as it is, remains part of a letter to the seven churches of Asia Minor.

The final part of John's introduction (1:9–20) introduces us to the book's visionary content. It also provides the beginning of the story, since John recounts his vision in narrative fashion. John names the seven congregations for the first time in this portion of his text. He tells of hearing a voice that instructs him to write down what he sees and to send the contents to the seven congregations. Since the rest of the book from this point forward contains John's vision narrative, that evidence is the most important data that suggests the whole book is a letter. The instruction to write what he saw directed John to record his entire vision. He is only instructed to write the seven individualized messages because each audience is not present to hear it directly from him. Those messages, nevertheless, are prophetic in content,

---

28. Klauck, *Ancient Letters* 299.
29. Witherington, *Revelation*, 14–15.

not *epistolary*. John's arrangement of the whole Apocalypse fits these prophecies seamlessly into his complex work of literature to make them part of his apocalyptic, prophetic, rhetorical, and narrative letter.

Revelation 2–3 claims to be messages directly from Jesus the Messiah. John cannot and does not take credit for such words. Throughout the Apocalypse, John credits himself as the recipient of a vision, as the one who has heard the words that the Holy Spirit spoke to the seven congregations, as a prophet, and as the author of the book. He does not take credit, however, for writing Revelation 2–3. These messages are the very words of the Messiah. John is merely the messenger. We understand that God is one in three persons, but John did not have that kind of language or theology available to him. Because trinitarian theology was not formulated for at least a century after the completion of the NT, we can miss the significance of John's claim that a prophetic *oracle* originated from the Messiah. It means the same thing as saying it originated from God. Thus, he claims already in the beginning of the book that God the Father and Jesus the Messiah are one, just as the *Shema* (the center of all Jewish monotheism) says "*YHWH* is your one and only God."

The *oracular* content of Revelation 2–3 targets the seven congregations directly. John shows throughout the rest of the book that he has intimate knowledge of each church, but he uses the divinely inspired images from the seven prophecies to make that knowledge known. As such, I will not offer further comment on the seven *oracles* here. I encourage us to view John's repetitions of *oracular* images in the body of the letter as a wake-up call to attract special interest to the congregants who directly received that imagery. For that reason, we will work with the individualized prophecies whenever we reach one of these wake-up calls.

Chapter 2

Worship in the Heavenly Realm (Rev 4–5)

4 ¹ After these things, I looked and behold: A door was open in heaven. And the earlier voice like a trumpet that I heard speaking with me said, "Come up here, and I will show you what must take place after these things." ² At that moment I was in the Spirit, and behold: A throne was placed in heaven with one seated on the throne, ³ and the one seated on the throne was similar in appearance to a stone, specifically jasper and sardis, and a rainbow was around the throne similar in appearance to an emerald. ⁴ Also, twenty-four thrones were around the throne, and on the thrones twenty-four elders were seated, dressed in white clothes with golden crowns on their heads. ⁵ Then lightnings, rumblings, and thunders proceeded out of the throne, and seven flaming torches, which are the seven spirits of God, were in front of the throne; ⁶ also in front of the throne was something like a sea of glass, like crystal. And four living creatures full of eyes in front and in back were in the midst of the throne and around the throne.

⁷ Now the first living creature was like a lion, the second living creature was like an ox, the third living creature had a face like that of a human, and the fourth living creature was like an eagle in flight. ⁸ As for the four living creatures, each one of

them has six wings and is full of eyes around and within, and they have no rest during the day or during the night, saying "Holy, holy, holy is the Lord God Almighty who was, who is, and who is coming." [9] And whenever the living creatures give glory, honor, and thanksgiving to the one seated on the throne who lives forever, [10] the twenty-four elders fall before the one seated on the throne, worship him who lives forever, and cast their crowns before the throne, saying: [11] "You our worthy, our Lord and God, to receive glory, honor, and power because you created all things and by your will they exist and were created."

5 [1] Then I saw a scroll—written on the inside and on the outside—in the right hand of the one seated on the throne. [2] I also saw a strong angel proclaiming with a loud voice: "Who is worthy to open the scroll and to untie its seals?"

[3] Indeed no one in heaven, on earth, or under the earth was able to open the scroll or look into it, [4] so I began weeping greatly since no one was found worthy to open the scroll or to look into it. [5] Then one of the elders said to me, "Do not weep. Behold, the lion of the tribe of Judah—who is the root of David—prevailed. He is able to open the scroll and its seven seals." [6] Then between the throne and the four living creatures and among the twenty-four elders, I saw a Lamb standing like it had been slaughtered, having seven horns and seven eyes which are the seven spirits of God sent into the whole earth, [7] and he went and took it out of the right hand of the one seated on the throne. [8] Then when he took the scroll, the four living creatures and the twenty-four elders fell down before the Lamb, each one holding a harp and golden bowls full of incense, which are the prayers of the saints, [9] and they sang a new song: "You are worthy to receive the scroll and to open its seals, because you were slain and redeemed people for God from every tribe, tongue, people, and nation by your blood, [10] and you made them a kingdom and priests for our God, so they will reign on the earth." [11] Then I looked and heard the voice of many angels around the throne, the living creatures and the elders, and their number was myriads of myriads and thousands of thousands, [12] saying in a loud voice: "The Lamb who was slaughtered is worthy to receive power, wealth, wisdom, strength, honor, glory, and praise." [13] Then every creature that was in heaven, on the earth, under the earth, in the sea, and all that is in them heard them saying, "Praise, honor, glory, and dominion be to the one seated on the throne and to the Lamb forever and ever." [14] Then the four living creatures said, "Amen." And the twenty-four elders fell down and worshiped.

1. JOHN AND THE HEAVENLY REALM (REV 4:1-3)

1.1 Vision Order

As John adjusts his focus from the seven congregations in the earthly realm to realities of the heavenly realm, he uses the phrase "after these things" to make that transition. John uses this technique commonly throughout his apocalypse to remind his audiences of the order in which the vision appeared to him. Although my translation above uses past tense language (as do most translations), most of the Greek verbs in the passage are present tense verbs. John's language reflects a phenomenon known as the historic present. He communicates a past event as if he is going through it when he writes or dictates. This is not unique to the Greek language; you can look at many parts of this present book and realize that I write this way too. This language imitates a manner of speaking when recounting history or discussing the past in general. This is exactly what John intends to do with his vision. That does not mean that we should expect a chronological account of historical events. It means, rather, that we should expect a chronological account of one historical event: John's visionary experience. That account begins in Revelation 1:11. The first ten verses of the book are John's introductory way of explaining he was about to recount a vision in a historical manner. Once he specifies the initial words he hears from "the voice like a trumpet," his account of that vision has begun. My reasoning for using the English past tense in my translation to render historical present verbs is to help explicitly show the difference between the historical nature of John's report and the ahistorical nature of the vision itself.

While John orders his vision to demonstrate a historical encounter with God, the content of the vision has little to no historical value. In other words, many of the events in Revelation are not intended to be taken literally. These events help John present a symbolic reflection of reality, but they are not themselves bound to ordinary existence. This provides more reason for John to use historical phrases like "after these things" to order his vision. What he saw reflects reality but does not display reality. Using phrases like this, however, he constantly reminds listeners of his conviction that his visionary experience was a factual, historical one. If the vision is the factual, historical event he claims it is, then John's vision is indeed of divine origin. Also, if the vision is divine in origin, then the content is truth that transcends time and place, whether or not it consists of a literal set of facts.

1.2 Seeing what John Sees

John says, "I looked and behold" as another historical marker, but it is not only a historical marker. Just as it communicates to the audience the order in which John experienced his vision, it also presents an invitation to the audience to see the vision for themselves. John is about to explain what he saw. With each part of John's vision, he offers a new introduction, like this one, through which he indicates what he wants listeners to imagine.

1.3 The Door in Heaven

This imagery of a door is found twice during the seven prophetic messages to the Asia-Minor congregations. As such, each of those two congregations should find special significance for themselves when they hear that imagery repeated later in the book. First, the divine message to Philadelphia involves a perpetually open door that was established by God himself. God reveals himself to the congregation in Philadelphia as the one who sustains them, as symbolized by that door that nobody has the authority to close. Conversely, to the congregation in Laodicea, God describes himself as one knocking on a closed door. In a message that calls for repentance, the symbolism places unrepentant people as those who have locked themselves in and kept God out. Nevertheless, God remains on the other side of that door, willing to extend his forgiveness and to restore relationship between himself and the people inside. They must only accept their need for him and turn away from the beliefs and actions that keep them separated from him.

1.3.1 The Open Door and the Church in Philadelphia

When Philadelphia's congregation heard the symbol of an open door in heaven repeated, they would have likely associated it with their own open door and the one mentioned in Isaiah 22:22. In Revelation 3:8, the congregation is told, "I know your works; behold, I have placed an open door before you that no one is able to close, because you have little strength, yet you have kept my word and did not deny my name." Here in Revelation 4:1, the congregation hears that John sees an open door. Is John about to explain what that door symbolically means for the believers in Philadelphia? Yes and no. The door that John saw open is the door into the heavenly throne room. Since the prophecy told Philadelphia's congregants about the door God had opened for them, 4:1 indeed refers to God's presence perpetually available to that congregation. God made it impossible for anyone to take them out of his presence. They would be able to constantly access the presence of God both in this age and in the age to come. So, the door indicates an invitation into God's presence, but it was not a direct promise for an individual congregation. Revelation 4:1's door remains open not only to God's presence but into the entirety of the heavenly realm. Philadelphia's congregation could thus discern that entrance into the heavenly realm is for them, but not necessarily in the present age. John experienced heavenly realities that he invited the congregants to enter imaginatively. To enter that realm in actuality (at least in an *ecstatic* sense) was only for John at that time. It pointed, nevertheless, to an eventual time when the heavenly and earthly realms in their entirety will be united (what the end of Revelation entails).

Isaiah 22:22 is the Bible's first use of "open door" language. In Isaiah's prophetic context, the symbol is used as a promise of God's future for Judah following a period of oppression at the hands of its own governmental leaders. *YHWH* pronounces coming judgment against corrupt leaders and a prosperous future for the faithful remnant. Revelation 3:7 presents Philadelphia with access to "the one who has the key of David." That key also accompanies Isaiah's prophecy. Philadelphia's congregation exhibited great perseverance as they remained faithful to God in the midst of a political and social environment that was hostile to their faith. To say that they dwell "where Satan's throne is" means that they suffered at least in part because of their own governmental authorities. This political environment placed them in a similar situation as Judah when addressed prophetically with their own promise of access to the "key of David." Revelation clarifies that the crucified and resurrected Messiah possesses the "key of David." Thus, the Philadelphian church would have understood any reference to an "open door" as access to some degree of messianic authority while being subjected to a corrupt and demonic regime.

1.3.2 *The Open Door and the Church in Laodicea*

Laodicea's congregation should have had a much different reaction to re-hearing the door imagery than Philadelphia's would have. The theme of judgment dominated the prophetic message for Laodicea's stagnant spirituality expressed through an unwillingness to partner with God in the building of his kingdom on earth. Jesus told them, "Behold, I stand at the door and knock; if anyone hears my voice and opens the door, then I will come to him and dine with him and he with me" (Rev 3:20). The Laodicean congregation consisted largely of people who knew that God was calling them to holy and fruitful lifestyles. They were reluctant to follow that call because it could involve the sacrifice of their wealth. Different members of the congregation would have imagined the open door differently. This distinction is based on how each individual in the congregation responded to the indictments in the prophetic message that was given to them earlier. The prophecy demands that Laodicean hearers open the door. Therefore, those who were willing to open the symbolic door of Revelation 3:20 would have likely taken a different meaning to the "open door" of 4:1 than those who were unwilling.

The prophetic message to Laodicea's church criticizes the congregation more than any of the other six *oracles*. "I know your works: You are neither cold nor hot. How I wish that you were cold or hot! Thus, because you are neither cold nor hot, I am about to vomit you out of my mouth" (Rev 3:15–16). This harsh statement alludes to the city's geographical features. Pools produced water with a minimum heat of 95°F useful for cleaning and medicinal purposes. Cold waters from Colossae flowed into Laodicea; they were clean enough for drinking. Water that was anywhere between the "hot" or "cold" designation had stagnated. It induced nausea and vomiting.[1] The prophecy addresses a geographical phenomenon that the congregation knew intimately. Therefore, we can easily surmise that the message assumes the "hot" and "cold" designations as equal degrees of usefulness for differing purposes. For Jesus to wish that the congregation had been one or the other indicates a desire for fruitful labor from them. Since they are described as "lukewarm," they remained unable and unwilling to accomplish any of the works God has called them to. They succumbed to spiritual laziness.

Because Revelation 3:14–22 consists not only of a list of evils but also a summons toward changes, we must presume that at least some of the people who heard this call heeded it. For such audience members, to imagine an open door in the heavenly realm is to experience the fullness of their repentance. Repentance is not sinlessness or moral perfection, but it requires a change of pursuit. What a person pursues first in life indicates the god they worship. God called members of the Laodicean church to trade their pursuit of comfort and wealth with a pursuit of God. As such, some who received this divine confrontation must have determined to follow the command. They would have sought after God and his plans rather than the things that kept them comfortable but rendered them complacent and useless regarding God's kingdom. For those who made this trade, an open door in heaven would represent God's willingness to welcome them back into relationship with him, to forgive them for their wandering and idolatrous pursuits.

---

1. Hemer, *Seven Churches*, 187.

Although the message of Revelation 3:14–22 must have been very persuasive (full of hope for those who would pursue God, yet full of fright for those who would continue in their complacency), the hardness of these hearts apparently reached quite deep. Even though God's love often manifests itself through strong discipline, it is uncommon to find Scriptures addressing believers as harshly as his comparison of this congregation to stagnant water. The lengths to which Laodicea had despised God's justice were not likely penetrable for all members of the congregation. Some, if not most, of the congregants likely responded to the prophetic message in a way that was unwilling to leave their pursuit of their own desires, of ease, and of riches. As such, they would have held on to the idols of self-interest, laziness, and luxury that prevented them from living lives entirely devoted to the worship of God. For them, an open door in the heavenly realm would have been connected to the closed door involved in the confrontation. The door of Revelation 4:1 leads to the true riches, purpose, and rest that can only be found in God's presence. It is a door that cannot be closed. The door Laodicean congregants were confronted with earlier, however, was one on which God knocked. If they refused to repent (to open the door on which God was knocking), they would not be able to experience the open door that leads to what they actually desire instead of the superficial comforts they presently enjoyed. Therefore, hearing about an open door in heaven serves as yet another opportunity for repentance for those still unwilling to pursue God foremost, to worship him alone, and to sacrifice personal needs and desires when necessary to that mission.

This discussion of how congregants in Philadelphia and Laodicea would have likely responded to hearing about the open door does not imply that they alone found meaning in the image. They would have realized the most personal meaning because of the previous use of the symbol directed squarely at them. All who heard, nonetheless, would recognize the context of this open door as one of invitation into God's throne room. They would have recognized that John invited them into an imaginative realm in which they would try to see the throne vision for themselves. They also would have recognized an invitation into God's presence in a present, spiritual sense and in an anticipatory sense for a future when God's presence on earth will be all-encompassing, just as it is in heaven during the present age.

1.3.3 *The Open Door and Contemporary American Delusions*

The open door is a symbol of entering God's presence and being willing to worship him alone. The whole throne room/worship scene unpacked in Revelation 4–5 carries many messages that are necessary for today's Christians in the United States to grasp and obey in order to pursue God as required. We will discuss this in much more detail as the worship scene unfolds, but here we can recognize that many American Christians must heed the messages that especially Laodicea would have received from this symbol of the open door.

Very few Americans find themselves in the genuinely difficult circumstances of Philadelphia in which it is challenging to be a Christian and to meet daily needs. That statement is especially true for white Christians. Nevertheless, many American Christians (especially white people) think of themselves as "poor, wretched, etc." Such believers claim religious persecution if someone makes fun of them, disagrees with them, or does not allow them to have their way. These people have obviously never been to a part of the world where people are daily placed in bodily harm and the fear of death because of their devotion to Jesus. These American believers confuse their own will with the will of God. They may assume that American entitlement (their perceived rights as American citizens) and the will of God are well aligned with each other, though they are not. In her discussion of this cultural phenomenon as related to the so-called "war on Christians," Elizabeth A. Castelli insightfully writes: "This trend mobilizes the language of religious persecution to shut down political debate and critique by characterizing any position not in alignment with this politicized version of Christianity as an example of antireligious bigotry and persecution."[2]

Many of these same individuals appear to think they are in poverty, although there are entire people groups in other parts of the world who have less money than most of the United States's poorest citizens. Many throughout the world think of the American poverty line as great wealth.[3] Because of these factors, many of the people in the United States who call themselves followers of Jesus desperately need to heed the message behind this open door that the Laodicean church was confronted with. Again, this material is particularly relevant for white Christians, since real poverty does exist in the United States, but it disproportionately effects people of color.

The wrong assumptions of poverty and persecution indicate pursuits of personal comfort, wealth, and prestige. These pursuits have changed dramatically since the election of President Donald Trump. A billionaire as president who makes big claims about what he has done for the economy (even though everything he has taken credit for was being established before he took office) helps to feed the pretensions of those who felt like they

---

2. Castelli, "Persecution Complexes," 154.
3. Kochhar, "Global Middle Class," graph 1.

were entitled to more monetarily than they were able to accumulate before Trump. All indications show that such people experienced no increase in their income and benefited very little (if at all) from his tax cuts.[4] Nevertheless, they believe his promises, even though he has never shown any signs of keeping them in a meaningful way. Instead, his 2016 campaign gave a voice to their perceived poverty. Believing that they would have a president who hears and understand their problems, Trump allowed their delusion to grow, so they perceive him as the one who saves them from poverty.

Similarly, Trump has given a voice to the delusion of religious persecution in the United States. He created silly conflicts like the "war on Christmas" that do not account for any facts (like the tendencies of public, secular environments to play Christmas music as early as October, music that at least uses the word "Christmas" alluding to Jesus as the Christ or Messiah, if not sacred hymns that blatantly celebrate his birth).[5] The "happy holidays" greeting simply recognizes that the season stretches out so long that it overlaps with other holidays, both religious and secular. What many American Christians have defined as religious persecution is the growing expectation to speak in a politically correct way that does not offend. Most Americans are not typically bothered by hearing the phrase "merry Christmas" or even by genuine expressions of faith, so long as they do not feel pressured to share in the actions or beliefs expressed. Therefore, Trump's irresponsible rage against political correctness feeds delusions of those who claim religious persecution.

White Christians remain a political majority in the United States, meaning that they hold the most power to influence the country's culture. This fact challenges most claims of religious persecution amongst American Christians. It is not necessary to do anything more than watch a half hour of television to recognize this truth. Very often, contestants on talent competitions sing traditional Christian hymns. If we lived in a land that tolerated oppression against Christians, such actions would not be allowed. Even if someone fell through the cracks of censorship, the singers would not be afforded the opportunity to progress in the competition but would be severely punished. Nevertheless, many such singers have won *American Idol*, *The Voice*, etc. This example is only one among countless others that can be found that show how widely acceptable Americans find expressions of Christian faith and values, whether they follow Jesus or not.

When Christians demand their rights of religious expression or free speech, they do not reflect any real need being denied them but rather the

---

4. Goodkind, "Trump's Tax Cuts," paras. 9–11.
5. Mazza, "War on Christmas," para. 3.

desire to avoid being bound to political correctness. To the contrary of many American Christian tirades, political correctness can create inroads for believers to share their faith. It became an issue as related to Christianity because so many unbelievers perceived Christians as "shoving religion down their throats." That problem is the fault of Christians, not political correctness. Not too many Christians want to be perceived in this way, so a more politically correct attitude can encourage us to become friends with unbelievers. It can empower us to proceed cautiously in how we discuss matters of faith and to live out our faith before unbelieving friends and neighbors in an unassuming manner. When we do so, we fulfill the command of Matthew 5:16 to be a light to the unbelieving world through good works.

Of course, political correctness can be taken too far. It often was in the postmodern era that began to die in the 1990s. Since our culture has transitioned to a post-postmodern era, however, even people who appear antagonistic to religion have begun to rediscover the pursuit of truth. We no longer live in a society that widely says, "nothing is absolute" or "everything is true as long as it does not contradict my truth."[6] So, Christians can no longer use postmodernism as an excuse for why people do not seem to listen to them when they share the gospel. Many centuries before our culture began valuing political correctness, the church father Saint Francis of Assisi summed up perfectly what American Christians need to learn: "It is no use walking anywhere to preach unless our walking is our preaching."[7] If we respond to our culture's call to most forms of political correctness in such a way, it can help our witness. Complaining and blaming others for Christian persecution—when no evidence of any such thing in the United States exists—blemishes the name of Christianity, the name of Christians, and even the name of the Christ we worship in the sight of unbelievers.

The apostle Paul recognized this before Saint Francis. Paul knew that being a Roman afforded him significant rights in the empire. Yet, he expressed willingness to lay down those rights to ensure that he never offended others in ways that could prevent their reception of God's salvation. He accomplished this goal in many ways according to 1 Corinthians 9:8–23. When he was with Jews, he followed Jewish religious rituals and laws that he otherwise would not have as an apostle to the gentiles. When he was with Romans, he participated in any Roman civic practices that did not necessitate idolatry. He was willing to enter the culture of the people around him, so long as he maintained a good conscience before God and people.

---

6. Turner, *City as Landscape*, 9.

7. Saunders, "Francis of Assisi," para. 3.

Therefore, if Paul could become "all things to all people in order that by all means I may save some" (1 Cor 9:22b), it should not be difficult for us to treat people as they want to be treated. For example, when Asian Americans say that the word "Oriental" should be reserved for rugs and food and never used for people, how difficult is that request to respect?

When Christians refuse common decency, they place themselves as being more important than the other. By condemning political correctness, they demand rights for themselves that are very likely to turn people away from the message of the gospel. Ironically, they actually demand a redefined type of political correctness and perpetuate the otherwise dead postmodern movement. They do so by partnering with the "alternative facts"[8] of right-wing extremism and by assuming that anyone who disagrees with them is against them or even hates them. When we give into this hypocritical form of political correctness that claims to despise political correctness, we become like the offenders Mahatma Gandhi referred to when he said, "I don't reject Christ. I love Christ. It's just that so many of your Christians are so unlike Christ. If Christians would really live according to the teachings of Christ, as found in the Bible, all of India would be Christians today."[9] When people outside the church can accurately indict believers like Gandhi did in India, those believers blatantly offend Paul's teaching and lifestyle. Paul teaches us, probably better than any other Jesus-follower in history, how to live like Jesus.

For Paul, suffering is a mark of a believer's relationship with Jesus (Rom 5:1–6; 8:15–17; Phil 3:8—9; 2 Thes 1:5; 2 Tim 1:8–14), a sign of church unity (1 Cor 12:26; 2 Cor 1:3–7; Eph 3:13; 2 Tim 2:2–3), and something to rejoice about (Rom 12:12; Col 1:24). For Peter, suffering can be a blessing and a demonstration of worship to God (1 Pet 3:14–18a). The author of Revelation views suffering as a reality Christians must accept as part of their normal experience (Rev 2:10 is most explicit, while this theme runs throughout the whole book). Demanding rights—including the right to override political correctness—rejects the required embrace of suffering, clinging instead to self-centered desires. Therefore, demanding rights, instead of willingly forfeiting them for the sake of others, denies God's demand for self-sacrifice.

The prophetic message to Laodicea's church mocks congregants for their upside-down view of their place in the world as related to suffering. "You say, 'I am rich, have grown wealthy, and have no need.' But you do not know that you are wretched, pitiable, blind, poor, and naked" (Rev 3:17).

---

8. White House Press Secretary Kellyanne Conway coined this term on January 22, 2017 on *Meet the Press*: see https://www.nbcnews.com/meet-the-press/meet-press-01-22-17-n710491.

9. Stroud, *Knights Templar*, 162.

Those ancient believers thought they were well off financially, physically, relationally, and spiritually, although the opposite proved true. As American Christians, we are also vulnerable to an upside-down view of our place in the world. Many once perceived their financial situations as insufficient, even if their actual lot in life has not changed, their perception has shifted dramatically, because a president gave credence to their complaints. They express an ideology that Donald Trump is the one to save them from the poverty and persecution they think they have endured. They express the belief (likely unintentionally) that God has abandoned them when they do not get what they think they need. They know they are, or at least used to be, "wretched, pitiable, poor, blind, and naked," but they think it is because they do not have what they want or what they pray for, but since Trump 'makes America great again,' they no longer worry about these perceived problems as long as they have Trump.

To some extent, all American Christians think God is supposed to intervene to make us happy, comfortable, healthy, and to give us "just enough" financially (although our idea of "just enough" is usually absurd when compared with the rest of the world). How we react toward disappointments when God does not intervene the way we expect tells a great deal about our spiritual maturity or lack thereof. The type of American Christian we have discussed here has placed his/her hope in the United States's greatness, not in God's. It is as if they say that they can no longer trust God to meet their needs, but they will trust Trump to do so.

This anti-Christian type of Christianity in the United States stems from the pursuit of the American Dream. Many congregations have been infiltrated by this wrong pursuit. Whether called the prosperity gospel or a health and wealth gospel, those who disseminate such a message encourage the worship of self and riches, not of God. Such preachers may be extremely deceptive, even (or perhaps especially) to themselves. They are usually genuine in their belief that they fulfill God's will for their lives and that their teachings align with the gospel message. We find the key to discerning if we have fallen prey to this deception when we ask ourselves about our pursuits. What we pursue first in life represents what is most important to us. Any priority that overrides our pursuit of God is an idol. So-called prosperity churches use the Bible constantly and sometimes interpret it appropriately, but when their interpretations are erroneous, they often spread idolatry. This idolatry can cause people to believe that if they do not have "enough" or if they feel disrespected by others, that they are not right with God. It is easy to see, then, how such beliefs can morph into a pursuit of the American Dream instead of a pursuit of God, all while using the name of Christianity to form a cult of wealth and/or personal reputation.

Former Republican strategist Stuart Stevens, who still considers himself a Republican, wrote a book titled *It Was All a Lie*.[10] Through articles and interviews promoting that book before its release, he reveals what he sees as a secret agenda of the GOP that he believes paved the way for Trump's presidency; that agenda connects directly to the wrong pursuits of many American Christians. Stevens perceives that the GOP has aggressively encouraged the persecution complexes we have been discussing. According to him, the GOP's secret agenda has evolved into a government similar to Soviet Communism through Trump. Trump wrongly compares his opponents to Communists to take the attention off of his own actual Communist-like behavior. Nevertheless, Stevens appears to suggest that the party itself was victimized by enough cultural brainwashing to not realize that even before Trump, it was becoming

> the character doesn't count party . . . the deficit doesn't matter party, the Russia is our ally party, and the I'm-right-and-you-are-human-scum party. Yes, it's President Trump's party now, but it stands only for what he has just tweeted . . . [it] exists only to advance itself . . . [and for] the acquisition and maintenance of power . . . [through provoking and taking advantage of] accumulated white grievance and anger.[11]

Stevens confesses that the Republican Party had been courting white Christian votes through lies and conspiracy theories for many years, as part of its descent into moral bankruptcy. In other words, Trump did not create the problems that Stevens writes about; Trump exposed them, worsened them, and used them as the foundational doctrines for the religious cult he formed.

Stevens's confession finally owns up to the reality that the party has encouraged lies about both political parties and that those lies have influenced fears and gullibility in voters. My greatest concern is how those lies have impacted US churches and tainted its witness to the world through syncretism with the cult of Trumpism and broader nationalism. For an example that fits our purposes, perhaps you have heard that Democrats have a hidden agenda to close the church in the promotion of tolerance for all other religions. If you have heard that rumor or any like it, then it is important to listen to Stevens's confessions that shows what a lie these conspiracy theories are. He suggests that the only recent political leader who poses any real threat for the freedom of religion that our country values so much is Donald Trump. According to Stevens, Trump demonstrated this assault

10. Stevens, *All a Lie*, forthcoming.
11. Stevens, "Wake Up," para. 5.

against the freedom of religion first and most dramatically by the ban of people from Muslim-majority countries from entering the United States in February 2016. I would add to Stevens's confession my own argument that the Democratic Party is as thoroughly influenced by nationalistic religion as the Republican Party is. Therefore, although Democrats might understand and apply those freedoms differently than the Republican Party, they would neither stand in the way of anyone's worship nor attempt to control the church. To do so would blatantly contradict the words of the founding fathers, shattering nationalistic convictions along with the illusion of the separation between church and state.[12]

By exposing these hidden agendas of the Republican Party, Stevens also exposes two false dichotomies that exist in many predominantly white portions of the church in the United States. First, he helps to illustrate how deeply many Americans connect their political affiliation with their identity in Christ, separating the church into groups of liberal and conservative Christians. Granted, these designations remain appropriate when dealing with theological matters (i.e., liberal Christians do not hold the same value of Scripture's authority as conservative Christians do), yet do not apply to politics. I hope that my book is also helping to break the power of that dichotomy, as I attempt to show throughout that conservative biblical interpretation and conservative politics are often at odds with each other.

The second dichotomy common in many United States churches today that Stevens helps expose is the false differentiation between holiness and social justice. This dichotomy is a biproduct of an individualistic culture. We can easily assume that holy living is an entirely personal matter. If we 1) defend people who determine that "character doesn't count," 2) give into the "I'm-right-and-you-are-human-scum" mentality, 3) accept or excuse every hateful presidential tweet, 4) take any part in the "acquisition and maintenance of power" for the mere sake of power, 5) or give into "accumulated white grievance and anger," we will not be able to follow the central tenet of holiness, which is love. We might think of ourselves as holy, because we keep ourselves disciplined to avoid breaking the Ten Commandments, yet Jesus said all OT law can be fulfilled by loving God and one another (Matt 22:36–40/Mark 12:31–33). Through this dichotomy, we risk following the behavior that Jesus condemned amongst a group of Pharisees in Luke 11:39–41. Luke wrote: "Now all you Pharisees clean the outside of a cup and a platter, but your inner selves are full of greed and malice. O foolish people,

---

12. Since Stevens's book was not yet released when I wrote this, my sources for his interviews, quotes, and opinion article were: Stevens, "2020 Election" and "Wake Up"; Harwood, "How the Republican Party Opened." For a full treatment of the topic, however, see Stevens, *All a Lie*.

the one who made the outside also made the inside, did he not? Therefore, give charitably to the poor out of what is inside of you; then behold, everything that belongs to you [i.e., your body and your inner being] is clean." So, without social justice, we cannot love, and without love we cannot be holy.

For many American Christians, we must understand the open door in heaven similarly to how the Laodicean church would have. If we pursue anything other than God as the answer to wretchedness, pitiable states, poverty, blindness, and/or nakedness, we worship a god of comfort and wealth. The door stays open for us as it did for Laodicea, serving as an opportunity for repentance. Like the church in Laodicea, this open door in heaven does not represent our first opportunity for change. Just as God specifically indicted Laodiceans in Revelation 3:14-22, so the Holy Spirit repeatedly convicts people of wrong priorities and unworthy objects of worship today. Some of us have become spiritually lazy and presumptive of the perverse idea that "God will forgive me no matter what," as if God is obliged to allow people to continue in error and disobedience without any repercussions. When such is the case, we risk becoming hardened to the Spirit's conviction and must be reminded again, as the open door reminded unrepentant Laodiceans that God keeps knocking. It is not too late for us to let him in, to repent, and to begin pursuing him again, but that will not always be the case. God's knocking eventually ends.

For those of us who have already received the call to repentance from a pursuit of the American Dream, we acknowledge the idolatry therein, and we turn toward a sole quest to follow God. Because we obeyed God in this way, we can receive the message of the open door, not as one that calls for repentance, but as one that rewards repentance. God invites us into his presence, where all our real needs and deepest desires are met because we seek him first instead of those needs and desires. We appropriately respond to that invitation through worship, as the rest of Revelation 4-5 outlines in great detail.

1.3.4 *What about Submission to Authority?*

As I wrote the last section, I could almost hear some readers ready to close the book if I do not quickly address the "biblical mandate to submit to authority." If you did not have that in your mind, you should be asking me to address the topic. Several portions of the NT demand obedience to leaders, and we must look at those passages to ensure that my proposals against nationalism and Trump's specific brand of nationalism are indeed well aligned with the Bible. The first thing we should notice about these passages is that most of them appear in the context of spiritual leadership, not secular governments (e.g., Titus 2:1—3:11; Heb 13:17–18; 1 Pet 5:1–11). Ruling out those kinds of passages, we are left with three passages that extend outside of Judeo-Christian communities, applied to governmental leaders. I found no fitting place for this discussion in the body of the book, however. Instead, in Appendix 2, I explain and defend an interpretation of each of the three remaining passages. In that appendix, I recognize biblical submission as a command toward a system, not a person. I argue that the Bible recommends but never demands, that believers obey any laws that do not compromise biblical justice as a way to keep a good witness before unbelievers. The Bible also instructs us with far more of a commanding force, especially in Revelation, to stand against individual leaders and administrations whose actions promote *syncretism* or are unnecessarily harmful to people whenever it is in our power to do so. This scriptural command is precisely the reason I take aim so squarely at specific political leaders. Although I attempt to do so in a bipartisan manner, the United States's political landscape at the time of writing was almost entirely controlled by Trump's Republican Party, thus creating a need for lopsided criticisms.

1.3.5 What Is Nationalism?

Biologist Robert Sapolsky wrote a fascinating article based on recent findings that demonstrate the brain's innate tendency toward tribalism. As a biologist and not a sociologist, he uses a different definition of "nationalism" than the one I use throughout this book. He defines it in terms of competition and tribal thinking. These characteristics are not necessarily negative or sinful. On the other hand, I will always refer to nationalism as sinful and idolatrous. Based on his biological view of nationalism, Sapolsky concludes: "Modern society may well be stuck with nationalism and many other varieties of human divisiveness, and it would perhaps be more productive to harness these dynamics rather than fight or condemn them. Instead of promoting jingoism and xenophobia, leaders should appeal to people's innate in-group tendencies in ways that incentivize cooperation, accountability, and care for one's fellow humans. Imagine a nationalist pride rooted not in a country's military power or ethnic homogeny but in the ability to take care of its elderly, raise children who score high on tests of empathy, or ensure a high degree of social mobility. Such a progressive nationalism would surely be preferable to one built on myths of victimhood and dreams of revenge."

Sapolsky's suggestion to use our natural tendencies for tribalism and competition for the good of all humanity finds parallels in Scripture. The twelve tribes of Israel each had distinctions in their roles of accomplishing God's plans (e.g., the Levites were responsible for temple maintenance and worship). Each tribe received an allotment of land according to its family background as a fulfillment of divine promise. Differences within that land are based solely on the population of each tribe. Diversity existed because the tribes had different purposes, yet Israel was one nation; God intended the tribes to reflect that unity, not to divide them. Division between Israel and Judah through a vast part of the OT demonstrates that God's chosen people were not always able to live within the realm of the healthy, idealized tribalism God had designed. Nevertheless, the ideal type of tribalism is a God-ordained social structure, not a nationalistic one (according to my definition of "nationalism").

Similarly, Paul instructs his audience in Rome to "outdo one another in showing honor" (Rom 12:10). As such, he directs Roman believers towards a type of competition that looks a lot like Sapolsky's proposal of what tribalism can be at its best. All the cultures of the ancient world embraced collectivism. They knew nothing about the Western individualism of the last two centuries. Their concept of "self" can be described by saying "I am who I am within my community." This mindset is squarely opposed to modern individualism's self-absorbed value of "being myself." Paul's call to compete in showing respect to others is a command for listeners to compare their selflessness with that of others. Following a sociological definition of "nationalism," I define the word as identifying one's personhood with his/her nation. Such ideology resists the type of positive tribalism that Sapolsky writes about.

1.4 Invitation into the Heavenly Realm

When John hears the voice that sounds like a trumpet speaking to him a second time, that voice summons John to witness the spiritual realm. The phrase "come up here" is accompanied by a promise regarding what he will experience. It points back to the opening of Revelation, where John explains that he saw events that must take place shortly. The invitation, therefore, calls John into the heavenly realm. The two foci of the vision are the forthcoming future for John's own time and absolute truth. These emphases are precisely why the vision begins with worship instead of details about *eschatological* judgment or Jesus's second coming. The angel invites John into a glimpse of heavenly worship. John does not merely observe that worship, but he participates in it and encourages his hearers to do the same.

1.5 In the Spirit

John reports that at the same moment as he received the invitation, he was in the Spirit. The temporal nature of the Greek construction used here might appear to imply John was only in this state briefly. Greek grammarian Daniel B. Wallace compares the tense of the verb to a snapshot capturing the single moment fully.[13] Even though John does not use a verb tense that indicates he was "in the Spirit" before or after this given moment, the context suggests that he remained in this state throughout his visionary experience.

In Revelation 1:10, John says he was "in the Spirit on the Lord's Day" implying worship. That verse is an introduction to his report of an *ecstatic* encounter with God that involves the *charismatic* gifts. This verse is an introduction to a *charismatic* encounter with God, specifically, a vision. The Holy Spirit is the source of such encounters and is himself the presence of God who lives in believers. The Holy Spirit, as the conduit of God's presence, shows John a different dimension of that same divine presence already at work in him.

1.6 Thrones and Politics

John envisions the placement of twenty-five thrones. One belongs in the center, and the rest placed around it subject themselves to it. This passage includes some of the more obvious imagery in the book of Revelation, since a lengthy and detailed worship scene follows. The Messiah sits on the single throne in the center, while worshipers sit on other thrones around him. The singularity of the throne in the center is a clear indication of God's sole worthiness of worship expressed though his Messiah, which is the main point of John's Apocalypse.

John's vision displays that God alone is worthy of worship. John could have expressed this in many ways to his audiences, as he does throughout the book. Nevertheless, throne imagery is the most common way he expresses that truth. Why a throne? Because this is Jesus's revelation. One of the most important characteristics of Jesus that the book unveils is his identity as King of Kings and Lord of Lords. It points out a political truth. Jesus's reign as Messiah King is greater than any king or other type of world leader throughout history. To have people on subordinate thrones indicates human involvement in God's political system in which Jesus is king over everything. Furthermore, the imagery explains that such involvement is the substance of the worship that God demands. We worship God by subjecting

---

13. Wallace, *Greek Grammar*, 554–55.

ourselves to him and remaining loyal to him as opposed to any earthly government or nation. We want all that we do and everything we say to bring him glory. We want to follow him, and we want to live in ways that will encourage others to do the same.

John sees thrones, because they reflect the earthly political realities with which he was familiar. The description of beautiful jewels and bright colors decorating the throne room might sound so splendorous and bright to us that we feel overwhelmed, especially those of us who do not even know what all those jewels look like. However, this description is actually mild and mundane compared to descriptions of the Roman imperial throne room that can be found from antiquity.[14] This restraint helps to show that the political reality John experiences in the vision is a transcendent one, greater in majesty and power than any Roman emperor could have ever imagined, yet with no need for an appearance that impresses people on a superficial basis. The imperial system at work throughout the whole era of the Roman Empire was one built on a pretention that it was the greatest authority in the world. Emperors were declared gods after their deaths, and a few even claimed divinity during their lifetimes (although most considered the latter to be improper).[15]

The throne in the middle of other thrones, therefore, shows that God alone is God, so no world leader possesses the right to claim divinity. Nevertheless, John's audience would have been familiar with emperors who were treated as gods. The individual prophetic messages of Revelation 2–3 demonstrate that each congregation had a different relationship with the Roman Empire and its imperial cult. Hearing the message of thrones placed in heaven would resonate with them all. Each hearer would likely have known instinctively if he or she was among those who commit syncretism, attempting to worship both the true God and any of the various deities abounding in the empire.

1.6.1 *Thrones and the Politics of Pergamum*

The prophetic message to Pergamum includes the first reference to a throne in Revelation that does not belong to God or his worshipers. John writes, "I know where you dwell–where Satan's throne is–yet you keep my name and did not deny my faith even in the days of Antipas my faithful witness who was killed among you where Satan dwells" (Rev 2:13). In the third century BCE, Pergamum was established as a Greek city. Attalus I reigned at the

---

14. Aune, "Roman Imperial Court Ceremonial, 6.
15. Corbett, "Paganism and Christianity," 850.

time, and his throne was in Pergamum. He went by titles such as "lord and savior" that carried the same divine and messianic connotations that the throne imagery in this portion of Revelation insists must be reserved for God's Messiah, not for any earthly ruler.[16]

Knowing this history behind the establishment of the city makes it easy to understand why the prophetic message to Pergamum referred to "Satan's throne" existing in the same city where the congregation was. Hearers who were part of that congregation would receive the revelation that they are part of a kingdom that transcends the earthly monarchy they knew. In that earthly empire, they had known some of the worst persecution that Rome perpetrated. The name Antipas (a shortened form of a common Jewish and Greco-Roman name) probably refers either to a victim of Nero's widespread persecution in the mid-sixties CE or one subjected to the more localized Christian oppression occurring later in isolated parts of the Roman Empire like Pergamum.[17] The church was commended for its faithful endurance in the midst of atrocities. They chose to worship at the throne of their God and his Messiah instead of the throne of their emperor.

Paul's letters to various congregations often condemn idolatry. In those letters, Paul expresses a conviction that something demonic is always at work behind any false object of worship, as informed by his OT knowledge (Deut 32:16–17; Ps 106:36–38). This connection between idolatry and demons existed beyond the OT and formed how all NT authors theologized, as evinced by *noncanonical* literature of the *Second Temple* period (*Jub* 22:17; *1 En.* 99:7; *T. Sol* 26:7). It demonstrates that Paul had centuries worth of precedent on which to base this conclusion.[18] Revelation's prophetic message to the church in Pergamum confirms Paul's belief, as the phrase "Satan's throne" alludes to all the demonic works that flowed out of the system of emperor worship. Thus, John provides an absolute contrast for believers in Pergamum between the throne in the prophecy addressed to them and the thrones of Revelation 4:2. While the prophecy lauds the congregation for its faithfulness in the midst of a location extremely unfriendly to monotheistic worship in 2:13, the next part of the prophecy rebukes the congregation for its willingness to tolerate some of the demonic works flowing out of "Satan's throne." An OT reference compares their actions with those of Balak and Balaam (Num 21–23). John's use of the story implies that the congregation has not fully heeded the words God has given to them. Further, their

---

16. Aune, *Revelation*, 180–81.
17. Koester, *Revelation*, 287.
18. Moses, "Love Overflowing," 26–27.

disobedience has contaminated other believers in their midst, just as happened in the OT story.

For Pergamum's believers to hear that John saw thrones placed in the heavens reminds them of their relationship to the location in which they live, since it includes Satan's throne. The thrones placed in heaven present the polar opposite of the one belonging to Satan, so to hear about these heavenly thrones calls Pergamum's hearers to continue worshiping only at God's throne and also to renounce the tolerance of idolatrous actions abounding around and among them. The language in the prophetic message seems almost contradictory. Jesus praises the congregation for their faithfulness to God in the midst of Satan's throne, but later he condemns their unfaithful behaviors. This paradox likely means that the assembly was trying to live in two worlds, subject to two thrones: God's and the emperor's. One of Revelation's clearest messages is its prohibition against all *syncretism* like that attempt. Nevertheless, God is patient, always guiding people toward the renunciation of idolatry and toward the sole worship of him.

1.6.2 Thrones and the Politics of Laodicea

Along with the message to Pergamum, Laodicea's message also includes throne language. Members of the Laodicean church, therefore, found special significance to their own situation upon hearing that John saw thrones placed in heaven. The throne in Laodicea's prophecy is a divine throne like the one in Revelation 4:2–4, unlike the throne in Pergamum's prophecy. In 3:21, Jesus promises the Laodiceans, "I will give to the one who conquers to sit with me on my throne, even as I also conquered and sat down with my Father on his throne."

Therefore, when a Laodicean Christian would have become aware of the thrones in Revelation 4:2–4, he or she should have associated it with the earlier message just for the Laodicean congregation. In order to have a part in these thrones being placed for worshipers around God's throne, Laodiceans must first conquer the complacency, idleness, and pretentions of self-sufficiency that Jesus had against them.

1.6.3 Thrones and the Politics of Contemporary American Readers

The United States is not a monarchy, so throne imagery does not mean as much to us as it did to John's audiences. However, because of the symbol's significance throughout Scripture, throne language exists in much of our worship. Hymns like "Crown Him with Many Crowns" point to the kingship of Jesus in ways we understand even though we do not live in an empire *per se*. Thrones are for kings and gods, so the thrones for worshipers in Revelation 4 signifies that those worshipers rule as kings with God, whether they are actual earthly rulers, marginalized citizens, or parts of any category in between.

1.6.3.1 Greco-Roman Paganism, Democracy, and The Throne of American Politics

Although the United States has no king, it shares many affinities with empires including the ancient Roman Empire that Revelation condemns. To use the same symbolism as the prophecy to Pergamum, Satan has a throne in American politics where religious and political realities are conflated. The United States replaces God as the subject of worship with the country's flag, military, president, or any other uniquely American representative or symbol. This risk of idolatry has existed since the country's foundation; this truth is on display at the nation's capitol. In the introduction to section 1.6, I mentioned that emperors were often named gods. That process is known as *apotheosis*. The Constantino Brumidi painting, "The Apotheosis of Washington" displays prominently in the capitol rotunda in Washington, DC. Brumidi modeled the painting after pictures from ancient Greco-Roman artifacts that show a recently deceased emperor joining the heavenlies to rule with the rest of the gods. The painting includes a rendering of many Greco-Roman gods and goddesses welcoming Washington to divinity. At the center of these heavenly proceedings is Libertas, the Roman goddess of freedom, after whom the Statue of Liberty was modeled. The decision to keep this portrait displayed in the nation's central political location represents a decision to declare George Washington and Libertas national gods. You can view the painting from different angles on the Wikipedia page for "The Apotheosis of Washington." You can also use the links to view pictures of some of the ancient *apotheosis* portraits that inspired the artist, so you can compare and contrast the two forms of idolatry.

Even though nationalistic religion is part of the founding of our country, it has never been realized as obviously in everyday life as it has since Donald Trump's election. Ancient Rome was commonly called "the eternal city." It was the center of the empire both politically and religiously. The attribution of eternity assumes not only that the city will last forever (an arrogant enough presumption on its own). The presumption also implies that the empire possesses some kind of inherent greatness that makes it superior to other nations and that no person, god, or circumstance can hinder or end that greatness. This presumption offers a perfect definition of nationalism. Nationalism is both a symptom of political arrogance and a religion. It places the given nation and its ideals as the center and driving force of a person's (or community's) life. It is the foundation of imperial cult, whether that of a literal empire like ancient Rome or a democracy that has given into imperial tendencies. Nationalistic expressions have always been present in the United States and have never been confined to a single political party. Further, their prominence has wavered to drastically different levels throughout the country's history.

Thrones are meant for bowing. People prostrate themselves before a person on a throne to demonstrate political loyalty, religious devotion, or both. Since we do not live in a bowing culture, it may be difficult to appreciate some of the throne language. Nevertheless, we too have our symbols of political loyalty and religious devotion. We do not bow to show deference to a person in power; instead, we are likely to stand in their presence or perhaps salute military professionals. We think of bowing, on the other hand, as a physical form of worship, whether or not we do it. Even more commonly, we tend to think of the heart as the seat of worship within a person. We commonly talk and sing about giving our hearts to Jesus and about our hearts being a throne for Jesus, since God's Spirit dwells within his people. Roman Catholics began the tradition that many believers follow of making the sign of the cross over the heart, signifying that same devotion and worship. Nevertheless, many of us also place our hands over our hearts to sing the national anthem or to say the Pledge of Allegiance. Such symbolism risks *syncretism*. We may talk about our hearts belonging to Jesus, yet through these symbolic actions and because of the words involved in both, we may give spiritual authority over our lives to an idol. Specifically, we can surrender to a personal vision of what we think the United States is supposed to be.

Much controversy has occurred concerning how people respond to the flag. Some Christians bizarrely accused NFL players of idolatry, because of their "take a knee" protest. As just stated, however, we do not live in a bowing culture. The protesters gave a very clear and completely secular definition for their symbol. Colin Kaepernick lucidly outlined his motivation for the protest as a movement against the national tendency of racially motivated police brutality. He worked out the plan for his protest with Army veteran Nate Boyer in an attempt to avoid offending veterans.[19] Thus, every aspect of his protest not only delegitimizes accusations of disrespect toward veterans, but also allegations of idolatry. Refusing to stand for the anthem

---

19. See Garcia, "Did a US Veteran."

represents an unwillingness to honor a governmental system that protesters believe has failed them. Their raised fists symbolize resistance against the evils of systemic racism. This protest is an entirely social statement, not a religious one, though it is a social statement that reflects the Christian value of love for all people. The non-religious nature of the protests, however, render allegations of idolatry completely ludicrous.

On the other hand, the entwining of religion and politics makes idolatry inevitable. Therefore, the real spiritual risk in this scenario belongs to the people offended by how others treat the flag. This offense places undue love and devotion in a mere symbol. The technical term for this sin is "iconography," a type of idolatry that the Ten Commandments explicitly prohibits (Exod 20:4). While protesters avoid worshiping the flag or the country, their detractors want to spiritualize political action by assuming that kneeling is only for worship. Since they possess this assumption, their popular bumper sticker boasting, "I stand for the anthem and kneel for the cross," is actually a confession that admits: "I try to worship two gods."

Paul's letter to the Colossians attends to this same problem. The whole letter is about the Messiah's sovereignty over pagan religions and even over some Jewish traditions, when those customs become habits that either oppress other people or attempt to hinder the inclusivity of the New Covenant. In Colossians 1:21–23, Paul encourages believers to continue shunning the idolatry commonplace in the Roman Empire. Paul even includes a caveat to the power of Jesus's redemption in this passage. Reception of that redemption depends on consistent hope in God and his Messiah that never wavers in favor of presumptuous hope in any source other than that of the gospel message.

Similarly, upon hearing about thrones placed in heaven, members of the assemblies in Pergamum and Laodicea were confronted with the question of whose throne they worship at—God's or the emperor's. American Christians must wrestle with this same question, even though we do not have an emperor. We have a flag, a set of values that the country was built upon, a president, a national anthem, a Pledge of Allegiance, and national gods deified in the capitol rotunda. These examples are only a few of many national symbols, people, and pursuits that can become gods, even for followers of Jesus. If we do not fully allow God to sit and rule in the thrones of our hearts, we will become guilty of *syncretism*. Because these national symbols are so ingrained in the ways in which we have been raised (for those of us who have lived in the United States our entire lives), it becomes easy to justify the worship of nationalistic idols. We might wrongly assume that they are not idols at all, but that God is glorified by our rigid cling to national heritage. When national political events like presidential inaugurations include church services, this phenomenon becomes particularly pronounced.

1.6.3.2 Thrones of US Nationalism and Interpersonal Relationships

Any kind of nationalism is harmful to all relationships. So far, we have discussed the harm it causes to vertical relationships (those between God and people). It also has the potential for great horizontal division. Now, you might be under the impression that ancient Israel was a nationalistic institution, because it was the chosen people of God. Indeed, God chose a nation out of all others to be his people on earth. However, from the very foundation of that special relationship between God and Israel, its purpose was for Israel to be a blessing to all nations (Gen 22:18). God never planned to have a single nation of followers, but he chose one people group to bring the inclusiveness of his reign to the whole earth. In the middle of judgment pronouncements against many nations that have oppressed Israel, Isaiah 19:18–25 interrupts the judgment theme to proclaim the purpose of that judgment. This purpose is international repentance, so that all people will ideally respond by forsaking idolatry, ending their harmful treatment of Israel, and worshiping YHWH alone. Only in this way could Israel accomplish its purpose as the people of God.

God indeed has a chosen people. Initially, that chosen people was ancient Israel and Judea. Since the time Judea was conquered by the Roman Empire, all Jewish people scattered throughout the world remain the chosen people. This designation is based on the concept of election in Romans 9–11. Although that text refers to all Israel (that is, God's chosen people throughout all ages) receiving salvation, it does not suggest that every individual of Jewish or Israelite decent receives the Jewish Messiah and his salvation. Nevertheless, Jews remain God's chosen people according to the divine election. Though God has a chosen people, he has had no favored country once ancient Israel ceased to be a nation. As such, nationalism (including nationalism in the current, secular nation of Israel) cannot accomplish God's will for people throughout the world but works against it instead. God's kingdom is global and unifying; anything apart from unification actively resists God's plans for the world.

The arrogance of American nationalism reaches much farther than the perverse sense of superiority over other countries. The times when nationalism has held the most prominence among American thought have also been the times of the most violence and hatred within the country. Andrew

Jackson's Trail of Tears that killed thousands of Native Americans flowed out of a belief that the land was only meant for people who shared Jackson's culture. Slave owners used biblical Scriptures to justify controlling, abusing, and killing people, because they believed they had rights as Americans and Christians over people who had been kidnapped from Africa, whom they considered to be their property. This spiritual and political phenomenon continued into the twentieth-century civil rights era, which was in part a fight between two conflicting interpretations of Scripture. Leaders fighting for civil rights began their demonstrations in churches and kept the genuine teachings of Scripture at the forefront of their fight. Their opposers, on the other hand, acted not out of faithfulness to the Bible, but out of devotion to their perceived entitlement, on which the country was founded.

1.6.3.3 Connection between the Thrones of Nationalism and Racism

Although its manifestations have changed, these sins of racism and nationalism, on which the country was founded, remain alive and deeply connected today. After the killing of George Floyd in Minneapolis that appeared to begin a national reckoning on race, white people protested and willingly proclaimed that "black lives matter" in an unprecedented way. White American Christians, however, have been far slower than other white Americans to accept the reality of systemic racism. Conservative Christian researcher Robert P. Jones founded the Public Religion Research Institute (PRRI) in association with the Southern Baptist Convention. The PRRI indexes levels of racism. The organization's index identifies white people who label themselves Evangelicals as the most racist people in the nation, albeit usually without recognizing their racist attitudes.[20] It is highly significant that the Southern Baptist Convention is involved with this index, since that denomination represents the largest number of white Americans who call themselves Evangelicals.

White Americans fall into the traps of racism and nationalism today when we neglect to understand that both evils were responsible for the creation of white supremacy. Much light has been shed on nationalism in recent years due to the concept of white nationalism that spawns from white supremacy organizations. Nationalism, however, is far broader than that application and has its roots in the founding of the country. Many see displays of white nationalism and think, "That's not me, so I can't be racist." By that assumption, white people delude themselves out of the responsibility we

---

20. Jones, "Racism among White Christians," para. 6–8.

must take to stand for our brothers and sisters of color. The PRRI's racism index shows that white Christians are twenty percentage points more likely than non-religious white Americans to deny the existence of systemic racism.[21] When we refer to something as systemic, we mean that it has infiltrated every aspect of our society. It impacts all of us, whether we are aware of it or not. For this reason, I caution all white Americans (myself included) against ever saying or thinking, "I can't be racist." On the other hand, because our society is so thoroughly ingrained with racism, it is better for us to all admit that we might be racist and work toward identifying the actions and attitudes that keep us that way. The former NFL player Emmanuel Acho has offered a helpful and very peaceable tool toward this end. His podcast series, "Uncomfortable Conversations with a Black Man," gently and lovingly confronts white Americans with ways we have been culturally brainwashed to perpetuate racism.[22]

Although Abraham Lincoln made the Emancipation Proclamation, the evils that began in slavery continue today in different forms and will continue until rooted out. Slavery is the reason systemic racism exists against black people in the United States. Historians have demonstrated how modern policing techniques began during the last days of slavery in the South to keep slaves in line. The North had a constable system adapted from the United Kingdom (which is still active and effective in the United Kingdom today). After the Civil War, however, the North replaced its constable system with a militarized policing plan that functioned almost identically to the antebellum South's system of keeping black people under their control.[23] Just as modern US policing has its roots in slavery, so did the segregation laws of the twentieth century.

Civil rights organizations in the 1960s began in churches, empowered by God to stand against real persecution. They organized according to principles of equity and love, not nationalistic worship. Many white Christians today, however, have fallen prey to the belief in an imaginary oppression that makes them particularly vulnerable to both nationalistic and racist sins. Such believers are blinded to the roles they have played in perpetuating both evils. Even though not all nationalism comes from white supremacy, all white nationalism has its roots in white supremacy. White Christians, therefore, risk giving into lies of white supremacy without realizing it. We do so when we do not understand the roots of our beliefs.

21. Jones, "Racism among White Christians," paras. 2–24.
22. See https://uncomfortableconvos.com.
23. Kapperler, "Brief History of Slavery," paras. 1–2.

It has become commonplace to label racism as the United States's original sin. In the book, *Reading Revelation Responsibly*, Michael J. Gorman offered partial agreement with that assessment though limiting it to the nation's original sin against humanity. He suggested that nationalism is a separate original sin that the nation has perpetrated against God since its establishment.[24] Because both of these sins are tied intimately to one another and to the founding of our nation, I think that we can take one step further back to diagnose a single original sin. Documents that accompanied the foundation of the United States included beliefs that all people possess "inalienable rights." At the same time, the creators of these documents owned slaves, through which they proved that they did not really believe that all people possess those rights. They upheld the desires of those who first emigrated to the United States seeking rights including the right to life and the freedom of religion. Nevertheless, they simultaneously denied those same rights to the indigenous people were here before them and to their slaves. We must realize that our country was not founded to be a Christian nation, as so many modern Americans believe. Rather, the founding fathers initiated their own religion centered around individualism, self-interest, and intolerance of other people. Such people determined that they and other people like them (i.e., the white people who came to the United States from Europe) were eligible for the rights they sought. They understood themselves to be entitled to rights that others did not deserve. Their evil sense of entitlement paved the way for both American nationalistic religion and all forms of American racism. If we understand entitlement as America's original sin, then I believe we can begin overcoming the wrongs that continue to flow out of it.

1.6.3.4 Thrones of American History

In attempting to disprove the notion that the United States is a Christian nation, I must point to the religious language in the Constitution and other documents connected to the country's origins. They reflect deism, not Christianity. Deism is the belief that accepts a divine creator who would never intervene in the world created. The philosophy leaves no possibility for redemption or forgiveness, but it gives humanity its own role to play in sustaining and reestablishing the created order.[25] Most of the founding fathers espoused deism (while a few, including Thomas Jefferson, considered themselves Unitarian), not Christianity. Displays at the Ethan Allen

---

24. Gorman, *Reading Revelation Responsibly*, 54.
25. Williams, "Deism," 190.

Homestead Museum clearly demonstrate these self-descriptions of the founding fathers.[26] This fact further illustrates the entitlement that the founding fathers possessed when they engaged in their own perceived god-like roles to form a new world. Their entitlement continues to plague us today.

The Mayflower Compact remains the source many use to defend the position that the United States was established on Christian values. Indeed, that document was produced by Puritans escaping England's King James I. It was created in 1660, however, while the United States did not become a nation until 1776. Independence from England made the United States a nation. Therefore, when searching for the nation's founding principles, we must look to the Declaration of Independence and other works of the founding fathers. The founding fathers produced these documents a century after the Mayflower Compact.

The Founding Fathers used and adapted the governmental aspects of the Mayflower Compact to inform their vision of a "more perfect union." Unlike those who created the Mayflower Compact, however, the founding fathers' arrogance and entitlement sought not only a new nation but also a new nationalistic, *pluralistic* religion. The Mayflower Compact that influenced them, nevertheless, made clear distinctions between church and state that many modern Christian Americans reject, instead allowing the Republican Party to control the church. The Mayflower's occupants fled a literal empire that intended to force how they worshiped God. They interpreted this governmental coercion as a form of religious persecution and made it abundantly clear in their document that they desired a secular government. For good reason, they did not want a government telling them how to worship God. They recognized, therefore, that a new nation should not be established as a country that promotes or presupposes the practice of any religion amongst those who enter.[27] So, even the Puritans that some modern Christians credit as founding the country as a Christian nation did not want the would-be country to be founded on any religion or religious values. If we truly shared this priority that the writers of the Mayflower Compact expressed, we would be far more effective in our work to fulfill the Great Commission. When we encounter people of a certain religion (usually Islam) or of an atheistic or agnostic persuasion, we often approach them with attitudes of fear and anger. We treat them as if they do not belong in our "Christian country." That kind of attitude, whether we express it verbally or

---

26. Displays at the Ethan Allen Homestead Museum in Burlington, Vermont demonstrate this vividly.

27. Philbrick, *Mayflower*, 1–33.

not, will turn unbelievers farther away from the gospel message and hinder the work of God's kingdom on earth.

1.6.3.5 Thrones of American History Infecting the Present

We already discussed Christians who think they are persecuted for their faith, because people do not want to listen to them, though that reticence from others most often reflects the Christians' attitudes. Other American believers think they are disrespected when they hear people around them speaking in a language other than English, even though the United States has no official language. Still others might think that their culture is being attacked when they witness customs or religious practices with which they feel uncomfortable. Whatever the assumptions are, these Christians feel entitled to make the United States into the nation they think it should be. The Ku Klux Klan embodied these same traditions and violently attacked African Americans (and others they deemed inferior) in order to protect their culture and heritage. Although modern white nationalists try to distance themselves from white supremacy, they do the same things. They use the same language of culture and heritage. As they do so, all white Americans become susceptible to cultural brainwashing that can make us active participants in both racism and nationalism without realizing it.

Two reasons help explain why white Christians rank so unfavorably on the racism index despite not participating in the blatant hate crimes that mark white nationalism. First, because many American Christians have given into anti-intellectualism, they are prone to attempt approaching complex problems with simplistic attitudes (see appendix 3 for a list of other complex issues that anti-intellectualism reduces to simplistic responses). Some, for example, respond to the Black Lives Matter movement negatively, because all lives matter. Actually, that truth that some Christians throw out cavalierly is precisely the point behind proclaiming the three words "black lives matter." Systemic racism promotes behaviors that demonstrate that black lives do not matter to all Americans. If black lives do not matter, then all lives cannot matter.

The fact that Black Lives Matter is not a monolithic organization also illustrates the problems of simplistic responses amongst white people. The protesters do not all have the same views regarding how to solve the problems of systemic racism. Reactionary people who are not likely to process data tend to suggest that the Black Lives Matter movement wants to defund the police. Some protesters promote that kind of policy, but far from all do.

WORSHIP IN THE HEAVENLY REALM (REV 4–5)   61

The concept of defunding the police terrifies people who do not recognize what the suggestion entails. It does not promote chaos but rather suggests that the United States (or parts of the country) should return to the constable system the North had before the end of the Civil War. Such a policy would help to remove some of the long-standing racist history that infects modern police departments. Other protesters promote reformed police departments that are well-equipped to overcome the racist tendencies so common in policing throughout US history. Either way, the goal is to save lives, including police lives.

Many white misunderstandings of the organization, on the other hand, somehow seem to credit it with the ability to make policy decisions. The government's job (not the job of the Black Lives Matter organization) is to decide which proposal saves the most lives. The Democratic Party is divided over which proposal will accomplish that goal, and the Republican Party generally supports police reform. President Trump, however, possesses one of the rare completely dissenting voices that wants to disown responsibility for systemic racism altogether. His voice has clouded any search for truth in the midst of this national crisis, just as it has with the other crises we have faced during his presidency. Trump is the king of offering simplistic phrases (not even full sentences) that condemn the other side (or sides). He hypocritically accuses his opponents of the very things he does. He encourages his supporters to think in the same way. As such, he gains control over the hearts and minds of people who would rather listen to him than pay attention to the facts. In the last chapter of this book, we will discuss how this type of control is a form of witchcraft that the Bible condemns. Christians who support Trump risk being recreated in the image of a new god—Donald J. Trump—instead of being formed in the likeness of Jesus. When Christians act like Trump and make his message the driving force behind aspects of their lives, they cannot help but give into all the racist lies he tells. When people claim that Trump is not racist, that claim yields assumptions that they cannot be racist. They accept Trump's innocence despite his blatantly racist words and actions, which then gain *influo* (see chapter 1, section 3.2.3) over their own lives.

The second reason Christians are vulnerable to unintended racism, as related to Black Lives Matter, is a sincere desire to avoid compromising too much with the world. A friend who is an excellent critical thinker told me things he discovered on the Black Lives Matter website that sounded quite concerning. If his assessment is correct, then Christians should not associate themselves too deeply with the organization but find other ways to stand against systemic racism. As I looked at the website, however, I found nothing remotely objectionable for a secular organization. Rather, I believe my friend has exercised too much caution in the struggle we all must endure regarding how much of the world to engage with and how much to separate ourselves from.

Our job, according to the Great Commission, is to make disciples. We cannot fulfill that command if we look too much like the world and engage with organizations that promote idolatry or encourage its participants toward immorality. We also cannot be faithful to the Great Commission if we disengage from people who live in unbelief and sin. The official Black Lives Matter website has a "What We Believe" section that includes nothing about religious convictions. It is a completely secular and inclusive organization. As such, it allows people into leadership that many Christians would understand as practicing sinful behavior. It in no way necessitates, however, that all protesters or organizational leaders abandon any religious or moral convictions.

My friend had two particular problems with the organizational beliefs. First, he expressed concern over the organization's strong pro-LGBT stance. It welcomes people of all sexual orientations and gender identities into leadership positions. In the final chapter of this book, I will present context concerning the Bible's attitudes toward that topic that will probably surprise most readers (it necessitated that I rethink my own views). In the meantime, however, I simply want to say that not all believers with a conservative view of Scripture reach the same conclusions regarding what the Bible teaches about LGBT matters. At this stage in the book, I ask you to consider the secular workforce. If you are looking for work in a Christian community, you obviously want to find an organization that aligns well with your views of proper Christian behavior. If you are looking for a secular job, however, hopefully you are looking for work that fits your job skills and financial needs, not a workplace that looks like a church. Your workplace should become your mission field. You will be able to fulfill the Great Commission because of the unbelievers you meet as you work. If your employer had discriminated against people based on religion, sexual orientation, or gender identities, then they would be stealing your opportunity to reach people with the gospel. We should take this same attitude into civic engagement over social justice issues.

My friend had another concern over Black Lives Matter, one that also concerned me before viewing the website for myself. It regards an issue that would be completely hypocritical if it were true. The organization was founded in response to the police brutality that has killed many black men and a few black women. My friend told me that the organization is feminist to the point of being anti-male. If it were truly anti-male, then it would be expressing the viewpoint that male black lives do not matter, defeating the whole purpose of its existence. My friend's perception came from the following portion of the organization's purpose statement:

> We dismantle the patriarchal practice that requires mothers to work "double shifts" so they can mother in private even as they participate in public justice work.
> We disrupt the Western-described nuclear family structure requirement by supporting each other as extended families and "villages" that collectively care for one another, especially our children, to the degree that mothers, parents, and children are comfortable.[28]

This statement certainly takes a strong stance against our male-centric culture, but it merely empowers women for the purpose of seeking equality between the sexes. The last phrase, "to the degree that mothers, parents, and children are comfortable," clarifies that the organization will not tell anyone how their families should function. Rather, the statement calls attention to the Western idea of the nuclear family that is indeed male-centric at its core. The biblical vision of the family is one of equality. Ephesians 5:21–33 (with special emphasis on v. 21) shows that the husband's familial headship reflects the culture of Paul's time but did not need to hinder the required equity between the husband and wife.

Additionally, church communities in the NT culture functioned like extended families and villages that shared responsibilities for raising children. My friend understood this aspect of the Black Lives Matter movement as a Marxist type of Communism. To the contrary, it appears more like a pursuit of community in the midst of a highly individualistic culture. It in no way expects conformity to any communal rules as Marxism would. Christians should be able to embrace the search for community that Black Lives Matter expresses. If necessary, believers can offer alternatives to aspects of Black Lives Matter communities that do not align well with Scripture as we work with the organization in fighting this worthy and peaceful goal (Please note that violence and looting has only erupted because of independent individuals and entities; Black Lives Matter has consistently condemned that behavior whenever it has accompanied their protests). Participation with the organization and its protests does not necessitate that we lay aside our biblical convictions. In fact, the local Black Lives Matter protests that occurred in Columbia, South Carolina following the murders of George Floyd and Breona Taylor began with protestors singing "Amazing Grace."[29] As such, it seems we can be a better witness if we engage with protesters, stand

---

28. See "Black Lives Matter: What We Believe," paras. 17–18.
29. Daprile, "Amazing Grace," para. 8.

with them, fight for the justice they need, and help them gain the voices in our culture that have been forcibly silenced for years. As white believers do so, they can spread the love of Jesus alongside African American brothers and sisters, partnering with other believers to obey the Great Commission. Furthermore, the organization expresses a "global Blackness."[30] That identity can reassure us that the organization possesses at least some protection from the vulnerability to a left-wing nationalism that could easily beset an organization like this one. It is centered on international justice and equality, not on partisan politics or on a vision of how the United States should operate.

The organization's belief statement includes language of "dismantling" and "disrupting" that disturbed my friend. Dismantling oppressive power structures, however, was one goal of ancient apocalyptic literature. Whether promoting radical changes through prayer and fasting or more direct types of confrontation, apocalypses always provide a way to nonviolently speak truth to power. If we believe that God hears our prayers and acts in response to our intercession for others, the gift of prayer gives us one such opportunity. Along with this desire for radical changes within systems that surround us, Black Lives Matter is actively and successfully revealing the truths of systemic racism. As they reveal this reality, many of us white Americans need to awaken to our own participation in the oppression that people around us have endured. Then we can join in a godly and nonviolent resistance that accompanies opportunities to spread the gospel. I highlight these factors of Black Lives Matter, because I believe we can understand the organization as a secular apocalyptic group. Christians can support their overarching goals in good conscience without necessarily agreeing with every detail of their beliefs. We can partner with an apocalyptic movement and reveal spiritual truth alongside the movement's revelation of sociological truth. Referring back to our earlier discussion on *influo*, the Holy Spirit must remain our greatest defense against giving into to any aspects of the organization that can hinder our witness. When filled and led by the Holy Spirit, Christians can be the ones spiritually influencing unbelievers in the Black Lives Matter movement. When such is the case, we do not need to worry about swerving in our own relationships with God.

1.6.3.6 Thrones of Political Racism

The prominence of white nationalism had been marginalized until the time of the 2016 presidential election. The beliefs and groups existed before, but

---

30. See "Black Lives Matter: What We Believe," para. 10.

they were kept so far underground that they were not capable of much visible damage. Throughout his presidential campaign, however, Trump stoked fears, promoted nationalism, and gave a voice to the hate that had previously been mostly hidden. Early in Trump's presidency, the Charlottesville Unite the Right rally that killed Heather Heyer demonstrated the results of the president's implicit call for nationalistic violence. The Neo Nazis there were vocal about their devotion to Trump and about their gratitude to him for giving a voice to their fears and persecution complexes. He became the scapegoat to justify their actions and their "Jews will not replace us" chant. Trump continued to refuse to condemn white nationalism but instead insisted that "there were very fine people on both sides."[31]

Through passivity of this sort, Trump paved the way for the drastic increase of hate crimes and homegrown, politically motivated terrorism that has occurred since Charlottesville. For specific numbers on this increase, see the Global Terrorism Database.[32] For 2017, the database counts nineteen terror attacks involving murder or attempted murder by white supremacists, far-right-wing nationalists, religious supremacists attacking Jews and Muslims, anti-LGBT entities, male supremacists, or anti-abortion extremists. The database specifies that pro-Trump extremists were responsible for at least three of those nineteen. In that same year, only three Islamic extremist attacks occurred in the United States, before Trump claimed victory over ISIL (see chapter 6, section 1.3.2, for my use of ISIL rather than the more common ISIS). In 2018, forty-seven similar homegrown attacks occurred in the United States. Of those forty-seven, pro-Trump extremists were responsible for at least sixteen. In that same year, only one Islamic extremist attack occurred in the United States, while ISIL perpetrated countless attacks in Muslim-majority nations (some of which occurred after Trump claimed to end ISIL). In other words, most of the terrorism occurring in the United States since Charlottesville has resulted from people who cling so tightly to an ethnocentric ideology that it has become their god.

I understand that much of my discussion risks making nationalism sound like a Republican ill. Donald Trump's presidency has made forms of nationalism so obvious that they create the most powerful examples. Furthermore, I wrote the entirety of this book between the 2016 and 2020 elections. I do not suggest, however, that Christians who do not identify with the Republican Party (either as Trump redesigned it or as the truly conservative organization it used to be) are immune to the risk. I will offer one example from the other side. When I was in a short interim period

---

31. Watson, "Trump on Charlottesville."
32. See www.start.umd.edu/gtd/.

before a major life change, I found time to consume more news media than I wanted to (something that ended up being important in order to write this book). During that time, I watched the hearings to confirm Supreme Court Justice Brett Kavanaugh. I cannot count the number of times New Jersey Democratic Senator Cory Booker used the word "sacrosanct" to describe various US political institutions and civic duty during that hearing. When Booker ran for president in 2020, he continued that habit throughout his campaign. Booker claims to be a Christian, and I in no way intend to say whether he actually is or is not. I do not know him. I have no idea what is in his heart. I can tell, though, because of his appropriation of that word for something that originated from humanity and not from God, that he has fallen prey to nationalistic *syncretism*.

For us to imagine thrones being placed in heaven with John, we must recognize that only God or country can sit on the throne of any individual's heart. We must choose to shun the idolatry, arrogance, and racism associated with nationalism in any form in which we may have entertained it. This requires a great deal of introspective prayer that remains fully open to the Holy Spirit's conviction, since much of this idolatry and oppression of others is ingrained in our culture. In most cases, it is far less obvious and more patriotic than the Charlottesville display. As such, we may not even realize we have any involvement in it. To become part of the throne room scene with John, then, we must renounce any form of nationalism and other religious syncretism, preparing room for God to reign over every aspect of our lives.

The book of Revelation includes liturgical sections interspersed throughout. I intend to treat this book in a similar manner. Our first liturgy provides an opportunity to meditate on Scripture and to sing praise to God that helps us to pinpoint any ways the United States has replaced God on the thrones of our hearts either individually or corporately. Thus, you can use these liturgies whether you are reading alone or using the book as part of a Bible study.

Liturgy 1: Repentance and Renunciation of Idolatry

1. Sing the hymn, "Crown Him with Many Crowns." Matthew Bridges (music) and George G. Elvy (text, "Diademata"), "Crown Him with Many Crowns" (1851).

2. Recite Ps 20:8–9 [Note that these verses connect to the Hebrew text; English translations place this text at Ps 20:7–8; this translation is my own]:

> Some boast in the chariot and some in horses, but we boast in the name of the LORD our God. They totter and fall, but we rise and stand upright.

3. Make this passage your own prayer. Replace the objects of boasting that do not apply to your present surroundings with those that do. For example, you can say, "Some boast in the military and others in the government, but we boast in the name of the LORD our God. They totter and fall, but we rise and stand upright." Pray in this way multiple times until you have included all the things you recognize as unworthy objects of worship in your setting. Other possibilities can include (but are far from limited to): "Some boast in their guns and others in their wealth, but we boast in the name of the LORD our God" or "Some boast in the Republican Party and others in the Democratic Party, but we boast in the name of the LORD our God."

4. As you pray in this way, pay attention to any uneasy feelings associated with one or more of the potential idols you mention. This discomfort may be the Holy Spirit's nudging to alert you that the statement "but we boast in the name of the LORD our God" is not true for you right now. If that happens, confess the objects of worship you have fallen prey to and offer them to God. Then, verbally commit yourself to no longer boast in that wrong object of worship. Then try to pray the same proclamation, "Some boast in . . . but we boast in the name of the LORD our God." Do so repeatedly until you are certain that the statement reflects your deepest convictions.

5. Sing the worship song "Give Us Clean Hands" as a declaration of repentance and reception of God's holiness. Charlie Hall, "Give Us Clean Hands," SixSteps Music, 2000.

6. Respond to the Holy Spirit. This response will look different for each person or group. I will share my own experience of receiving freedom from nationalistic *syncretism* that will hopefully help. When I was in the seventh grade, one of my classmates was Jewish. I asked her why she never stood and recited the Pledge of Allegiance with the rest of us. She responded, "Because I don't worship a flag." At that young age, though I was a Christian, I assumed too much of a separation between Judaism and Christianity to be bothered by her statement. I merely

thought she was expressing a conviction that does not apply to the NT. That conversation might have been the only time I ever even talked with that girl. I do not remember her name or anything else about her. Yet over ten years later in 2004, I went to an NBA game with a friend. When the national anthem began and everyone around me stood up, I suddenly and randomly remembered those words she said to me. I had not thought of the encounter since the day it happened, yet I knew God was calling me to avoid participation in the activity. I stayed seated for a few notes. I reluctantly stood up at the urging of my friend, not wanting to make a scene over something that seemed so odd in the moment. I refused to sing and to put my hand on my heart. Since that day, I have not been able to attend any sporting event or other environment in which the anthem will be played in good conscience. In time, I received it as the Holy Spirit's conviction to flee from nationalistic worship. The Spirit may direct you in a completely different way than he led me, but the important thing is to listen obediently to whatever he might say during this time.

7. Finish responding to the Holy Spirit through meditation on the hymn, "Rise Up, O Saints of God." This hymn centers us on our calling to be representatives of the Messiah who are committed to social justice. Forness, Norman O. (music and text), "Rise Up, O Saints of God" (1936).

1.7 THE PEOPLE OF THE HEAVENLY REALM (REV 4:4–8A)

The main character of this throne room scene is the one seated on the throne. Nevertheless, other characters appear throughout the Apocalypse, and we read about some of them for the first time in this passage. The person who sits on the throne unquestionably represents Jesus. The identities of the others John witnesses, however, are much more difficult to pinpoint. Many scholarly debates have offered different possibilities of who the four living creatures and the twenty-four elders might refer to. Revelation is both a prophecy and an apocalypse. These two genres often require layers of interpretation and carry the potential for multiple referents for any symbol. Therefore, we should not expect a single correct answer to the question at hand.

In the following two sections, I will present many possibilities, some more likely than others. These are the first two of this book's several "Critical

Thinking Exercises." Later exercises will tend towards opposite sides of an issue that will encourage you to wrestle with preconceived notions on various topics. They will encourage you to deeply consider both sides of various issues. With these first two, however, I intend to ease you into the process, since it only requires you to wrestle with the likelihood of each possibility.

I present one section for each group of characters. Each begins with a table that outlines some of the most prominent ways of identifying the living creatures and the elders respectively.

Critical Thinking Exercise 1: Twenty-Four Elders

Categories for identifying the characters:	List of interpreters and their time of writing, followed by the specific identity that each interpreter ascribes to the characters:
Biblical Figures or Writings	1. Victorinus (200s): The Law and the Prophets (*ANF* 8:347–50). 2. Oecumenius (500s): Each elder corresponds to a specific OT figure.[33] 3. Andreas (500s): The twelve tribal patriarchs and the twelve apostles (*PG*, 106.253). 4. André Feuillet (1964): The witness of OT heroes.[34]
The Church	1. Martin Luther (1528) and John Wesley (1755): All deceased saints, with an emphasis on martyrdom for Luther.[35] 2. R. C. K. Lenski (1935); William Barclay (1976): The entirety of the church from all eras.[36]
Other Significant Interpretations	1. R. H. Charles (1920), G. B. Caird (1966), and Robert Mounce (1977): A gathering of angelic beings.[37] 2. G. A. Krodel (1989): Participants in an entirely future event of worship at the *eschaton*.[38] 3. David E. Aune (1997) and Grant Osborne (2002): Priestly orders.[39]

This table shows a variety of options available for understanding the identity of the twenty-four elders. As you look at the list, you can probably think of ways that several of them make sense with the context of Revelation. As such, we should not expect only one correct answer. Only Krodel's *hermeneutic* is

---

33. Hoskier, *Oecumenius*, 23.
34. Feuillet, "Twenty-Four Elders," 183–214.
35. Backus, *Reformation Readings*, 9; Wesley, *Notes*, 703–5.
36. Lenski, *Interpretation*, 172–75; Barclay, *Revelation*, 152–54.
37. Charles, *Revelation*, 1:129; Mounce, *Revelation*, 135. Caird, *Revelation*, 63.
38. Krodel, *Revelation*, 158.
39. Aune, *Revelation*, 229–30.

mutually exclusive. If the elders are part of something that has not yet been initiated, then it is impossible to argue that they symbolize any part of past or ongoing history. For that reason, we should determine that his suggestion is the weakest. We can wrestle with the rest of these possibilities, nevertheless, without expecting a single answer.

The late Jesuit scholar Fredrick J. Murphy offered another possibility to consider beyond the self-explanatory options in the table. His proposal attends to 1) the symbolic aspects of apocalyptic literature, 2) the necessity of a relevant message to the audiences of both prophetic and epistolary literature, and 3) the sociological realities to which the book of Revelation alludes. He refers to the twenty-four elders as a metaphor for earthly rulers who sacrifice their reign to the one whom they recognize as sovereign. Their attention to God's all-surpassing power as evident in the work of creation (Rev 4:10–11) further illuminates the humble recognition of God's reign being higher than all manner of human authority.[40]

Murphy's suggestion connects particularly well to the political realities that surrounded Revelation's first audiences in Asia Minor. After many chapters that condemn the actions of corrupt earthly kings, Revelation 21:24 suggests that some earthly rulers will submit themselves and their reign to God. As such, Murphy's assertion is valuable to us primarily for the contrast it provides to the majority of the earth's rulers. There are a few (though very few) world leaders (probably in all generations) who genuinely attempt to lead in deference and surrender to the sovereign King of kings and Lord of lords. Despite this value, nevertheless, we must be careful not to elevate it (or any of the other identifications listed here) as the only right answer to the question of who the twenty-four elders represent.

---

40. Murphy, *Apocalypticism*, 106.

Critical Thinking Exercise 2: Four Living Creatures

Theological Allegory	1. Irenaeus (ca. 130 to 202): Both the four Gospels and four elements of Jesus's ministry (royalty, priesthood, humanity, and the Holy Spirit).[41] 2. Victorinus (200s): The Gospels, four aspects of salvation history (birth, death, resurrection, and ascension), and a demonstration of universal worship.[42] 3. Augustine (ca. 354 to 530): The Gospels.[43] 4. Joachim of Fiore (ca. 1135 to 1202): The four senses of Scripture (historical, theological, moral, and allegorical) and the four orders of the church (Roman Catholic ministerial designations of pope, bishop, priest, and deacon).[44] 5. W. Scott (1900): Judah, Reuben, Ephraim, and Dan.[45] 6. J. F. Walvoord (1966); A. F. Johnson (1981): Divine attributes of splendor, strength, capacity for intellect and spirituality, and freedom.[46]
Natural Allegory	1. Oecumenius (6th c. CE): The four elements of nature.[47] 2. Henry Barclay Swete (1918), George Eldon Ladd (1972), and Robert W. Wall (1991): The entirety of living creation.[48]
Historical Interpretation	1. R. H. Charles (1920), Austin M. Farrer (1964), and G. R. Beasley-Murray (1978): Depictions of Babylonian mythology's zodiacal sigs as related to Ezekiel's similar vision.[49] 2. G. B. Caird (1966): Pictures of Assyrian and Babylonian royalty.[50]

You likely noticed the overlap present in this table. Especially amongst the early church fathers, interpreters tended to have more than one explanation for the symbol. As such, many have taken these creatures to represent the four Gospels along with other referents. Many of Revelation's earliest interpreters possessed an affinity for allegory. They would understand almost anything in Scripture as representing something else. Later interpreters (especially those around the time of the Protestant Reformation) found

41. Irenaeus, *Haer.* 3.11.8.
42. Brighton, *Revelation*, 126–27.
43. Augustine, *Cons.* 1.9.
44. Joachim, *Lib. Conc.* 25v, 67v; *Expositio* 17–8.
45. Scott, *Revelation*, 126.
46. Walvoord, *Revelation*, 106; Johnson, *Revelation*, 641–42.
47. Hoskier, *Oecumenius*, 73.
48. Swete, *Apocalypse*, 134; Ladd, *Revelation*, 73–75; Wall, *Revelation*, 94–95.
49. Charles, *Revelation*, 1:133; Farrer, *Revelation*, 91; Beasley-Murray, *Book of Revelation*, 117–18.
50. Caird, *Revelation*, 63–64.

this allegorizing to be excessive and dangerous. Indeed, it can be dangerous when applied to historical works like the Gospels, Acts, or biblical epistles. A prophetic apocalypse, on the other hand, may have a historical grounding as we discussed earlier, but it transcends any historical setting. As a result, its language cannot always align with that of the other biblical genres. With that in mind, we are wise to listen to the church fathers' allegorical interpretations for some aspects of Revelation. Like them, we should not assume that symbols have a single referent, as we would when identifying symbols in other biblical genres.

All of the interpretive identifications in the graph have some merit. Contrary to *hermeneutical* patterns for almost all other scriptural matters, however, the current scholarly ideas for the identifications tend to be the weakest. They lean towards those I categorized as historical interpretations in that table. Although prophecies and apocalypses certainly point to historical realities, we must be cautious to avoid assuming identities that the original audiences might not understand. Linking the figures with Assyrian or Babylonian mythology and history works well for the books of Daniel and Ezekiel when similar creatures appear. Yet, those documents were produced for audiences that would have more familiarity with those legends than John's audiences. Since Revelation is written to followers of Jesus who were surrounded by the Roman Empire, they had access to the legends (i.e., orally-transmitted stories that can be either true or fictional) of the OT, the Gospels, Acts, Jewish apocalypticism, and Greco-Roman mythology. Revelation's four living creatures are very similar to those found in OT books. As such, the original OT referents may indeed have Assyrian or Babylonian points of reference, yet John would have likely considered those antecedents to be antiquated. He used them with the intention of pointing his audiences to the matters with which they were most familiar: Jesus's life and ministry, the OT, the burgeoning Christian movement, etc. The church fathers make this point better than many modern biblical scholars in part because they were not bound to black-and-white thinking that requires one right answer. They found no conflict in identifying these characters in several different ways. Neither should we.

2. THE WORSHIP OF THE HEAVENLY REALM (REV 4:4-11)

In between the two initial descriptions of the separate sets of characters in this passage, John lists cosmic disturbances that he witnesses in Revelation 4:5. This same list appears many times throughout the Apocalypse. In each setting, it appears to be a way of linking the heavenly and earthly realms. John uses them to explain that what happens in the heavenly realm impacts daily occurrences on the earth. John's experience with the elders and living creatures clearly takes place in the heavenlies. An angel guides John's tour showing him realities he had never encountered before. The lightnings, rumblings, and thunders indicate a relationship between the two realms. This interjection of cosmic disturbances interrupts the introduction of characters but precedes any activities of those characters. Since those activities are acts of worship, John indicates that the worship he experiences in the heavenly realm must also occur in the mundane.

John provides a liturgical order in this passage much like the OT instructions for temple worship. The demands of temple construction include cherubim, altars, and many other features that evidently mimic God's heavenly throne room. The *Pentateuch* provides directions not only for building the Temple but also for worshiping and sacrificing in it. The worship demanded there presents an earthly example of what worship looks like in heaven. Similarly, when we recite the Lord's Prayer, we do the same thing when we get to the third clause. The phrase, "let your kingdom come and your will be done on earth as it is in heaven," implores God to unite the heavenly and earthly realms in the present age. We know from Revelation 21–22 that the fullness of this unity will not happen until the end of the current age. Nevertheless, the kingdom of God and the will of God can be realized on the earth in the present age through worship. Therefore, through the list of cosmic disturbances and a liturgical ordering, John suggests that we can all join in the heavenly worship that he reported.

2.1 The Seven Spirits and Church Activity

John makes many references to "lightnings, rumblings, and thunders" in Revelation. This first instance is the only one to add the imagery of the seven flaming torches. The torches are among the rare symbols in Revelation that John explicitly defines. Nevertheless, explaining the torches as representing the "seven spirits of God" may sound so cryptic that it does not clarify anything for us. This thought would be true if John did not bring up "the seven spirits of God" in other parts of the Apocalypse. Since he does mention the "seven spirits" elsewhere, we can learn who or what the torches represent.

John's first mention of the "seven spirits of God" comes in Revelation 1:4. As part of the *epistolary* introduction, he offers a "grace and peace" *beatitude* similar to those of Paul's introductions. While Paul often credits God the Father and Jesus as the source of the blessing, John offers a threefold *beatitude*. John's grace and peace comes "from the one who is, who was, and who is coming; from the seven spirits that are before his throne; and from Jesus Christ the faithful witness, the firstborn from among the dead people, and the ruler of the kings of the earth." Many traditions assume that the *beatitude* is trinitarian, referring first to the Father, second to the Holy Spirit, and finally to the Son. Ancient Jewish and Christian numerology associates "seven" with completion, so John could have used the symbol to point to the fullness of the Holy Spirit or the completeness of the Spirit's ministry. This label is problematic, however, because John makes other clear references to the Holy Spirit as a single Spirit. Also, since the NT writers did not think in terms of trinitarian theology like later theologians would, we should not expect John to use that kind of language. Rather, the word "spirit" can carry multiple connotations. Since 1) there are seven churches, 2) each church has a messenger, and 3) the Greek word *angelos* can mean either "angel" or human "messenger," it is simplest to think of the "seven spirits" as each congregation's pastor.[51]

2.1.1 Seven Spirits and Sardis's Church Activity

The prophetic message to Sardis also includes a statement about the "seven spirits." "The one who holds the seven spirits of God and the seven stars says this" (Revelation 3:1b). This passage reveals Jesus in the same way as Revelation 1:20. The earlier verse explains explicitly that the "seven stars" represent the seven churches. Mentioning the "seven spirits" and "seven stars" again implies that God has special interest in ensuring that its congregation recognizes messianic revelation. The number "seven" appears many times in Revelation as we have already established, but the number of completion should hold even greater significance for this congregation. God rebukes Sardis as he says, "Come alive, and strengthen the remainder that is about to die, since I have not found your works complete before my God" (Rev 3:2).

The Greek word that translates to "complete" can also be rendered "perfect," as many translations read for the message to Sardis. The two words can be synonyms, although our culture tends to forget this aspect of the word "perfect." Of course, "perfect" can also connote doing a job scrupulously and getting every detail right. As a result, we can misread this prophecy (along with many other biblical encounters with the English word "perfect"), assuming that the congregation possesses multiple moral flaws. Though the prophetic message suggests moral failing later with the statement about "some who have not defiled their garments" (Rev 3:4), the text

---

51. Koester, *Revelation*, 363; deSilva, *John's Way*, 97n12, 169n9.

does not deeply connect that failure to the congregation's lack of completion. The reason for the rebuke at this earlier juncture is explained in the end of Revelation 3:1, "I know your works: You have a reputation that claims you live, but you are dead." A congregation develops a misleading reputation by being active. Activity does not give life. The majority of Sardis's Christians at the time must have had bold plans for big activities intended to bring the life of God to the Roman Empire. For Jesus to say, "I hold the seven spirits and the seven stars" suggests that their ideas might have been good but were not fully aligned with those of the Messiah (the one who holds them). The church's ministry might have been based entirely on good and godly intentions, but they did not complete their deeds. They must have planned in one of the following ways that did not align with the purposes of God: 1) Their plans were not informed by the Holy Spirit, 2) their programs placed their own desires (noble as they might have been) above those of their Lord, or 3) they became distracted so as to not finish their projects. Jesus does not rebuke their plans. Because of either their approach in decision-making or in working out their plans, they evidently did not reach their goals. Jesus rebukes the congregation's lack of completion. Thus, it has died figuratively. Jesus commands the church to come back to life, that is to receive life from the only one who gives life. Then, the Holy Spirit could empower Sardis's believers to complete the works they were called to accomplish.[52]

When John repeats the symbol of the "seven spirits" in Revelation 4:5, he encourages believers in Sardis to think about their own call to completion, wholeness, and life. In this verse, the "seven spirits" accompany the cosmic disturbances that represent the convergence of heaven and earth. This convergence reminds them of their responsibility to allow God to form and direct their community's life. Then, all activities that flow out of that formation constitute worship and serve as signs of spiritual life. With mere activity, however, the congregation would remain dead. Connecting the "seven spirits" with the unification of heaven and earth encourages the congregants to unite their earthly actions with heavenly, angelic worship. Only then can all their actions truly be worship to God. They must not assume they can do anything worthwhile apart from his leading.

2.1.2 The Seven Spirits and American Church Activity

The message conveyed to Sardis through John's repetition of "seven spirits" displays one of the easiest connecting points to American Christianity. This message is so universal it does not possess the cultural and temporal weight

---

52. Johnson, "Always on the Brink," 2.

that most of Revelation's symbols do. God calls all congregations, all Christian families, and all believing individuals to completed work. Many OT figures accomplished great things for God but did not finish well. The message in using the symbol of the "seven spirits," here, reminds us that we must make sure all ministerial activity we pursue is led by the Holy Spirit so we can bring it to completion. Partnering with God as he builds his kingdom on earth must be our top priority at all times. When we discern the specific deeds that God has called us to complete, we must not allow anything to distract us from finishing well.

Congregations of all denominations present good plans to fulfill the Great Commission, yet many of those plans go unrealized. Professional and lay ministers in all capacities suffer burnout. John's literary link between the "seven spirits" and the unification of the heavenly and earthly realms serves as a tool to help us fight against these two common problems. To know that God's kingdom is present is to know that an angelic army led by God himself is at work around us. Even though the symbol of the "seven spirits" probably does not refer to the Holy Spirit, it still can remind us that the Holy Spirit dwells and works within us—in the church and in individual believers.

Different denominations have different emphases regarding the ministry of the Holy Spirit. The emphases are all grounded in Scripture, but if we do not balance them, we can have lopsided theology. Some Protestant teachings (especially Baptist, Wesleyan, and Charismatic/Pentecostal) can unintentionally lead us to think that the Holy Spirit's empowerment is solely a personal blessing. If we think that way, then we will not involve ourselves sufficiently in the ways God works through community. We will put too much pressure on ourselves to complete the Great Commission in ways that will lead to burnout and much unnecessary pain in relationships. Without the church (that is, the whole church, not any given congregation or denomination), it is impossible to finish the works God has called us to complete. Nevertheless, Catholic and mainline Protestant denominations can accidentally lead us toward the equally wrong thinking that the Holy Spirit only works in gathered churches. If we think the Holy Spirit only empowers Christians during gatherings, we potentially miss out on opportunities to spread the gospel through our daily interactions with people that others in the congregation might not know. We risk idealizing those moments of encountering God corporately and *sacramentally* so as to limit worship to those times. That limitation risks missing the truth that all Christians are called to worship God at all times and in all places. We can do so through our actions, our words, our obedience to God's word and Spirit, and through our relationships with other people. When we submit our whole lives to God, our corporate and individual relationships with the

Holy Spirit empower us to know the will of God, to carry it out to completion, and to do so joyfully.

2.2 The Worship of the Four Living Creatures

Each group of worshipers offers a different liturgical expression of praise. John recounts the liturgy he heard from the living creatures first. The threefold repetition of the word "holy" was as familiar to Revelation's first hearers as it is to us today. We find this liturgical construction first in Isaiah 6:3. Isaiah's prophecy, though not an apocalypse *per se*, provides an apocalyptic vision with a heavenly *ascent* like apocalyptic authors wrote about. That *ascent* for Isaiah allowed him to see an expression of heavenly worship similar to what John records. Ascribing holiness to God in this repetitive fashion appears to have been common throughout all stages of Jewish and Christian worship since the initial reception of Isaiah's prophecy.[53]

The words that follow "holy, holy, holy" for Isaiah's seraphim are somewhat different than those of John's living creatures. Unlike John, Isaiah records personal involvement in the worship he sees. Isaiah expresses repentance in 6:5: "Woe to me, because I am undone. Indeed, I am a man of unclean lips, and I dwell amongst a people of unclean lips, yet I have seen the king—*YHWH* of hosts." Isaiah also participates in a *sacramental* activity in the following verses: "Then one of the seraphim flew to me, and he took a hot coal with tongs in his hands from the altar, and he applied it on my mouth. Then he said, 'I have applied this on your mouth, so it removes your guilt, and your sin is atoned for.'" John, on the other hand, does not record how he participates in the heavenly worship.

John certainly had familiarized himself with OT Scripture prior to writing Revelation. That familiarity does not mean, however, that we should understand his allusions to the OT in exactly the same way as his source material used it. John saw something that was similar to what the author of Isaiah recorded, but it was not the same thing. The apocalyptic prophetic characteristics of both passages necessitate a direct message for their audiences. Since Revelation's initial audiences were distinct from Isaiah's, John's use of similar imagery probably points to something different than Isaiah's.

---

53. Humphrey, *Grand Entrance*, 81.

2.2.1 The Worship of the Four Living Creatures and Pergamum's Singers

Keener's *IVP Bible Background Commentary* is an accessible work that provides historical and cultural context for each book of the NT. He explains that the worship of the four living creatures reflects not only a heavenly phenomenon but also a Greco-Roman imperial one. Choirs in Pergamum arranged themselves like John's animals and sang hymns structured like the one found in Revelation 4:8. They did so to worship the deceased, deified king Augustus.[54] John's vision, therefore, includes two examples of literary parody. This form of worship originated with Isaiah's vision. John's similar vision of the spiritual realm attacks emperor worship as a parody of true worship. The true worship that John sees, then, is itself a parody of Roman emperor worship. This dual parody announces that God alone deserves this attribution, that no emperor is worthy to be named "holy." Revelation's singers explain creation as a reason to ascribe holiness to God. As God made all things, he is separate and above them all. Singers in Pergamum credited Emperor Augustus as being separate from and greater than the created order. John, thus, shows the folly in worshiping a mere human being or any other part of the created order.

The prophetic word to Pergamum's congregation refers to the city as the place where Satan's throne dwells in Revelation 2:13. This worship scene, therefore, points directly to Pergamum's liturgical role in the imperial cult. It also broadly condemns any songs that attribute divine holiness to any figure other than God. We must distinguish here between divine holiness and general holiness. *YHWH* commands the Israelites to "be holy since I am holy" (Lev 11:44). The NT repeats this mandate under a New Covenant framework in 1 Peter 1:15. Peter specifies: "Be holy in all your conduct." This distinction sees divine holiness as separation and transcendence above all else. It recognizes human holiness as the appropriate response to experiencing divine holiness. Divine holiness made the sacrifice of the cross possible. Our response must be one that aligns with God's moral order. As such, it is not inherently idolatrous to refer to a person as holy, as long as personal holiness is understood as a morally responsible reply to divine holiness. Any attribution of holiness outside of this context consists of idolatry.

---

54. Keener, *IVP Bible Background Commentary*, 725–26.

2.2.2 The Worship of the Four Living Creatures and American Patriotic Music

Nationalism often produces liturgies parallel to the ones for which Jesus rebukes the city of Pergamum. Any belief that a nation is greater than others assumes that the nation transcends the attributes of others. Such a worldview makes an arrogant separation between one's own country and every other part of the world. It places people of a given nationality above other created humans, deeming one nationality holy. We can recognize this tendency in many patriotic songs but none as obviously as the relatively modern "God Bless the U.S.A. (Proud to Be an American)." Lee Greenwood wrote and popularized this song in 1984. Each phrase offers worship to the country and ironically corresponds with the Christian hymn, "My Hope Is Built on Nothing Less," which Baptist pastor Edward Mote wrote in 1834.[55] Therefore, we can use these two anthems to find a modern parody that distinguishes between acceptable and unacceptable worship similar to John's use of literary parody. Because of the time in which it was written, I can freely quote from the Mote hymn without delaying publication for copyright purposes; the same is not true for "God Bless the U.S.A." Therefore, I recommend you find a recording of that song or a transcription of its lyrics to help follow along with the rest of this section.

The first verse of Greenwood's song declares that the US flag gives Americans reason to keep living during the darkest of circumstances because of the liberty and security that the flag represents. This parallels the third verse of Mote's hymn that includes the line, "His oath, his covenant, his blood sustain me in the raging flood. When all supports are washed away, he then is all my hope and stay." Greenwood suggests that something separates the United States from other nations, and he derives hope from that distinction. That hope empowers him to rejoice in the worst of circumstances. His song calls people to worship the American ideal of freedom through a claim that nothing in the world can remove it. This belief is exceedingly arrogant and ignorant. The United States is not invulnerable to attack. Any attack on the nation strips some of its freedom.

To say that liberty cannot be taken away ascribes spiritual transcendence to the United States. Furthermore, John finishes his description of the worship by indicating that "the one who lives forever" is the recipient of the worship. This statement likely mocks the idea that Rome was the "eternal city." God is the only one who lives forever, since he had no beginning. Greenwood suggests, to the contrary, that the United States

---

55. Greenwood, "God Bless the U.S.A."; Mote and Bradbury, "My Hope Is Built on Nothing Less."

possesses everlasting rights and freedom similar to what many members of the Roman Empire believed about the city of Rome. John clarifies that only God—through Jesus's work, death, and resurrection—can offer the kind of hope "God Bless the U.S.A." assumes. The end of the chorus for "My Hope Is Built on Nothing Less" says, "all other ground is sinking sand." The hope Greenwood contends for in his song is built on two arrogant and ignorant assumptions: his country can give him a reason to keep living when circumstances are at their worst, and the freedoms associated with being an American will last forever. These convictions are excellent examples of "sinking sand" that provide no real or lasting hope.

The chorus of "God Bless the U.S.A." attempts to make nationalistic pride sound desirable. Declaring oneself proud to be American may not sound dangerous or sinful. Nevertheless, the declaration identifies people with their national heritage. If a person said, "I'm proud to be a Christian" or "I'm proud to be a Jew," ideally that would mean, "I'm proud of the God who created this world, has accomplished so many great works for his people, and who has a great future for those whom he calls his own. I am proud to be called his," as opposed to a boasting in religious affiliation. The first kind of pride I described in the last sentence aligns with what Paul often calls "boasting in the Lord." Pride in religious affiliation, however, assumes a false sense of superiority over others. Out of that superiority, people risk refusal to reconcile with past and present evils that have been committed in the name of Christ. As such, this pride risks tolerance of the unnecessary historical violence of the Crusades and the current bitter divisiveness between denominations that causes dissention throughout the whole church. Pride in religious affiliation prevents us from being the witness of love to unbelievers that we are called to be (John 13:35). Hypocrisies matter no longer when boasting in one's religious affiliation.

Similarly, to assert pride in being American identifies oneself with a past and a present that includes some noble deeds along with some blatantly evil ones. It risks embracing everything that the United States stands for and everything it was founded on. If we assume that nationalism and slavery were only problems for the founding fathers that do not impact our current generation, then we unknowingly tolerate and perpetuate these sins. As every other nation in the world, however, the United States was built by humans on human principles. To express pride in being American elevates oneself above people who are not American. At worst, it even implies, "I'm proud to be identified with a nation responsible for slavery, the Trail of Tears, internment camps for Japanese Americas after WWII, the separation of children from their legally asylum-seeking parents at the southern border, and the other atrocities it has committed throughout its years." At best, it is to pride oneself in leaning fully on "sinking sand."

The hymn we are comparing and contrasting with Greenwood's anthem has a clause in its first verse that says, "No merit of my own I claim, but wholly lean on Jesus's name." To pride oneself in American identity claims a part in the massive sense of entitlement and self-aggrandization that paved the way for some atrocious acts of hatred. It expects the guarantee of certain rights because of national identity. This entitlement suggests that being an American is a personal merit that offers many selfish benefits. To identify oneself with Jesus, however, means laying aside self-centered assertions of greatness and giving up rights (both real and perceived).

The chorus of Greenwood's song also offers worship to veterans. It claims that their deaths give life to Americans. I in no way want to express ingratitude for people who have risked or lost their lives to protect others from grave harm. Nevertheless, assuming that the gift of life can flow from a veteran's sacrifice to other Americans assumes that such people are life-givers. They must exhibit something otherworldly, or holy. It credits veterans with the same things the four living creatures and twenty-four elders clarify are only true of God. Such veneration makes veterans gods much the same way surviving Greco-Roman warriors were treated. Marches of those victorious in imperial battle involved legions of patrons ready to glorify the conquerors.[56] The physical actions of this ancient cultural phenomenon parallel the assemblies many elementary and high schools force their students to attend every Veteran's Day. These festivals train children to "give glory" to veterans in the same way that the four living creatures "give glory" to the Messiah.

Again, I wish no disrespect against those who have fought in battle. I am certainly grateful to my grandfather who fought in WWII. As such, I understand war to be necessary in some rare cases. Whether a given war is a necessary evil (like WWII to stand against murderous schemes being enacted throughout the whole world) or an unjust waste (like I would argue for most US wars, but that subject is for another book), it seems better to classify veterans as heroic victims rather than merely heroes. All warfare is caused by injustice, and those fighting are always among the victims of that injustice. It may be the injustices of dictators like Hitler, Mussolini, and Hirohito in WWII. Alternatively, it could be the injustices of a government that learns there are no weapons of mass destruction as previously thought but continues to demand the same military action as if that presumption was true (the second Iraq War). In either scenario, the soldiers are victims. To focus

---

56. Hope, "Dulce et decorum," 35.

on heroism without victimhood risks elevating their military accomplishments to the status of divine sacrifices. A soldier's work deserves our respect, but we must not exalt it as a life-giving sacrifice. When soldiers' lives end, their military service has no impact on whether or not God will receive them in heaven to await resurrection. The second verse of "My Hope Is Built on Nothing Less" states, "his anchor holds beneath the veil." But "God Bless the U.S.A." gives veterans the spiritual authority of being the anchor that keeps Americans living the lives to which they believe they are entitled.

The end of Greenwood's chorus implies that sacrificial deaths impart a spiritual reward on all who are willing to receive. Of course, there has been only one fully sacrificial death. The spiritual benefits of Jesus's sacrificial death only became apparent after his resurrection. The marks of the American religion are the courageousness to die (whether for a noble cause or an unjust one) and the reception of rights through the worship of people who expressed that courage. The final verse of Mote's hymn contrasts with Greenwood's presumption by its expression of real spiritual reward. "When he shall come with trumpet sound, O then in him shall I be found, clothed in his righteousness alone, faultless to stand before God's throne." We must trust in the only completely sacrificial death and the resurrection that followed that death as our source of hope for the resurrection of all the Messiah's followers. Resurrection, then, is the only source of real and lasting hope.

In section 1.6.3 of this chapter, we looked briefly at how Paul's letter to the Colossians sends a similar warning against dependence on any source of hope that does not come from the gospel. In Colossians 2, Paul furthers this warning with regards to his audience's pagan surroundings. The "elemental spirits of the universe" in Colossians 2:8 refer to the worship of created things at the expense of appropriate worship of the Creator. "God Bless the U.S.A." promotes the worship of aspects of the created world, whether the natural landmarks of states praised in the song (in the verses I have not worked with here) or the deeds of people created in God's image. These aspects of the song suggest that as people who desire to wholeheartedly live for Jesus, we must recognize that "God Bless the U.S.A." is a pagan hymn that promotes idolatry through nationalism.

2.3 The Worship of the Twenty-Four Elders

Immediately after John recounts the worship scene of the four creatures, he does the same thing for those identified as elders. Like the living creatures, the elders sing, but they offer a more physical form of worship first. They prostate themselves before the throne and cast down crowns before the one sitting on that throne. This pattern (a physical symbol of submission, followed by offering gifts, and concluding with extolling words) dates at least as far back as the twenty-third century BCE. It ascribes honor to a person in authority. Its historical attestation is intermittent, but nonetheless significant, as it demonstrates a long precedence for such actions with which John's audience was apparently familiar. As such, it paves the way for the audience to see multiple associations between the worship of the elders and the actions of their own cultural surroundings.[57]

John's use of this pattern is significant for understanding what worship looks like in the heavenly realm. We have already discussed the actions of bowing or prostration that can either be sacred or secular expressions of loyalty. Gift-giving, of course, can also fit either purpose. The words spoken, however, are the climax of the progression. This climax in the text makes the scene unequivocally worshipful. The elders declare the Messiah worthy of worship on the merits of his involvement in creation with God the Father.

2.3.1 The Worship of the Twenty-Four Elders and Roman Imperial Crowns

All portions of the Roman Empire valued crowns, also called wreaths. Many people would render their wreaths to others in a fashion similar to the elders casting theirs before the messianic throne. This act could be done for religious or social purposes. Different contexts allowed for different means of removing wreaths and giving them to others. Defeated rulers surrendered to their conquerors by casting down crowns before them.[58] Roman followers of the Persian god Mithras would receive wreaths, place them on their heads, and then remove them to symbolically name Mithras as their crown.[59]

John's cultural environment (and that of the seven congregations in Asia Minor) involved the use of such wreaths for many varying purposes. Thus, Romans, Jews, and Christians all had experience with crowns and would have been culturally entrenched with the norms regarding the use of them. University of Notre Dame professor David E. Aune offers seven categories for the broad ways in which John's audiences would recognize the action of the elders: 1) to bestow honor on another person, 2) to recognize a great achievement, 3) celebration, 4) a symbol of one's submission

---

57. Aune, *Revelation*, 288. Cf. Westenholz, *Kings of Akkade*, 95; Tadmor, *Tiglath-Pileser III*, 225; Exod 35:21–35; 4QDeut[a] 32.43; Matt 2:11; Acts 4:36–37.

58. Tacitus, *Ann.* 15.29.

59. Tertullian, *Cor.* 15.

to another, 5) a religious practice, 6) to signify a martyr's reward, and 7) a representation of immortality.[60]

Aune's broad categories make it easy to recognize how the action of casting crowns fits within the Revelation 4 worship scene. As the elders lay down their wreaths before the Messiah's throne, they follow the preceding worship of the four animals to "give him glory." They recognize the great achievements of creation and redemption. They celebrate their deliverance from the power of sin and death accomplished at the cross. They indicate their surrender to God and his Messiah. They worship God liturgically. They give Jesus the reward of honor for his martyrdom. Also, they take part in the immortality of God the Father and Jesus the Messiah through the promise of resurrection.

2.3.2 Roman Imperial Crowns and the Church in Philadelphia

In Revelation 3:11, Jesus tells Philadelphia's congregants, "I am coming quickly. Hold fast to what you have so that no one removes your crown." The prophetic message to Philadelphia's Christ-followers contains only commendation. These congregants have remained faithful in some extraordinarily difficult situations. So, the command Jesus gives them diverges significantly from the directives to other congregations. Jesus did not tell Philadelphia's believers to repent, surrender, or obey. Instead, he told them to continue doing what they were already doing. The prophecy promises them that if they hold fast, they will keep their crown. This statement implies they already had a crown.

The crown promise is preceded by a reference to a door kept perpetually open to them in which to experience God's presence, a list of the ways in which they had stayed firm in their commitment to the Savior, and a divine promise to protect them from a forthcoming time of distress that would impact the entire world (probably the destruction of Jerusalem that occurred in 135 CE). The promise of the crown is followed by a temple-related promise, but the temple was destroyed in 70 CE and has never been rebuilt. The message's final promise seems to clarify the temple promise: "I will write on him [on the person who conquers] the name of my God and the name of the city of my God (the new Jerusalem that comes down from heaven), and my new name" (Rev 3:12b). Revelation 21–22 expounds on the New Jerusalem that Jesus will establish at his second coming. That New Jerusalem has no need for a temple. Just as the presence of *YHWH* stayed perpetually in the Jerusalem temple, so God will be ever present—presumably physically

---

60. Aune, *Revelation*, 172–76.

through Jesus—in the New Jerusalem. In that sense, Jesus is the New Jerusalem's temple rather than a building. Jesus calls each of Philadelphia's congregants a "pillar in the temple." This label must signify that the congregation's devotion to the Messiah prepares its members for their roles in the New Jerusalem. John may use contradictory language (a temple in the New Jerusalem according to Rev 3:12, but no temple in it according to 21:22), but his imagery adds up. Both passages refer to the New Jerusalem as the center of the restored earth in which Jesus rules eternally. Revelation 3:12 operates under a broad rendering of temple that does not necessarily need to be a building, while Revelation 21:22 alludes specifically to the Jerusalem temple building.

Since John clarifies earlier that Jesus is the source of the words for the prophetic messages in Revelation 2–3, the name of his God and his own new name are one in the same, *YHWH* (see this chapter's section 4.2 for more on *YHWH* as name of God given to Jesus). This part of the prophecy connects to the "open door" promise of always having the presence of God available to the congregation both in the present and coming ages through Jesus. The "name of the city of my God," on the other hand, does not consist of something that already existed for them, since it will arrive with Jesus's second coming. As such, the beginning of the message with its "open door" and the end with the reference to a "new Jerusalem" suggest that Jesus's words to Philadelphia are all about resurrection. When we look at the seven different categories for giving crowns outlined above, the most logical one that Philadelphia would have anticipated is a symbol of immortality. Since resurrection to eternal life is the main subject of the prophetic message for the congregation, they would have probably understood the reference to "crowns" in Revelation 4 as a call to continue faithfully worshiping God. Jesus has already approved of their worship, so they could join the heavenly surrender of crowns. To lay their crowns before Jesus would be the only way to keep their crown (their immortality). Thus, they could ensure that nobody unworthy steals their crowns by way of encouraging them to transfer their devotion and faith to a source other than *YHWH*.

2.3.3 *The Worship of the Four-Living Creatures and American Christians*

The seven categories for Roman crown-casting reveal not only what worship looks like in the heavenly realm but also what it should look like on earth. The wide variety of reasons for offering wreaths signifies that not all wreaths are necessarily for worship. Nevertheless, all can be part of a worship setting as they commonly were in Roman pagan environments. As such, this portion of the worship scene must cause us to ask ourselves, "Who or what do we surrender to"?

In previous sections, we discussed the United States's financial prosperity in different contexts. Within this discussion, since we live in an extremely wealthy nation, we must ask ourselves how we use our wealth as individuals, families, and Christian congregations. When our emphasis is entirely on buying or saving, we surrender to the god of the American Dream. Our money must be a prominent way in which we worship God. The OT Law demanded a tithe (10 percent) of everything (including money and goods). The NT presents a higher demand. The message of the entire NT is that God gave his all to humanity through his Son. Receiving that gift from God requires us to give everything back to him. Everything about who we are as individuals must likewise be God's. If everything we have and everything we are belongs to God, then we can follow in God's love. "God so loved the world that he gave his only Son" (John 3:16). If everything we are and everything we have belongs to God, then we echo that love and give it freely to the world. The Western individualism that surrounds us emphasizes what belongs to "me." It demands "my rights." Neither the cultures of the Bible nor most cultures around the world today think in these terms. For us to enter this worship scene with John, we must stop presuming upon anything as our own and become willing to give everything to God through freely giving in a communal sense (i.e., "what's mine is yours" as in Acts 2:44, not Communism).

As we see the twenty-four elders give their wreaths to God, we must also lay down our lives at the throne. This surrender means we become willing to partner with God as he builds his kingdom on earth. In order for our finances and our belongings to be his, we must determine to use everything we have in life for the purposes of his kingdom. Every thought, desire, and plan must align with his kingdom purposes. Only when our worship is marked by surrender to the King of kings and Lord of lords, can our lives be realigned in this way. For us to lay our crowns at the feet of Jesus means to give up the notions of self and to live so as to build up the worldwide community of believers, draw unbelievers into relationship with God, and restore justice to the fallen world wherever possible. We proclaim God's worthiness to rule over his whole creation as we allow him to rule over our lives. We are no longer our own. We belong to God, and we belong to the family of the global church. Thus, we must lay our lives down to him through living for others and not for ourselves.

Liturgy 2: Joining the Worshipers of Revelation 4

Each part of this chapter's section 3 corresponds well with a hymn or worship song. So, the liturgy here is simply to sing each of these songs. First, "All Things Rise" matches the discussion on the convergence of heaven and earth. Second, "Holy, Holy, Holy" follows the same liturgical pattern that John saw the twenty-four elders follow and also alludes to that worship scene. Finally, "My Hope Is Built on Nothing Less" responds to Jesus's sacrifice in like manner to the four living creatures.

1. Sam Yoder, "All Things Rise," VinyardSongs, 2015.
2. Reginald Heber (text) and John Bacchus Dykes (melody, from "Nicaea"), "Holy, Holy, Holy," 1861.
3. Edward Mote (text) and William B. Bradbury (melody), "My Hope Is Built on Nothing Less," 1837.

3. THE SCROLL, JESUS'S WORTHINESS, AND REIGNING WITH GOD (REV 5)

3.1 The Scroll's Content

Scrolls were the predominant form of written communication in the ancient world. As we discussed in chapter 1, though, the ancient world always preferred verbal interaction to written. As a result, written documents from this time period usually served as replacements for face-to-face discussions when distance or other factors made such conversations impossible. Scrolls throughout Scripture reflect this value. They were expensive to produce and thus used only for the most important of documents. The OT reports their efficacy for governmental records (Ezra 6:2), prophetic messages (Jer 36:2–4; 45:1; 51:60–64), and urgent interpersonal correspondence (Jer 36:6–19). Their content demanded to be read aloud and heard (see Isa 29:18–21), since no one possessed the idea of reading silently until many centuries after the Bible was written.

OT authors also make symbolic references to these documents. In Psalm 7:7, David refers to a scroll on which his pursuit of and obedience to *YHWH* are eternally etched. Ezekiel recounts a vision involving a scroll quite similar to the one in Revelation 5 (Ezek 2:9—3:10). Ezekiel and John both have apocalyptic prophetic experiences in which an angel tells them to eat a scroll (Rev 10:9–11), representing the condemnatory nature of the message that each visionary was charged with conveying. Immediately after this heavenly worship, John takes his readers to earthly judgment via the unveiling of the seven seals.

Revelation 6–18 focuses on divine judgment. John places his description of eating the scroll in the middle of all this judgment, indicating that he has much more warning to do before completing this most difficult part of his mission. As prophets, both Ezekiel and John must warn people concerning the eventual consequences of sin, so as to call for repentance. Yet, their job was to send the message. Neither was responsible for whether or not anyone actually repented. Revelation is only twenty-two chapters long, so over half of its chapters detail God's retribution against the unrepentant. This characteristic certainly contributes to why so many people fear the book. Nevertheless, the point of it is to encourage people toward repentance. It provided that opportunity for its original audiences, and it does the same for today's readers, thus offering hope. Revelation's first five chapters set the stage for this call to repentance as they point to God's glory. They agree with the rest of the Bible that God is the perfect embodiment of both love and justice. These dark and violent scenes are preceded by everything an audience needs to hear to know that judgment flows out of God's love for his people.

Since Revelation 5's seals represent the first set of judgments in Revelation 6:1—8:4, the scroll must contain judgment. John says that the scroll has writing on both the inside and the outside. This reflects ancient legal texts, particularly the last will and testament. It shows how God's love for his people and his judgment work together. We can see, then, that the scroll's writing contains God's will for the earth as expressed through judgment. It offers proof that people can know God's will, even on a cosmic level. Yet, the unveiling of God's will (the unsealing of the scroll) clarifies that God's will can only be complete on the earth after all sin ceases.[61]

Revelation's first four chapters constantly highlight Jesus's death and resurrection as the way in which God dealt with sin. This incarnational miracle was the beginning of what the Bible calls the "last days." Jesus's sacrifice makes forgiveness available to all, but just like the people who heard Ezekiel's message, the recipients must respond through faith marked by repentance. We still live in a fallen world. That divine work at the cross ended sin only on one level; sin still pervades throughout the whole world. The complete removal of sin, then, requires judgment against the unrepentant. Evil's eradication means that God will meet every need for his people and restore the entire created order to health. Then, the will of God will be fulfilled.

---

61. Koester, *Revelation*, 383.

3.2 Jesus's Worthiness to Open the Scroll

Revelation 5 concerns itself primarily with proclaiming the worthiness of the one seated on the throne. John gives many different names and attributes for Jesus yet clearly indicates that each one refers to Jesus. When the worshipers announce Jesus's worthiness to open the scroll, they mean that he is worthy to know, to declare, and to take part in the completion of God's will. The Revelation 5 worshipers attribute this worthiness to Jesus based on the merits of his sacrificial death and resurrection through language of a slaughtered lamb and conquering hero.

This worthiness echoes Philippians 2:9: "Therefore, God also exalted him [Jesus] and gave to him the name that is above every name." Many modern worship songs declare that Jesus itself is the name above all names. Many believers (especially the Pentecostal circles I have been part of) encourage others to invoke the name Jesus during distressing events. Such believers assume that speaking the name Jesus will bring God's presence into the situation, because Jesus is "the name above every name." Likewise, believers of all stripes in the United States have the tendency to tack on "in Jesus's name" to the end of prayers as if they are magic words, since Jesus is "the name above every name." I fear that those who sing such songs or promote such activities do not understand what it means that God gave Jesus "the name that is above every name."

First of all, the context of the Philippians passage is much the same as the one in Revelation 5. Paul proclaims in Philippians 2:1–8 that Jesus is worthy of something that is bestowed on him because of his sacrificial death. Therefore, the name God gave him could not be the name he normally went by. Before his birth, prophets had already said he should be named Jesus. He was called by that name as long as he walked the earth. As such, the name Jesus is not the "name above every name." The name Jesus is a Germanic pronunciation of the Greek name *Iesus*, which comes from the Hebrew name *Yeshua*. *Yeshua* means "*YHWH* is salvation." In English, the name is rendered as Joshua. The name is so common that we see two different translations of it (Joshua and Jesus) multiple times each in Scripture. In Matthew's account of the trial that led to the crucifixion, he goes to great lengths to distinguish between the two people named Jesus in that story. Matthew makes definite distinction between "Jesus Barabbas"—the robber who was released—and "Jesus who was called the Messiah." The name Jesus is also identical to Jesús in Spanish, among many other renderings from many other languages. So, if Jesus is the name above every name, then the criminal Pilate released possessed the name above every name, Joshua is the name above every name, Jesús is the name above every name, and countless other forms of the same name count as the name above every name. This line of reasoning is heretical, so Paul must have meant something different when he said that "God gave to him the name that is above every name."

Jesus's prayer for his disciples as recorded in John 17:11–12 offers further clarity to this matter. The name given to Jesus elicits the response of worship. In Philippians 2:10–11, Paul explains the divine rationale for the name given to him. That purpose is so that "at the name of Jesus [i.e., the name God gave to Jesus according to the passage a few verses earlier], every knee should bend . . . and every tongue confess that Jesus Christ is Lord." Only God is worthy of the kind of praise that would cause every single person to bow before him and name him their master. This means that the name God bestowed on Jesus must be God's own name, the divine name, *YHWH*, the name God revealed to Moses at the burning bush (Exod 3:13–15), the name that is unquestionably above every name. The name is inherently part of Jesus's earthly name since the name Jesus means "*YHWH* is salvation," yet the meaning of that earthly name applies to all people, not just one.

Paul and both Johns (the Gospel writer and the author of Revelation) predated trinitarian theology, something that did not surface in its complete form until the eighth century CE. They held cautiously to traditional Jewish monotheism. To say that Jesus is God would have been very difficult for them. Yet, they all do so in roundabout ways through discussion of the divine name bestowed on Jesus. Their careful manner of speaking about Jesus as God ensures that they uphold Jewish monotheism.[62] John's record of experiencing worship that says Jesus is worthy to open the scroll offers further depiction of the Apocalypse's main point: Jesus is worthy to be worshiped, because God has given him his own name. In other words, Jesus the Messiah is one with God and always has been, since the reason God gave Jesus his own name (his death and resurrection) has always been part of the divine plan. Granted, we are likely to think in terms of time when we speak of someone giving something to another, but the bestowal of the name is part of the Triune God's very nature, not something that happened at a particular point in history. As the recipient of God's own name, Jesus can reveal God's will to the whole world, and he is worthy of the worship that God alone deserves.

3.3 Lion of the Tribe of Judah/Root of David

Revelation 5 accomplishes two literary goals. It portrays a worship scene and tells a story. That story does not seem to connect as directly to the seven

---

62. Walther, "Address in Revelation," 171.

churches as the Revelation 4 worship scene does. In Revelation 5, John narrates the pursuit and discovery of one worthy to open the scroll. John's story reflects an ancient Hebrew tradition of depicting heavenly courts (e.g., 1 Kgs 22:1–38; Isa 6:1–13) and includes three descriptions. Each description is steeped in OT symbolism. As such, we find a rare chapter in Revelation that seems to momentarily leave behind Greco-Roman imagery and focus entirely on Jewish history and culture.[63] Each messianic description provides a clearer picture of what it means to affirm that Jesus is Messiah, that he possesses the divine name, and that he is worthy of worship. We have already discussed the "lamb" imagery that dominates the passage, but we must also attend to the other images that John mentions but immediately abandons.

In Genesis 9:9, Joseph imparts a blessing on his son Judah in which Joseph names Judah a lion. Each of Joseph's twelve sons became one of the twelve tribes of Israel. John connects two OT titles for the Judean tribe. The Greek structure of Revelation 5:5 clarifies that the two names represent the same person. Isaiah 11 speaks of a coming Messiah and the Messiah's kingdom. The name "Root of David" makes its first biblical appearance in the same prophecy and refers to the coming Messiah. Both Judah and David appear in Matthew's opening genealogy of Jesus (Matt 1:2–17). John apparently combines the two names in order to ensure his audience knows he refers to Jesus as the Messiah. The "lion" attribute naturally refers to victory in battle as it did for Joseph when he blessed his son. Jesus accomplished victory in spiritual warfare by his death and resurrection. Being Judah's lion and the messianic descendent of David means that Jesus can complete the victory implied in Joseph's blessing. As a result, only Jesus is worthy to reveal the *eschatological* victory involved in God's will.[64]

3.4 Sending Seven Spirits

In section 3.1 of this chapter, we looked at how John uses the symbol "seven spirits" as another way of referring to each congregation's pastor. In that portion we discussed Sardis's lack of finished, Spirit-led work and the tendency of American Christians to emphasize part of the Holy Spirit's ministry (within the church or individual believers) to the exclusion of the other. This emphasis paves the way for unfinished works, attempted works that are good on the surface but not aligned with what the Holy Spirit has revealed,

---

63. Aune, *Revelation*, 335. For a survey of various viewpoints on the how much of the background for Revelation 4–5 is Jewish and how much is Greco-Roman, see Archer, "*I Was in the Spirit*," 25–30.

64. Beale, *John's Use*, 120, 239.

and in some cases ministerial burnout. In Revelation 5:6, John uses the imagery again. This time the Lamb's seven horns and eyes symbolize the "seven spirits." If we understand the "seven spirits" as the complete ministry of the Holy Spirit, as some do, then seeing those spirits as part of the Lamb connects to a type of trinitarian theology that risks anachronism. However, if we understand "seven spirits" as representing each church's pastor, as I suggest, then the act of sending the spirits gives further credence to the connection between the work of the kingdom and worship. When we understand kingdom work as worship, we should desire to grow in knowledge and wisdom of God's will both communally and individually. Such a pursuit unifies the church with God and helps it accomplish God's will. When we approach that pursuit with a humble spirit that is willing to look for any gaps between our will and God's, then we can come to discern his will. If we want God's will more than our own, we will obey when we know he has spoken. Anything done out of humble obedience is an act of worship.

3.5 New Song

The worship in Revelation 5 continues the theme of victory through the elders' "new song." Some of the most important examples of biblical worship involve composing and/or performing a "new song." Each one accompanies a divine act of deliverance in which God and his people conquer in some way or another. The songs of Moses (Exod 15:1–19) and Miriam (Exod 15:20–21) both follow God's defeat of Pharaoh and the other Egyptians who abusively enslaved Israelites. These hymns name the specific divine actions that led them to safety. Coinciding with the consistent OT directive to tell of God's deeds to their children and to people of other nations, Exodus's author seems to use these songs as an instruction for worship. The text places the record of the songs immediately after the description of deliverance. Therefore, it encourages hearers to always recognize God's work in their midst through offering words and songs of praise that can be remembered and taught for all future generations.[65]

Similarly, several hymnic passages direct worshipers to "sing a new song" that expresses God's good works for them (Ps 33:3; 96:1; 149:1; Isa 42:10). David's hymns most commonly include this instruction. David also mentions singing new songs himself. In Psalm 33:3, he professes that God directly gave him the song to sing; in Psalm 144:9, he promises to perform a new hymn to God in response to the personal deliverance he experienced. The OT calls for music in worship many more times than we have room to

---

65. Viljoen, "Die betekenis," 213.

discuss here. For our purposes, we must notice that hymns (whether "new songs" or established ones) function in two important ways in Scripture. First, singing about God's work is an act of worship. Secondly, the content of the songs teaches worshipers about God's worthiness and thus teaches them how to worship.

As a "new song," Revelation 5's hymn distinguishes itself from those of Revelation 4. John follows the OT tradition of recording the song written in connection to the deliverance that prompted the song. Again, the worshipers deem Jesus worthy of opening the scroll because of his sacrificial death and resurrection. The hymn that accompanies that knowledge expresses gratitude for the act of deliverance itself and for many of the ongoing *eschatological* blessings that flowed out of it. In the last section of this chapter, we will concentrate on the one such blessing explicitly declared in the hymn.

3.6 The Reign of God's People on the Earth

Revelation 5 offers two reasons for its claim that Jesus is worthy to open the scroll. So far, we have only dealt with Jesus's role in past redemptive history. The other reason is Jesus's role in future redemptive history (or at least the future from John's perspective over 1,900 years ago). "You made them a kingdom and priests for God, so they will reign on the earth." Since *eschatology* refers to the last days, and because the last days began with Jesus's earthly ministry, NT *eschatology* is far more extensive than most American Christians realize. The NT's central *eschatological* moment is the outpouring of the Holy Spirit that ushered in the church age (Acts 2) as empowered by the Messiah's death and resurrection. While many NT authors discuss the second coming and its attending resurrection of all people (e.g., John 5:25–29; 1 Cor 15:35–58), they concern themselves far more with either past salvation history or their present ministerial situations. Revelation emphasizes future *eschatology* far more than other NT works. One of John's *eschatological* motive is to connect Jesus's death and resurrection with his eventual return to take his place as king over the earth.

The Messiah's eternal, earthly kingship offers the most hope of anything the NT promises for believers. Much of Western Christianity has lost its way *eschatologically*. For most of us, our hope centers on the promise of going to heaven when we die. However, the Bible barely speaks of the state after death. References to an intermediary state between death and resurrection appear, but vaguely. They create no reason to build theology or even exercise much hope. All we know for certain about that state is what we can glean from Paul's statement that he "would rather leave the body and so be alive with the Lord" (2 Cor 5:8).

Even though we know this intermediate state must be preferable to the present, sinful state of the earth, it still leaves the body dead. All biblical *eschatology*, on the other hand, points back to Jesus's resurrection and forward toward a general resurrection. That latter resurrection of God's people ushers in Jesus's earthly reign. Jesus's second coming will not be momentary (or for a thousand years as some interpretations of the Revelation 20 millennium suggest). Jesus will not gather his people for the purpose of taking them to a heavenly home. Instead, Jesus will return to establish his eternal kingdom on the earth, in which he will reign with his people, making this very earth their home. When he does that, he will fulfill the hopes of all creation (Rom 8:18–25).[66]

The concept of a rapture that has inundated much of Western Christianity often perpetuates the overblown hope of going to heaven. Some rapture theologies understand an eternal, otherworldly existence as the source of all *eschatological* hope. The word "rapture" appears nowhere in Scripture. The concept comes from 1 Thessalonians 4:13–18. That apocalyptic passage reveals something significant about Jesus's second coming for the pastoral purpose of encouraging people regarding grief. Unlike John's Apocalypse, the audience of 1 Thessalonians consisted predominantly of gentiles.[67] As such, Paul addressed an audience who did not possess a Jewish apocalyptic worldview when he said that at the second coming, all living Jesus-followers will be "caught up in the clouds together with them [with those who have died] to meet the Lord in the air, and so we will be with the Lord forever" (1 Thess 4:17). Paul describes himself as being "all things to all people in order that by all means I may save some" (1 Cor 9:22b). He manifests this self-perception through his communication with the Thessalonians. In order to encourage gentile Christians to reject idols and fully conform to the image of Jesus, Paul uses imagery they would have understood. As pagans, many of them already believed in afterlife and some type of finality for the earth, but their perceptions of both were colored by fear regarding vengeance of the gods. Paul, therefore, intends to express a monotheistic type of *eschatology* that was foreign to his audience using images that would not be foreign to them.[68]

In addition to this authorial consideration, we should also pay attention to the motion and location of the gathering in 1 Corinthians. While

---

66. See Wright, *Surprised*.
67. Ascough, "Thessalonian Christian Community," 312.
68. Ascough, "Question of Death," 529.

returning to the earth, living saints are gathered from scattered locations throughout the world to meet God in a heavenly location only to join him as he returns to the earth. According to Wright, "the point is that, having gone out to meet their returning Lord, they will escort him royally into his domain."[69] The rapture, then, finds its purpose in initiating the reign of God's people with God in the earthly location that other portions of the Apocalypse refer to as the New Jerusalem.

We must recognize that the 1 Corinthians passage marks the only point in Scripture that uses this language. If we read it without the context provided above, then it contradicts the Bible's many consistent *apocalyptic* statements that point to an earthly resurrection at Jesus's second coming. Instead, we must admit that our Western Christian cultures have failed us with all of its "heaven" talk. When we base our hope for the future on Jesus's coming to the earth, we find real hope. We also avoid the risks of escapist mentalities associated with some rapture theologies. We do not expect God to get us out of "great tribulation" but to intervene in the midst of it. We anticipate the time when God will establish an eternal kingdom on earth that has permanently erased all the sin, death, and decay that the world has been subject to since the fall. We anticipate an end to all suffering that makes many agonies of the present age worthwhile. Since John says that God's people "will reign on the earth" with him, we await the time when we will be a completely unified body that actively participates with all divine activities. At that time, our desires will perfectly align with God's. In this future, we find real hope.

Many hymns and worship songs that originated in the West exacerbate the problems of our *eschatological* misunderstandings. Nineteenth-century pastor Thomas Salmon sent a poem written by his mentor William Walford to *The New York Observer* to inquire if the paper would want to publish it. Fifteen years later, after the deaths of both Salmon and his mentor, composer William Bradbury who put that poem to music, the paper published the hymn "Sweet Hour of Prayer." The hymn carries a beautiful message about the presence of God through prayer as a strong shelter in the midst of all of life's troubles. Its last verse, however, counteracts everything theologically profound and everything encouraging about the first three verses. Much of the final verse is so esoteric and super-spiritual that it makes no sense. At best, it is laughable to modern listeners who do not speak that way anymore. At worst, it marks one of the earliest messages to promote a disembodied eternity that accomplishes nothing more than escaping the troubles of the world. Thus, it played a significant role in shaping the same

---

69. Wright, *Surprised*, 133.

dangerous *eschatology* that permeates much of the church today. In his last verse, Walford wrote: "Sweet hour of prayer! Sweet hour of prayer! May I thy consolation share, 'till from Mount Pisgah's lofty height, I view my home and take my flight. This robe of flesh I'll drop and rise to seize the everlasting prize and shout while passing through the air, 'Farewell, farewell, sweet hour of prayer.'" This view of life after death offers as much hope as old cartoons that picture a character in heaven, sitting alone on a cloud, and playing a harp. Biblical *eschatology*, on the other hand, centers on bodily resurrection, an earthly reign with Jesus, and an intimate community of redeemed humanity from all generations. Heaven, then, is merely the intermediate state, the realm in which God dwells and his deceased saints await resurrection. That state is not eternal. Bodily resurrection in a renewed earth is eternal. We find real *eschatological* hope in this promise.

3.6.1 *The Earthly Reign and the Church in Thyatira*

The prophetic message to the congregation in Thyatira includes the promise, "As for the one who overcomes and keeps my works until the end, I will give him authority over the nations, and he will shepherd them with an iron rod, like clay jars are shattered" (Rev 2:26–28). Thus, congregants would have probably heard the Revelation 5:10 promise as something specifically for them. Thyatira poses the most difficulty of the seven cities for which to reconstruct a cultural context during the time in which John's Apocalypse would have been read to the seven audiences. Scholars have only established two certain aspects of the city at the end of the first century CE: its renowned military and its trade guilds.[70] The type of authority promised in the prophecy could relate to both.

Both military activity and trade guilds united with the Roman Empire's religious practices. Trade guilds consisted of social interaction amongst people who shared a given skill. Such gatherings involved meals, so they inevitably ate foods sacrificed to Greco-Roman gods. Wealthy Christians in Thyatira (and other provinces) found monetary and social value in these organizations.[71] The prophetic message to Thyatira pointed toward these people in the rebuke, "Nevertheless, I have this against you: You tolerate the woman Jezebel who calls herself a prophet, and she teaches and deceives my people to commit sexual immorality and to eat foods sacrificed to idols" (Rev 2:20). Paul's letters seem to make allowance for eating foods sacrificed to

---

70. Hemer, *Seven Churches*, 106, 108.
71. Thompson, *Revelation*, 122–23.

idols, so long as it does not lead to another person's crisis of conscience (1 Cor 8:1–13), while John's Revelation seems to condemn the activity altogether.

Do Paul and John disagree, or do other factors make the situation more complex than it appears? No convincing evidence exists that can fully answer this question, so I offer a partial answer based solely on the genre and rhetorical aims of each author. Paul wrote NT letters. John's Revelation is also an *epistle* but mixed with many other ancient genres. In Revelation, statements against eating foods sacrificed to idols appear only in the *oracles* to the individual churches in Asia Minor. As prophetic messages, John would not understand these as his own words in any sense. Surely, he viewed the whole experience as divine inspiration towards his Apocalypse, yet he remained deeply involved in the process. He generally chose the words to describe what he saw. Exceptions to this rule exist only when John claims that God directly told him what to say verbatim. So, John would say that the portions about eating foods sacrificed to idols were not his own words but Jesus.' Does that mean that Paul was wrong and misunderstood God's will for his audiences? Of course not. It merely refers to two distinct audiences. Paul's needed unity. John's needed holiness. Therefore, the safest determination we can make is that the Bible does not make an absolute statement against eating foods sacrificed to idols but that certain people were more liable to idolatry than others were when partaking in those meals. In other words, eating foods sacrificed to idols is not in and of itself idolatry, but it can lead to idolatry. Faithful Thyatiran congregants received the promise of authority in Revelation 2, not necessarily because they refused to eat foods sacrificed to idols. Rather, Jesus promised them authority, because they refused to do so in an idolatrous manner and because they remained sexually pure. Since that authority promised is founded on holiness with regards to monotheistic devotion and sexual practice, to hear that they "will reign on the earth" suggests that their holiness of character and faith will grant them authority in the realm where such holiness and monotheism is valued (i.e., in the church).

All of the NT was composed during the era known as the *pax Romana* ("peace of Rome"). This peace was accomplished hypocritically through conquest. The Roman Empire's authority was vast because of its previous victorious warfare. During the *pax Romana*, the empire enjoyed the fruits of its conquest. Therefore, it was not necessarily a peaceful time for those living under imperial rule who were not citizens of the empire. Many monotheists certainly found little peace during this era. The imagery used in the message to Thyatira points to this reality for them. They were "shepherded," not in the more common biblical sense of the word (e.g., Ps 23 or NT references to Jesus as the "Good Shepherd"), but rather in the sense that others lorded over them and tried to make them conform to the ways of the empire. Although little is presently known about Thyatira's situation in the empire, we do know that the city had a strong military presence. Since we also know that the congregation was addressed during the *pax Romana*, we know that military activity centered on keeping the perceived peace. Imperial authorities did so by ensuring that people throughout the empire lived in accordance with the plans of the empire. Local leaders enforced these plans very differently, but the bigger the military presence in any area, the greater the likelihood for control over the city's people. As such, we can surmise that Jesus followers in Thyatira were shepherded by some unfeeling people who wanted only to protect the lifestyle of the *pax Romana*. The Roman Empire's largest commodity was slaves. Although we cannot determine any percentage of how many Jesus followers in Thyatira were enslaved, we can recognize that they were likely to be bound in some sense, whether they were literally slaves or not.[72] So, for the city's church members to hear that they would reign on the earth must have meant a type of reversal for them. Their prophetic message declared that they will "shepherd them with an iron rod, like clay jars are shattered." Instead of being bound by others, they would become the shepherds.

3.6.2 *The Earthly Reign and American Christianity*

We are tempted to read about reigning with God and assume that this is an entirely future-oriented promise. Certainly, both NT and OT prophesies clarify an *eschatological* dominion of God that will involve God's people. However, just as Thyatira received a promise for greater authority within the church of their present age, so God continues to reign on the earth today. We pray, "Let your kingdom come and your will be done on earth as it is in heaven." This prayer has two dimensions: the future and the present. Ultimately, God's kingdom will fully come, and God's will certainly shall be done on earth as it is in heaven. That fulfillment waits for another age. In the present age, nevertheless, we pray this prayer precisely because we see evil in the world that has not subjected itself to God's reign. The Christian life is a life of submitting to God's authority, learning his will, and partnering with him to accomplish his will in this age. Wherever truth, love, and justice outshine the darkness pressing throughout the world, it provides evidence of God's kingdom on earth in the present age.

Both the prophecy to Thyatira and the statement about reigning with God on the earth in Revelation 5:10 suggest that holiness serves as a prerequisite for involvement in that rule. Human holiness requires both

---

72. Diehl, "Anti-Imperial Rhetoric," 39–43.

undefiled worship (i.e., not mixed with idols or idolatrous pursuits) and worthy relationships with others that reflect the love God has demonstrated to all people (Phil 2:3–11; Matt 22:31–46), which includes sexual purity (also part of the message to Thyatira in 2:20). God indeed desires to give his people greater influence both inside and outside the church in order to bring increasingly more people into his kingdom. For us to reign with him in this way means that we must first be consistently committed to acting like people who have been transformed into the image of Christ.

We live in a culture without polytheistic religiously inspired trade guilds, so we do not face the challenge of whether or not to eat food sacrificed to idols. Nevertheless, just as such sacrificed food is not inherently idolatrous but can lead to idolatry, the same is true for almost anything in life. As we discussed the American Dream earlier, the pursuit of financial wellbeing can be a god. Of course, neither money nor earthly goods are idols, but they can lead to wrong pursuits and thus to idolatry. They can become gods even though they are not so inherently. We must be careful to never limit the possibilities of what can be gods for us. Even church or interpretations of the Bible can become idols if we decide that our pursuit of such a thing is more important to us than our pursuit of God, his kingdom, and his will.

We can find a relatively close modern parallel to foods sacrificed to idols in guns. Gun ownership for the purposes of hunting or even protection does not necessarily constitute sin. It certainly does not imply that an average gun owner is going to murder someone. When politically conservative people (even Christians) engage in hotly contested debates over gun control, however, their language tends to lend itself toward idolatry. They lean on the Second Amendment as if it is a sacred, God-breathed promise. In truth, it is a right that the Constitution's authors granted for a particular purpose within their own time. The founding fathers knew nothing of semi-automatic handguns or any of the other weapons that are central to modern gun control debates. To demand such a right without evaluating the original intentions of the document is to give oneself to the idolatrous American entitlement we have been discussing.

Furthermore, those who maintain this right without acknowledging the facts around it tend towards a completely unempathetic, self-centered view of the world. Of course, the NRA's adage "guns don't kill people, people kill people" is correct in theory. If you encounter someone who has lost a family member due to gun violence that could have been prevented by proposed gun control measures, do you really want to assert your right to that person? Hanging on to this right is not only anachronistic and thus intellectually dishonest, but it also presents a grave danger for dividing people in the church. Those clinging to their perceived rights demonstrate that they do not care enough about the needs of others. As such, it is quite similar to the concept of eating foods sacrificed to idols. If owning a gun will not cause other people around you to have a crisis of conscience or to question your faith in Jesus, then it may not compromise your relational holiness. Nevertheless, because we live in a nation that has become so bombarded by gun violence, it is difficult to imagine any setting in the United States in which people who own guns for any purpose other than hunting do not risk that compromise. So, Christians clinging to their Second Amendment rights must prayerfully remind themselves of Philippians 2:1–11 and 1 Corinthians 13 to discern whether or not their innermost pursuits are aligned with love or idolatry.

The NRA functions in some ways like a Roman imperial trade guild. The organization receives hundreds of millions of dollars per year (something that could not be said of trade guilds). It uses its money in order to build its community of like-minded people and to spread its message so as to attract others to their cause. Trade guilds were also purposed in community-building and outreach that would bring business to the tradesman as well as new members. A Gallup poll in 2018 found that 60 percent of Americans across party lines approve of stricter gun laws.[73] Such legislative change does not necessitate the NRA cease to exist; it would only require it to return to its earlier message of responsible gun ownership. Nevertheless, the organization became increasingly vocal during the 2016 and 2018 elections, in which it took strong aim against sensible gun restrictions.

In 2016, wherever then-candidate Trump rallied, he repeated the NRA's unfounded fears that Democrats were going to take all their guns away from them. Yet, research demonstrates that most people want restrictions (what Democrats actually attempt to accomplish). Because US politicians within both major parties are split on how to interpret the Second Amendment, their emphasis is always on how to avoid gun violence, not on limiting anyone's right to gun ownership. This fact suggests that the NRA has tried to control how the country and its politicians view the topic of guns, even if polls show that they are not very successful at gaining that control. They are successful, however, at gaining the control of a small portion of faithful Americans. Such people have undergone the same shift from promoting responsible gun ownership to demanding rights no matter whom it might harm. Thus, they appear to have been brainwashed by the NRA cult. Since many of these people profess Christianity, it is important for such believers to harshly evaluate their spiritual states and learn to renounce any rights that have become gods for them so as to surrender them for the good of others and for the sake of their own relationships with God.

73. "Gallup Historical Trends," graphs 3–4.

In discussing the United States's gun cult, conservative Evangelical leader Rob Schenck encourages believers to consider the difficult ethical dilemma of whether or not Christians should own guns. He argues that private citizens without law enforcement duties have no genuine Constitutional or spiritual right to bear arms. He promotes gun use only for those trained and responsible for public safety. For the rest of us, he asserts that the decision of whether or not to purchase a gun inherently involves the choice of deciding that one will kill another human if he/she finds it necessary. "The contemplation of taking another human life requires that we dehumanize certain people in our minds and hearts.... We must mentally place them into a 'disposable class.'"[74] Although we cannot conclude with certainty that gun ownership for private citizens is sinful, we must think very hard about this matter Schenck proposes. If our guns are for the purpose of hunting, then we are prepared to kill animals, having determined that they are disposable. As long as Christians eat or give away what they kill for the purpose of eating, then the animal itself may be disposable, but God's creation is not wasted. To own a gun for any purpose other than hunting, however, demands that we view certain human lives as worth wasting. That belief demonstrates that the NRA and the greater gun cult in the United States has infiltrated the church that is supposed to be marked by its regard for human life.

Liturgy 3: Worthy Is the Lamb

1. Simply pray aloud the opening of the Lord's prayer: "Our Father in heaven, let your name be sanctified. Let your kingdom come; let your will be done, even on the earth as it is in heaven" (Matt 6:9b–10).

2. Meditate on the last sentence you just prayed. Consider what you know about God's will in the present time. Reflect on any new ways you can begin partnering with God's kingdom. And confess any ways in which your habits, attitudes, morality, or decisions may hinder God's will. If alone, consider journaling; if in a group, brainstorm with one group member designated to write down every thought that group members bring up.

3. Sing "Revelation Song" by Jennie Lee Riddle, Lakeland, TX: Gateway Worship, 2006.

---

74. Schenck, "Should Christians Own Guns?," 14–18.

4. Sing a "new song." I am not suggesting you stop everything you are doing and compose a tune even if you have no musical experience. Rather, I want you to follow the example of the elders and sing a song that praises Jesus for his victory over sin and death that makes us victorious. And for many of you, this gospel song adapted from Psalm 18 will be new. Oleta Adams, "I Will Love You," Detroit: Harmony Records, 1997.

5. Invite God's reign in your life through singing a hymn that we normally reserve for Christmas but actually applies better to *eschatological tension* than it does to the Messiah's birth. Isaac Watts (text) and Lowell Mason (melody), "Joy to the World," 1719.

Further Reading:

For John's vision ordering and reasons for communicating as he does:
David A. deSilva. *Seeing Things John's Way: The Rhetoric of the Book of Revelation.* Louisville: Westminster John Knox, 2009.

For the symbols and histories of the seven congregations:
Hemer, Colin J. *Letters to the Seven Churches of Asia in Their Local Setting.* JSNTSup 11. Sheffield: Sheffield Academic Press, 1989.

For the United States's foundation on self-interest, entitlement, and nationalistic religion:
Noll, Mark A. *The Old Religion in a New World: The History of North American Christianity.* Grand Rapids: Eerdmans, 2002.

For biblical worship:
Humphrey, Edith. *Grand Entrance: Worship on Earth as in Heaven.* Grand Rapids: Brazos, 2011.

For the Trinity and Holy Spirit in Revelation:
Koester, Craig R. *Revelation: A New Translation with Introduction and Commentary.* New Haven: Yale University Press, 2014. Pertinent pages: 36–39; 216–20; 377.

For OT language and imagery in Revelation:
Beale, G. K. *John's Use of the Old Testament in Revelation.* Sheffield: Sheffield Academic Press, 1988.

For resurrection as the church's hope for the future:
Wright, N. T. *Surprised by Hope: Rethinking Heaven, Resurrection, and the Mission of the Church.* San Francisco: HarperOne, 2008.

Chapter 3

The Seven Seals (Rev 6:1—8:5)

6 ¹ Then I looked when the Lamb opened one of the seven seals, and I heard one of the four living creatures like the sound of thunder, saying: "Come." ² So I looked, and behold a white horse with one seated on it having a bow, and a crown was given to him, and he went conquering, in order to be victorious. ³ Then when he opened the second seal, I heard the second living creature say, "Come." ⁴ So another horse—a fiery red one—came, and it was granted to the one seated on it to remove peace from the earth, even with the result that they will murder one another; thus, a large sword was given to him. ⁵ Next, when he opened the third seal, I heard the third living creature saying, "Come." Then I looked, and behold a black horse with one seated on it having a scale in his hand. ⁶ And likewise, I heard a voice seemingly in the midst of the four living creatures, saying, "A quart of wheat for a denarius [a day's wage], three quarts of barley for a denarius, and do not harm the oil or the wine." ⁷ Then when he opened the fourth seal, I heard the voice of the fourth living creature saying, "Come." ⁸ So I looked and behold, a pale green horse, and the one seated atop him had his name—Death—ascribed to him. Then Hades followed after him, and authority was given to him over a fourth of the earth in order to kill by the sword, by hunger, by pestilence, and by the beasts of the earth. ⁹

Then when he opened the fifth seal, I saw under the temple the souls of those who had been slain because of the word of God and because of the testimony that they were giving. [10] Then they cried out with loud voices: "For how long, O Lord—the holy and true one—will you not judge and vindicate our blood from the ones who dwell on the earth?" [11] Then a white robe was given to each of them, and it was told to them that they will rest a little while longer until the time arrives when their fellow slaves and brothers are about to be killed as they also have been. [12] Then I watched as he opened the sixth seal, a great earthquake occurred, the sun became black like hairy sackcloth, the full moon became like blood, [13] the stars of heaven fell to the earth as a fig tree throws off its unripe figs by the wind shaking greatly, heaven was split apart like a scroll rolling up, and every mountain and island was removed from their places. [15] Also, the kings of the earth, the high-ranking officials, the tribunes, rich people, poor people, all slaves, and all free people hid themselves in caves and in the rocks of the mountains. [16] And they said to the mountains and the rocks, "Fall on us and hide us from the presence of the one seated on the throne and from the wrath of the Lamb, [17] because the great day of their wrath has come, and who is able to withstand it?"

7 [1] Then after this, I saw four angels standing at the four corners of the earth, controlling the four winds of the earth in order that the wind cannot blow on the earth, on the sea, or on any tree. [2] Then I saw another angel coming up from the rising sun, having the seal of the living God, and he cried out in a loud voice to the four angels that were granted authority to harm the earth and the sea, [3] saying, "Do not harm the earth, the sea, or the trees until we have sealed the slaves of our God on their foreheads." [4] Then I heard the number of the sealed people, 144,000, sealed from each tribe of the children of Israel: [5] From the tribe of Judah, 12,000 sealed; from the tribe of Ruben, 12,000; from the tribe of Gad, 12,000; [6] from the tribe of Asher, 12,000; from the tribe of Naphtali, 12,000; from the tribe of Manasseh, 12,000; [7] from the tribe of Simeon, 12,000; from the tribe of Levi, 12,000; from the tribe of Issachar, 12,000; [8] from the tribe of Zebulun, 12,000; from the tribe of Joseph, 12,000; from the tribe of Benjamin, 12,000.

[9] After these things, I looked and behold, a great multitude which no one was able to count from every nation, all tribes, peoples, and tongues, standing before the throne and before the Lamb, clothed in white robes and having palm trees in their hands. [10] And they cried out in a loud voice: "Salvation belongs

to our God who is seated on the throne, to the Lamb." ¹¹ And all the angels stood around the throne along with the elders and the four living creatures, and they fell on their faces before the throne and worshiped God, ¹² saying, "Amen. Praise, glory, wisdom, thanksgiving, honor, power, and strength belong to our God forever and ever, Amen."

¹³ Then one of the elders answered, saying to me, "Who are these people clothed in white robes, and from where have they come?" ¹⁴ So I said to him, "My lord, you know." Then he said to me, "These are the people coming out of great distress, and they washed their robes and purified them in the blood of the Lamb." ¹⁵ For this reason, they are before God's throne, they will serve him day and night, and the one seated on the throne will dwell amongst them.

¹⁶ They will neither hunger nor thirst any longer, and neither the sun nor scorching heat will ever fall on them, ¹⁷ since the Lamb in the midst of the throne will shepherd them and lead them to a spring of living waters, and God will wipe away every tear from their eyes.

8 ¹ Then when he opened the seventh seal, silence occurred in heaven for about a half hour. ² Then I saw seven angels that stand in the presence of God, and the seven trumpets were given to them. ³ Then another angel came and stood at the altar having a golden bowl, and much incense was given to him in order that he will offer the prayers of all the saints on the golden altar before the throne. ⁴ Then the smoke of the incense, which represents the prayers of the saints, went up from the angel's hand before God. ⁵ So the angel took the bowl, filled it from the fire of the alter, and cast it to the earth; then, thunders, rumblings, lightnings, and an earthquake occurred.

1. THE HORSES AND THEIR RIDERS (REV 6:1-8)

In chapter 1, we discussed the role of divine judgment in apocalyptic literature. In chapter 2, we looked at the seven seals as a representation of God's will. God demonstrates mercy for his people through judgment of those who refuse to acknowledge God's authority and mistreat God's people. Revelation depicts the coexistence of God's judgment and mercy through each of its three *eschatological recapitulations*. *Recapitulations* are repetitions of material from different perspectives. Each one appears in a set of seven, also known as a *septet*. Through each *recapitulation*, the text gives different details about divine judgment beginning in John's own time and culminating with Jesus's second coming. John apparently intends to communicate each version of these events in a manner that addresses differing matters for the seven congregations. With the "seven seals," John presents the first of three *septets*. The Lamb opens the seal, and John writes, "behold." "Behold" indicates the specific things John saw in his vision. John saw warfare, murder, injustice, and death. Since the seals represent God's will, does this mean that the evils presented are aspects of God's will?

1.1 The First Seal: The White Horse

Modern readers sometimes assume that Jesus must be the first horseman, because the Bible often associates the color white with pure and divine characteristics. Further, Revelation unquestionably depicts Jesus on a white horse later in the book (19:11). If we were to conclude that Jesus is also the horseman of Revelation 6:2, then indeed God's will must involve bloodshed. This idea, however, contradicts the purpose of Revelation. By the end of the book, the will of God has been fully revealed. All war, sin, suffering, and death cease at the end. Although less obvious, each *septet* follows this same revelatory pattern. The four horsemen embody the same evils that God's will declares must end. The horsemen in this passage are not messengers of God's will; they are subjected to God's will via judgment.

A potential problem arises from the fact that the four living creatures (unquestionably godly figures that are around the Messiah's throne) charge the horsemen with their duties. When we look at the theme of judgment in the OT, however, we realize that this need not be an issue. God often used ancient Israel to exact his judgment on unrepentant people. Further, when Israel rebelled, God occasionally used Israel's enemies to bring judgment on his own people. So, the four living creatures fulfill their God-ordained tasks of subjecting these four evils to judgment along with the people committing them. This pattern parallels the plagues of Exodus. Through those plagues, God's judgment destroyed Egypt's gods along with the people who abused Israel. Revelation's first horseman conquers in battle; the second incites murder; the third commits economic and social injustice; the fourth represents all manner of death. The four horsemen together, then, represent the totality of human violence and destruction.[1]

---

1. Koester, *Revelation*, 393–94.

1.1.1 The White Horse and the Seven Congregations

The seven messages of Revelation 2–3 include warfare language, but it is much different from the white horse's warfare. The seven prophecies involve promises to the "conquerors" in each of the seven congregations. Those passages, however, refer clearly to spiritual warfare, not physical combat. The congregants must fight temptation, idolatry, *syncretism*, the evils prevalent in the Roman Empire, and the demonic realm. The messages never include any references to earthly warfare.

In the message to Pergamum's congregation, Jesus says he will fight against unrepentant congregants who continue in their ways of false teaching. He says, "I will wage war with you by the sword of my mouth" (Rev 2:16). The sword most likely represents justice and the word of God. By the sword, Jesus calls the churches to repentance. He wages war to protect them from falling away and to keep them alive in the presence of God. His warfare must not be one of bloodshed but rather one of moral and spiritual conviction purposed in engendering repentance.

Luther Seminary professor Craig R. Koester recognizes the four horsemen as a condemnation of all violent conquest.[2] Although the seven messages of Revelation 2–3 do not allude to this type of warfare, all of the congregants would have had experience with it in some way or another. They all lived in the Roman Empire, which prided itself in its military occupations. We can safely presume that if any of the congregations engaged in Roman imperial warfare, this would equate losing their spiritual battles. When the Lamb reveals the will of God through opening the first seal, he reveals that God's will entails an end to warfare.

1.1.2 The White Horse and the US Church Today

The message behind the white horse for the seven congregations coincides much more directly with a modern application than most of Revelation's symbols do. The symbol calls us to full engagement in spiritual warfare. It reminds us that our most fervent enemy is not human, no matter how cruel the people around us might be. The battle we must fight is against demonic spirits and anti-Christian ideologies that try to take root in the midst of our Christian expressions (Eph 6:12). It does not necessarily preclude the possibility of Christians fighting in physical warfare if necessary, but it does condemn unjust warfare that takes life for selfish, political, or monetary gains.

---

2. Koester, *Revelation*, 394.

1.2 The Second Seal: The Red Horse

Just as John presents the white horse as a condemnation against imperial military conquest, so the image of the red horse denounces anything that attempts to divide people with malicious intent. The passage begins with the general statement that the red horse will "remove peace from the earth." The Bible suggests that some schisms between people are necessary. Jesus even said, "Do you think that I came to grant peace on the earth? No, I say to you, but rather division" (Luke 12:51). This statement directly follows one of Jesus's most cryptic statements about his forthcoming crucifixion: "Now I have a baptism to be baptized with, and how much distress I am in until the time is complete" (Luke 12:50b). Jesus's statement about division precedes a comment about family members torn from one another (Luke 12:52–53). Since Jesus claims to be the source of this division, it echoes other Jesus sayings about carrying a cross and leaving everything to follow him. Of course, it does not literally mean that any family members should hate each other. Rather, it suggests that following Jesus can require some people to distance themselves from family, possibly even rejecting family members if those people hinder them from following Jesus sacrificially.

Paradoxically, the division that Jesus grants unifies his church and protects its holiness. Thus, it accomplishes a greater good through something intensely painful. The division that the red horse commits, on the other hand, possesses no potential for good. The horseman's divisiveness has no limits. It encourages people to commit murder in order to make the divide complete and irreparable.

1.2.1 The Red Horse and the Seven Congregations

The messages to Smyrna and Philadelphia both mention false Jews. Jesus came to earth as the Jewish Messiah. He came as a Jew for the Jews. He also came to fulfill the biblical reality, testified throughout the OT, that the purpose of the Jewish people is to be a light and a blessing to all nations (eg., Isa 49:6). Therefore, Jesus also came as a Jew for the gentiles. In Ephesians 2:11–12, Paul vividly describes how Jesus created a unified body amongst Jewish and gentile believers. All of Paul's letters demand that his audiences uphold that unity. Throughout his letter to the Romans, Paul seeks to end gentile beliefs of supersession (the idea that gentiles replaced Jews in the New Covenant). He also attacks the actions of Judaizers (people who attempted to force gentiles into OT Jewish practices, some of whom might have been gentiles themselves).³

In a book written for the University of Toronto's Studies in Christianity and Judaism, Michele Murray presents evidence that suggests strong pagan interest in aspects of Judaism in Rome. Her book is titled *Playing a Jewish Game*, as she suggests that many gentiles in the first century CE (some of whom became Jesus-followers) attempted to hypocritically play the role of Jews. She uses this evidence to conclude that most (if not all) of the NT's statements that can appear to be anti-Jewish are actually against gentiles who claim to be Jews but are not.⁴ I believe Murray overreaches with this conclusion. History shows that the division went both ways at certain times. Sometimes gentiles were the predominant guilty party; other times Jews were, but usually both were at fault. Also, the Greek word *Ioudaioi* that translates to "Jews" in Greek can also be translated, "Judeans." Most English translators leap to translate every instance of the word as "Jews." However, many of the attacks Murray refers to (especially in the Gospels) contextually target the people of a location (Judeans) rather than the people of a racial and religious identity (Jews).⁵ Murray is correct, however, in noting that the NT never attacks the Jewish people as a whole or any of their rituals as many interpreters since the time of the Protestant Reformation have assumed. Her insights are particularly helpful when looking at the messages to Sardis and Philadelphia.

Murray's discussion centers around a group of people known as Judaizers. Judaizers (whether Jewish or gentile) were legalists. They sowed discord by attempting to convince new gentile believers that in order to be saved they must subject themselves to circumcision and follow other OT laws. Both Luke (in Acts) and Paul (in his *epistles*) take strong stances against all forms of legalism. They make it abundantly clear that people receive salvation only through their reception of the work accomplished at Jesus's death and resurrection. Sin separates people from God; the lack of participation in a ritual does not. Unlike most of the NT's rebukes against *Ioudaioi*, the word must be translated "Jews" in the messages to Sardis and Philadelphia, as well as in Romans 2:17. These three instances all pertain to people who claim to be someone they are not. As such, a translation of location would not make sense. To say that they are Judeans when they are not would be like saying someone pretended to be French when he was not. Why would anyone do that? To be a "false Jew" or "one who calls himself a Jew" is to take on a role

---

3. Murray, *Jewish Game*, 2.
4. Murray, *Jewish Game*, 2.
5. Levine, "Third Quest?"

and to be a hypocrite in order to deceive others and self. This form of legalism assumes that gentile believers somehow replaced Jews in the plan of God. Further, it tries to convince people that everyone must follow specific directives in order to receive salvation. Such coercion treats both Judaism and Christianity as works-based religions, which neither are.

1.2.2 *The Red Horse and Legalism in US Christianity*

The gentile-Jewish divide still exists in the church today. Messianic Judaism has risen from a tiny minority to a global movement. Gentile believers are often unprepared to welcome Messianic Jews into their congregations. Some wrongly assume that Jews must give up some or all of their practices in order to follow their Messiah. Such Christians risk forgetting that 1) Jesus said he did not come to abolish the Law but to fulfill it and that 2) the OT repeatedly states that people of Jewish lineage are to carry out their end of the covenant perpetually. Others are afraid that Messianic Jews will try to convert them to Jewish practices. For a Jewish person to follow *Yeshua* as their Messiah means to accept the gift of *Yeshua's* sacrifice, just as it does for gentile Christians. For Jews, however, it also entails worshiping *YHWH* through remembering their special identity as God's chosen people. Messianic Jews have widely differing levels of observance to OT regulations; nevertheless, gentile Christians must respect that observance as an act of worship to God. A Messianic friend told me about his initial attempts to worship in gentile churches. The congregants tempted him with a religious test that assumed he could not follow *Yeshua* if he refused to eat ham. Christians that make such presumptions minimize the power of Jesus's sacrifice, as if they believe Jesus died so they could eat pork.

The church in the United States is fractured in many ways beyond the Jewish-gentile divide. We are often quick to assume that people who interpret portions of Scripture differently than we do must be heretics. We inappropriately assign full denominations to a category of "nominal Christians," even if we do not understand what such groups believe. Certainly, we must hold fast to the foundational truths of Jesus's atoning death that offers forgiveness of sins, his coexisting humanity and divinity, his resurrection that gives eternal life, his second coming and judgment, and the *eschatological* resurrection of all people. We must agree that the original words of the Bible (written in Hebrew, Aramaic, or Greek) comprise the word of God, inspired by God to human authors. These matters are black-and-white. Most of the Bible, however, includes gray area.

Modern Christians become guilty of the same sin that the "false Jews" committed whenever they add unbiblical limitations to who can be saved and who cannot. Some will say that total abstinence from alcohol is a requirement for being a Christian. Yet, the Christ that Christians are named after drank wine almost daily and turned water into wine as his first miracle. Certainly, many believers have good reason to abstain from alcohol and to believe that God has called them to that decision as individuals. When we take it beyond a matter of personal conviction, however, we become intellectually dishonest regarding what the Bible teaches, and we become spiritually corrupt in our relationships. Similarly, many in Pentecostal/Charismatic circles lack understanding about what ancient witchcraft and magic entailed. Out of wrong assumptions about something the Bible very clearly prohibits, some of these people label activities like role-playing games and Harry Potter fandom as acts of witchcraft that can disqualify people from the kingdom of God. In reality, however, those games and stories have very little (if anything) in common with the magic that the Bible prohibits.

Perhaps the most dangerous limitation on salvation in our current cultural environment relates to political affiliation. I have heard many white American Christians express a belief that all Christians are Republicans, because all Democrats are "baby killers." Though most are not quite that frank, a long conversation with somebody that includes discussion of both religion and politics will reveal if a person has joined the two together in a divisive way. Since the 1970s, many church leaders throughout the country have taught and perpetuated this belief, even if they do not explicitly say it.

First, the belief firmly upholds a nationalistic *syncretism* that worships the United States's political system. It does so by assuming something about what it means to be a Christian that can only apply to US citizens. Members of the US Republican Party must be US citizens. A belief that only Republicans can be Christians elevates the United States and its government above other nations. It gives a type of spiritual authority to the nation that no country deserves. When a person guilty of this *syncretism* is confronted with the idea I just presented, the likely response is something vague and defensive like, "but that's different." What is different? That retort makes no sense. It does not address the issue at hand, and it raises another significant question. Is God a different person to different countries? The assertion that Christians must be Republican is inherently (though unintentionally) ethnocentric and idolatrous.

Secondly, a 2017 survey found that 70 percent of US citizens profess Christianity. Only about 43 percent of white US citizens (the racial majority) profess Christianity, while 83 percent of African Americans do and 82 percent of Hispanics do.[6] A 2008 study found that only 5 percent of African Americans identify as Republicans. Less than 5 percent of US Hispanic citizens identified as Republicans, although almost half identified as right-leaning independents.[7] Since that time, Donald Trump's racially insensitive and xenophobic rhetoric has caused the numbers of both African American and US Hispanic Republicans to decrease further.[8] Since these surveys account for many non-white Christians who are politically liberal, the assertion that Christians must be Republicans and cannot be Democrats is inherently racist.

I am sure many who read this section will resist, because statistics can only point out how many people profess Christianity, not how many actually are Christians. That response is true, but the statistics are also staggering, and we are remiss to ignore them. They suggest that, in most US settings, we are significantly more likely to meet a black or Hispanic American who professes faith in Jesus than a white American who does so. White Christian Americans remain the political majority, even if non-religious whites comprise the demographic majority. This fact might also imply that white Christians are more likely to go to church and think of themselves as Christians simply because it is part of what the political majority does. It is more difficult for a political minority to be a Christian if his/her Christianity does not align perfectly with the Christian expressions of the majority group. I argue, therefore, that white people are far more likely than people of color to be the nominal Christians for whom these statistics cannot take account.

If nothing else, these statistics show us that there tends to be something wrong with white Christianity. Of course, that should be obvious, since the church is a global, united, and racially/ethnically diverse institution. The idea that Christians must be Republican, as far as I can tell, is a uniquely white phenomenon. When a belief cannot transcend a single racial group, we can tell clearly that such a belief has either no basis in reality or a very limited applicability. Since this belief is a matter of eternal salvation, it cannot be a question of applicability.

Finally, the primary reason behind this perverse belief among many white Christians is a generally well-meaning conviction against abortion. Almost all Christians, regardless of political affiliation, agree that abortion is evil except in cases of sexual assault and when the mother's life is at risk. Although no portion of Scripture explicitly states that life begins at conception, we can gain insight into how the earliest followers of Jesus

---

6. Zoll, "White Christians," paras. 2, 7.
7. Newport, "Democrats Racially Diverse," graph 1.
8. Chinni, "Republican Party ID Drops," graph 1.

interpreted and applied Jesus's teachings through the *Didache*. The *Didache* is a document of the early church, written at the same time as parts of the NT. It includes a passage that discusses murder in much the same way Jesus does but includes a clause that clearly labels the intentional and unnecessary killing of a fetus as murder.[9] In order to align with the beliefs of those who first applied the teachings of Jesus, we certainly should take stances against abortion. We do not, however, need to agree on the best way of handling the abortion crisis in order to be legitimate Christians. Those who make a correlation between how one votes and the legitimacy of one's faith wrongly assume that the only way to respond to the crisis is by voting for people who can illegalize abortion.

Ironically, studies are consistent and universal that whenever a nation or state legalizes abortion, the number of abortions in that location drops drastically. The United States saw such a decrease in abortions in the years that followed *Roe v. Wade*. From the 1980s forward, the number has fluctuated greatly but has never been as high as it was before the 1973 Supreme Court ruling.[10] So, if abortions are more common when illegal, then votes intended to encourage the illegalization of abortion are counterproductive. In other words, if a vote for a Democrat is a sin that makes a person a "baby killer," then those who vote Republican are also "baby killers." Further, under such a presupposition, Republican voters will be guilty of many more murders if their party of choice is ever able to build a Supreme Court willing to reverse *Roe v. Wade*. If Christians must vote Republican, this demand places American Christianity in a literal "damned if you do, damned if you don't" scenario. Most Democrats function under a pro-choice ideology, but Republican policies pave the way for large rises in the number of abortions. So, if a vote identifies an American spiritually because of abortion, then none will be saved.

We should also recognize that some pro-choice politicians use language when they discuss abortion that we should not judge too quickly. Many say they are personally and spiritually opposed to abortion but cannot support making the practice illegal. Based on the statistics, if these leaders mean what they say, then they are more pro-life than most anti-abortion advocates. Many Democrats use the euphemisms "reproductive rights" and "women's health." For many politicians, those euphemisms are probably nothing more than expressions of the idolatrous and deadly American entitlement we have discussed. For some, however, these words accompany plans and policies that help avoid situations in which women could feel that abortion is necessary.

9. *Did.* 2.2.
10. Levy, "Abortion Rates," paras. 1–3, graph 2.2.

These factors can indicate that some Democrats (even if only a few) might actually want to combat abortion. Because they recognize the paradoxical dilemma of the statistics, they do so as pro-choice politicians. In other words, pro-choice politics do not necessitate pro-death policies. The common idea among centrists of both parties that abortion should be legal, safe, and rare is probably the best anyone with anti-abortion leanings should expect from politicians. The rest is up to us.

These considerations on abortion help to point out that we should stop looking at the topic as a political issue and begin recognizing it as a spiritual matter. If we truly believe that all humans are created in the image of God and that the process of that divine creation begins at conception, we must treat it as a life-and-death matter. We must stop relying on politicians and politically motivated marches to do the work for us. Our relationships with other people can make a much bigger difference than any law can. Once we begin to take responsibility for ourselves by using the gifts, money, talents, and communities God has blessed us with, we can work together to make a real difference.

Some can open crisis pregnancy centers. Others can form community outreach activities that support life for the unborn without bringing politics into the equation. As churches, families, or individuals, all of us can seek out women who are struggling with the decision of whether or not to end a pregnancy. We can demonstrate God's love to these mothers and their babies. Of course, not all the mothers will make the decision we want them to. Nevertheless, if we form relationships with women who are considering abortion and lovingly extend truth and hope instead of judgment, we might eventually see an end to abortion in the United States. On the other hand, I guarantee that we will never see an end to this evil as a result of law or politics.

The red horse of Revelation is a source of division. Revelation's first audiences experienced division predominantly through religious confusion. Judaizers made false claims about what it means to follow Jesus. They tried to convince people that rituals and abstinence from neutral activities would activate their salvation. In the United States today, many segments of Christianity legalistically claim that in order to be a Christian, you must . . . [fill in the blank with each of the things discussed above, along with any other way you can complete this sentence from your own experience, since there are many that I did not have the space to cover]. This division partners with the demonic realm in its attempt to destroy the body of Christ.

1.3 The Black Horse

Throughout ancient literature, scales uniformly represent famine, because they were used to measure food allotments during times of famine. As John sees the horseman holding the scales, he also hears a "voice seemingly in the midst of the four living creatures" (Rev 6:6). Other portions of Revelation make it clear that the Lamb is seated on his throne in the midst of the four living creatures.[11] The voice declares prices for daily food staples (wheat and barley) that are between ten to fifteen times their normal price in the first century CE. The first horse represents warfare, and the second represents divisiveness. After warfare, ancients expected famine. Famine made inflation worse. Ancient warfare generally took precautions when conquering an area to avoid harming products such as wine and oil that could devastate the area's economy completely.[12] Parts of Asia Minor experienced these events at the time Revelation was written. The voice of the Lamb, thus, speaks words that coincide with the natural effects of war, famine, and inflation in the first-century Mediterranean world.

The voice also alludes to financial disparity in the Roman Empire. Parts of Asia were especially guilty of economic corruption at the time Revelation was written. Philadelphia, whose congregation Jesus praised for its faithfulness in dire circumstances, would have been most harmed by the disparity. Roman tradesmen made significantly more money from the items that were less necessary (like wine and oil) than from the daily necessities (like wheat and barley). Their decisions to prize the wine and oil over food had especially horrific consequences for children, as many died of starvation.[13] Since the four horsemen represent the beginning stages of judgment, the Lamb appears to make the pronouncement he does as a parody against Roman economic practices. He enacts the role of a corrupt governing authority preparing for the fallout after warfare in order to condemn the practices that yielded the disparity. The text warns that because the government's policies cause death, God will judge the perpetrators with the same harm that they caused. Rome will be subjected to famine, just as the text has already subjected it to the unjust warfare and unnecessary division that Rome first perpetrated. This judgment most likely occurred through the fall of the Roman Empire. Alternatively, the parody of the Lamb's proclamation could be a general pronouncement that assures God will right all wrongs at

---

11. Beale and Campbell, *Revelation*, 133.
12. Keener, *Revelation*, 205.
13. Kenner, *Revelation*, 204–5.

the end of the age. Since Revelation is so layered in its imagery, I suspect that both are equally accurate.

1.3.1 The Black Horse and the Ephesian Loveless State

Asia Minor had particularly heavy involvement in carrying out the financial policies of Rome.[14] Christians in Philadelphia and Sardis deeply felt the effects of famine and its subsequent perils. Unlike believers in other Asia Minor locations, many refused to take part in the economic corruption of the empire. The seven messages of Revelation 2–3 confirm that these two congregations maintained faithfulness to God in dire circumstances. Many amongst the other five congregations, however, apparently participated in aspects of imperial commerce that caused oppression. The Roman Empire was never shy about who it hurt, so believers would have known whether or not a particular economic activity would harm others. The five congregations that received rebukes must have acted complicity as if they approved of the blatant wrongdoing around them, because it would have benefited them financially.[15]

Jesus reprimands the Ephesian congregation for its lack of love. "You have disowned your first love" (Rev 2:4). This reproof suggests that the congregation had once been an exemplar of loving God and loving people. The symbol of the black horse appears to point most directly to this congregation's abandonment of the love they once expressed. They must have given that love in many ways. One such way would have been financial support to people in need. The more a congregant succumbed to the ways of the empire, however, the more comfortable he or she would have become from the wealth it afforded. That comfort paved the way for complacency. Complacency and love do not coexist well.

The Ephesian loveless complacency was not just a matter of personal benefit that harmed others, although that was most likely present. It is more relevant to the congregation's relationship with the empire, which extended far beyond economic matters. The more comfortable they became, the less they cared about their Christian responsibility to meet others' needs when they had the ability to do so. Through the symbol of the black horse, the Holy Spirit asked several questions of the Ephesian congregation. Each question has the same answer: "You cannot."

---

14. Kenner, *Revelation*, 205.
15. Beale and Campbell, *Revelation*, 133.

- How can you love people when you have the means to help others but do not do so?
- How can you love people when you support a governmental system that causes poverty?
- How can you love people when you support a governmental system that oppresses the people God created in his own image?
- How can you love people when you support a governmental system that promotes death through gladiatorial contests, exposure of infants to the elements, etc.?
- How can you love God when you do not love your neighbor?

1.3.2 The Black Horse and Contemporary US Churches

Although it looks much different than it did in first-century Asia Minor, economic disparity has been a reality in the United States for a long time. The saying "the rich get richer, while the poor get poorer" is nothing new in our country. Nevertheless, we must remember that the United States is still one of the wealthiest nations in the world (or at least it was at the time of writing). Many people below the poverty line in our country possess what people in many other parts of the world would consider to be wealth. That fact, however, does not make economic oppression within the United States acceptable. Ethnic minorities are disproportionately more likely to experience real poverty than white Americans. That tendency is another outflow of the United States's systemic racism. It means that the US government is systemically guilty of two economic sins: disparity within the country and unwillingness to share its wealth with others around the world. The sins of the overarching national system extend to individuals and churches through our attitudes about wealth and giving.

Like the Asia Minor congregations other than Sardis and Philadelphia, we can become involved in governmental corruption even if we have no governmental authority or connection. Unlike the congregations of Asia Minor, however, we can be lured into participation without being fully aware. When we emphasize being American, capitalist consumers, we chase the American Dream. We find ourselves entitled to whatever we might want no matter how it might hurt others. We are most vulnerable to this type of cultural brainwashing when we do not know we are causing harm. The black horse, therefore, offers a prompt from the Holy Spirit to assess ourselves using similar questions to those Ephesian believers needed to answer. All but one of the following questions have a direct parallel to those listed above. I have added an additional question to direct us toward individual lovelessness stemming from our individualistic culture's value of convenience. No first-century societies were individualistic or desired convenience, so these concerns could not factor into the rebuke of the Ephesian church's lovelessness.

1.3.2.1 How Can We Love People When We Have the Means to Help Others but Do Not?

This question most clearly ties to the economic nature of the black horseman's activities. Once again, we must remember how wealthy we are as a nation. As individuals, we must renounce any false ideas of poverty or financial struggle whenever we find ourselves in economic situations that appear wealthy to the rest of the world. Our love for God or lack thereof hinges on this kind of attitude. If we can see ourselves as financially blessed when we do not have everything we want, we can then see how God has provided for us and given us a great abundance far beyond what we need. As we receive these benefits as gifts from God, then we naturally want to respond by using the excess as an expression of love for others, which is a reflection of our love for God. It requires us to seek those who are in genuine need, whether around us or abroad and to give accordingly. How can we love others if we do not provide for their needs whenever we have the capability to do so? We cannot.

1.3.2.2 How Can We Love People When We Support a Government that Causes Poverty?

In the United States, both sides of the political aisle are equally concerned about the optics of poverty in the United States, if not the poverty itself. Some politicians make genuine efforts to end American homelessness and malnutrition (the real poverty that exists in the United States). Others, to the contrary, uphold the status quo so as to appear as if they are helping solve the problem when they are actually worsening it. Nevertheless, no US politicians I am aware of play any active role in causing poverty in the United States, though some perpetuate it. Recent political decisions, nevertheless, cause poverty elsewhere in the world.

 The world's poorest nations are becoming poorer, and middle-income countries are quickly sinking into real poverty (as opposed to the United

States's poverty line) because of climate change. Weather abnormalities have caused famines and prevented growth of the crops these nations once depended on. Their productivity decreases because of the overuse of fossil fuels amongst the wealthiest nations. Developing nations need fossil fuels in order to attempt building their economy. Wealthy nations, on the other hand, can securely transition to alternative forms of energy, ensuring that fossil fuels are only used by those who need them. That transition necessitates significant changes regarding what jobs in the power industry entail, but it does not pose a significant threat to the jobs themselves.[16] The Paris Climate Accord is an agreement amongst the wealthiest nations of the world to make this transition for the benefit of impoverished parts of the world. President Trump, however, took the United States out of that agreement in his desire to continue the status quo of American excess and entitlement. Trump made this exit official on November 4, 2019.[17] The decision, thus, has caused and exacerbated poverty and untimely deaths around the world. How then can we love people if we support a government that protects our comfort at the expense of millions of peoples' livelihoods and lives? We cannot.

1.3.2.3 How Can We Love People When We Choose Convenience over Wellbeing?

Beyond these governmental issues, all Americans, to some degree or another, contribute to the loveless harm of the poor on an individual basis. We habitually waste food, overuse natural gasses, trash items that can be recycled, and consume convenience food items processed with dangerous chemicals that emit greenhouse gasses. We do all of these things, because we have been culturally conditioned to do them. The concept of convenience has become an idol to most (if not all) Americans. When we make convenience a priority in life, we inevitably waste in ways that prevent other people from having their needs met. When we unnecessarily use natural gasses and when our trash is burnt, we are responsible for the gasses emitted that create or worsen poverty in other countries. This waste also contributes to changes in all environments, rapidly increasing respiratory diseases and destructive wildfires in wealthy nations. These last two effects of climate change can be felt in the United States. Doctors diagnose patients with breathing disorders at rapidly increasing rates.[18] Also, as of September 2020, the wildfires that

---

16. Davey, "Developing Countries," paras. 1–24.
17. Dennis, "Paris Climate Accord."
18. D'Amato et al., "Climate Change," 161–69.

commonly plagued California began destroying all three states along the West coast. Therefore, we demonstrate that we prize convenience even over our personal health.

If you read this section of the book as a skeptic concerning climate change, I encourage you to watch the 2006 documentary, *An Inconvenient Truth*. Despite the fact that its presenter once ran for president, the movie has no partisan political content. Al Gore merely shows slides of facts that scientists had presented in the years leading up to 2006. He worked with other knowledgeable people to analyze that data and make predictions of what the world would like in the near future.[19] I watched it about ten years after its production; I was still a skeptic until viewing the film with hindsight. All the predictions laid out for the following ten years had happened almost exactly as presented and within a fairly close timeline. The movie's title is particularly relevant to the discussion here, since we must become willing to forsake our idols of convenience in order to save lives. After all, how can we love when convenience is a higher priority than wellbeing? We cannot.

1.3.2.4 How Can We Love People When We Support an Oppressive Government?

If we truly believe that all people have been created in the image of God, we should have no tolerance for real oppression. Many white Americans, including Christians, assume themselves to be marginalized citizens, though truthfully their delusions render them partially responsible for the real marginalization that occurs. The Trump administration has changed immigration laws and prioritized its border wall in ways that have oppressed immigrants, just as he promised he would do. Trump has placed unreasonable expectations on people who need to enter the United States to escape dangerous and unlivable environments in Latin America.[20] As a wealthy nation, the United States possesses the capability to meet the needs of asylum seekers without neglecting the needs of its own people (including the homeless veterans that usually accompany sanctimonious complaints to make them sound more selfless and less like the excuses they are).

At the same time, Trump has attempted to redefine what it means to be a legal citizen of the United States. Many people throughout the country have legal status but have extended their stay because of lasting dangerous conditions in their home country or unanticipated life changes in

---

19. Guggenheim, *Inconvenient Truth*.
20. Anderson, "'Merit-Based' Immigration," paras. 1–2, 5–11.

the United States. This group represents a vast majority of what constitutes illegal immigration in the United States, not illegal border crossings. Past administrations of both parties worked towards finding paths of citizenship for such people. The Trump administration, on the other hand, seeks to make immigration illegal wherever beneficial to a white-nationalistic agenda. Trump has attempted to enact policies that hinder people who would want to enter the country if they do not fit his racist merit-based approach,[21] forcing them to continue living in oppressive societies. Beyond entry into the United States, his policies oppress people who already live in the United States, work here, raise their families here, and benefit their American communities.[22]

To raise the question of this section in new and more specific ways, how can we love people if we support a governmental system that turns away needy people from receiving the help it can offer them? How can we love people if we support a leader who criminalizes normal life for people whom he deems un-American? How can we love people if we accept the legitimacy of an administration that unrepentantly separated families and held children in cages at detention centers, when this policy exposed many children to disease and sexual assault and caused multiple deaths?[23] We cannot.

1.3.2.5 How Can We Love People When We Support a Government that Promotes Death?

Our contributions to climate change (through our daily activities and through our votes for people who could do something about it but refuse to) create poverty around the world. That poverty makes us responsible when people die as a result. Many of the breathing disorders mentioned in connection with the effects of climate change in the United States are deadly. The system's status quo has lulled us into an idolatry of convenience. Out of our worship for that idol, we sacrifice the lives of others through our waste. The Trump administration aggressively enforces an agenda that contributes to the effects of climate change, causes deaths among asylum seekers, and prioritizes the economy of the United States over anybody's life.

Trump vividly demonstrated that priority through his response to the 2018 murder of Jamal Khashoggi. Khashoggi was an American journalist

---

21. Keith, "'Merit-Based' Immigration Plan," paras. 1–4, 8–12.

22. Clark, "Illegalization," paras. 1–6.

23. Frazee, "Inside the Facilities," paras. 1–36; Silwa, "Family Separations," paras. 1–8; Gomez, "Children Report Sexual Assaults," paras. 1–5, graph 1.

originally from Saudi Arabia (a dual citizen). Saudi political officials murdered him. Evidence points toward Saudi Crown Prince Mohammad bin Salman's prior knowledge and consent of the murder. Out of his high value for the economic benefits surrounding his relationship with bin Salman, Trump refused to look at that evidence. He dismissed the insights and desires of Congress, including those from a majority of his own party. In an interview with Right Wing Watch, televangelist Pat Robertson rebuked Republican lawmakers for making too much of Khashoggi's killing and not enough of Trump's financial agreement with Saudi Arabia. Although he later disavowed the statement, Robertson said, "You don't blow up an international [economic] alliance over one person."[24]

Many American Christians have given into a hypocritical belief like Robertson expressed that appeared long before the Trump administration. The belief that equates being pro-life with being against abortion allows us to appropriately condemn one way in which people can promote death (abortion) while accepting other forms of murder or potential murder. As I have outlined in this section, the Trump administration operates a pro-death governmental system. To a far lesser degree, the Republican Party has had pro-death policies for decades by rushing into wars and denying climate change. No overarching pro-death agenda, however, could be recognized in either party prior to Trump's presidency. Trump gave many hints of that agenda in his 2016 campaign. The Republican Party, however, never ceases to hold on to its so-called Evangelical support because of the party's pro-life label. This points to a deficiency of love in many American churches. Like Robertson, many Americans act as if "one person" is not valuable enough to deserve life. Proponents of this belief support and vote for pro-life politics that are mostly pro-death in practice during the age of Trump.

The COVID-19 crisis most dramatically demonstrates some American Christians' Trump-induced lovelessness. Listening to the words of President Trump instead of medical experts has turned life and death matters into partisan political statements. On many occasions, Trump referred to the virus as a minor problem that Democrats overblew and exploited. At the same time, however, he expected people to believe that the coronavirus is a very real crisis manufactured by China. Of course, both cannot be true, and neither are, which means Americans who listen to Trump on this matter prefer a lie to the truth. Although much was still unknown about the disease at the time of writing, the CDC, WHO, and nearly all medical professionals agreed that some data is conclusive. That data includes:[25]

---

24. Mantayla, "Pat Robertson," paras. 1–4.
25. See "How to Protect Yourself & Others."

- Contagious people spread the virus through the air by respiratory emissions (coughs, sneezes, speaking, etc.).
- People can have COVID-19 without developing symptoms, making it difficult to identify all who carry and spread it without aggressive testing measures.
- It spreads quickest when groups of people do not stay six feet apart from anyone with whom they do not live.
- Face coverings help to curb the risk of spreading. They offer limited protection for the one wearing the mask (unless it is a surgical mask or face shield) but are invaluable for potentially asymptomatic people to have relatively normal lives without infecting others whom they could potentially kill.

This list consists of established facts. Unless seeking Trump's approval, health officials have never wavered on any of them, after each had received broad medical acceptance. Yet, throughout the country, many Trump supporters (including Christians) appealed to their American sense of entitlement to avoid taking responsibility for life-and-death matters. When the CDC and local governments demanded a hiatus on all physical gatherings, these particular Christians complained about the government taking their freedom of religion. First of all, if the government had actually removed any rights, then it would be the fault of the current governing authorities. At that time, all those decisions were based on the recommendations of the CDC. The CDC is an institution that the federal government oversees; as the head of the federal government, any removal of rights would have been Trump's fault. Nevertheless, Trump supporters blamed Democrats for taking their religious freedoms from them, even in states where Republican governors made the orders. Christians who complained about losing the freedom of religion not only neglected to accurately assess the current political landscape but also American history. A study of the country's previous experience with a global pandemic—the influenza pandemic of 1918—could have helped us learn from the responses of earlier Christians.

The 1918 pandemic forced church buildings to close for services throughout most of the time before a vaccine became available. In some locations, pastors and priests wrote their sermons in newspapers in an attempt to keep their church bodies connected.[26] They proved that the church did not and could not close. Assemblies of God congregations throughout the world began corresponding via mail through the denomination's *Christian*

---

26. Garrison, "What Clergy Said," paras. 1–2, 5–7, 12–15, 21–23, 26–29.

Evangel (now *Pentecostal Evangel*) magazine.[27] They also proved that the church did not and could not close. The Churches of Christ denominations continued ministering by converting their church buildings into hospitals. They worked with health and government officials to ensure their buildings met all safety measures for the purpose of effectively treating influenza patients.[28] They too proved that the church did not and could not close. Most other denominations and local churches in the United States proved this same truth in different ways by being creative and surrendering to the love that their urgent situation required. Nevertheless, some protested and assumed the government was stealing their freedom of religion. Those protests included many illegal church gatherings, several of which killed attenders on the spot.[29]

COVID-19 is not a flu of any type (despite one of Trump's favorite lies to repeat about the disease). As such, it spreads and infects people much differently. We have never seen crowds that include people dying while still gathered as they did in 1918, but we have seen many similar protests in the names of Christianity and religious freedom. We have seen pastors force congregations together in ways that caused eventual deaths amongst their congregants. Such pastors often claimed religious persecution in attempts to get out of legal jeopardy. Some even took pride in their actions as if they were suffering for the Lord instead of creating avoidable suffering among their own flocks.[30] Their actions communicate willingness to sacrifice their own congregants' health and lives in order to have church the way they used to. That sacrifice appeases the idol of self-interest; it cannot please the God who is love. It is a self-centered and self-serving reflection of American entitlement.

Thankfully, we have also seen many responses to the outbreak similar to the creative efforts in 1918 that have helped the church continue to minister to its people and reach the lost. No technology existed in 1918 that could bring physically separate people together. We have so many tools at our disposal because of recent technological advancements that nobody has any excuse to complain about churches being closed. Creativity and technology have helped the church not merely continue in a difficult time, but even grow. Livestream services have made ways for people to attend church who normally would not. Several pastors I know have reported higher attendance than any in-person services they had ever held. Some

27. Isgrigg, "How Pentecostals Responded," paras. 3–4.
28. Hicks, "How Churches of Christ Responded," paras. 1–9.
29. Yount, "Churches Closed in 1918," paras. 5–12.
30. Kaleem, "Megachurch Pastors Defy Coronavirus," paras. 1–18.

have even said that they have had visitors from countries that experience real persecution for their faith, who found new difficulties expressing their worship during the pandemic. Churches that have the technology to add interactive components to their services, such as virtual prayer rooms, have grown significantly larger among the pastors I know. Of course, I have only provided circumstantial evidence for the church growth of a few congregations. Nevertheless, the evidence helps to illustrate the principles that 1) the church of Jesus Christ cannot close, and 2) if we are willing to relearn how to love people during a strange season, God will abundantly bless those efforts.

The American entitlement that led to complaints about churches closing also led to the bizarre phenomenon of politicizing the responsible and loving action of wearing a mask. The facts demonstrate that the act prevents the spread of the coronavirus, making asymptomatic carriers far less likely to infect others. Thus, masks save lives. Yet, some claim they have the right to choose for themselves whether or not they wear a mask. These same people most often claim to be Christians and usually maintain beliefs that women do not have the choice over whether or not to terminate a pregnancy. They rightly understand one act of deadly entitlement while simultaneously partaking in another act of entitlement that is potentially deadly itself. Likewise, they tend to approve of laws that prohibit smoking in public, though secondhand smoke is far less likely to be fatal than spreading COVID-19. They do not admit or recognize the hypocrisy in their attitudes toward life and death matters.

Such a claim about masks demands a perceived right over who lives and who dies. Those who fight for this right communicate that they feel entitled to endanger and even kill other people. The facts of COVID-19 determine this reality. It is not an opinion. In the first chapter of this book, I discussed one facet of critical thinking as evaluating and interpreting data. Some facts, however, require no interpretation. They are absolute, black-and-white matters. One plus one will always equal two. The COVID-19 facts listed earlier are among those absolutes. There is no way to interpret them any differently than the way the words read. This same principle also applies to most of the facts available about climate change that I addressed in earlier paragraphs. If the decision to wear a mask can potentially save someone's life, then my decision to exercise my right, refusing to wear one, makes me guilty of murder before God if someone dies of the disease while I am an asymptomatic carrier. Likewise, if I decide to worship the god of convenience and neglect taking the appropriate personal actions that can help curb climate change, I play a role in the deaths due to preventable natural disasters and starvation. I admit that the necessary actions to stop climate change are the most difficult adjustments for me to make in order to love the way Jesus calls us to. I live in a constant cycle of repentance, always trying to change my destructive behaviors, even as I recognize that I have a long way to go.

While many of us wondered for a long time if President Trump was clueless about the facts of COVID-19 or spreading misinformation for personal political gain, his supporters listened to him. I have been hard on the individuals who make pro-death decisions, yet I do not want to lose sight of the brainwashing that occurred. Some Trump supporters assumed that these were not black-and-white issues. They reached this assumption naturally, because the president constantly changes how he responds to the crisis and because Fox News has downplayed it as much as Trump has. Once the tapes of his conversation with Bob Woodward surfaced, however, no room for questioning Trump's motives remained. We heard with our own ears the admission of our president that he knew and believed the established facts concerning the virus. He articulated these facts to Woodward even before the whole country knew them. After he made his knowledge known to Woodward, he encouraged businesses not to shut down when the CDC recommended closures because of the same knowledge Trump possessed. Trump chose the economy over life, as he often has. Later, Trump told supporters not to wear masks or social distance and even called them to his rallies without the proper precautions (though Trump took drastic precautions to protect himself that eventually were not enough). Since Trump usually maintained far more than the prescribed amount of distance from others, it was not always necessary for him to wear a mask. Yet, he discouraged the whole nation from wearing masks, even when circumstances demand the action. He promoted political division over the objects.

With regards to masks, Trump uncharacteristically decided that winning a perceived political battle was even more important than the economy. The knowledge concerning masks that Trump held back from his followers empowers people to be in public in as safe a way as possible. If Trump had been upfront about that knowledge, he could have avoided much of the economic fallout that occurred. Since he lied, many businesses are still making (at the time of writing) the difficult decision to keep extremely limited hours in order to avoid mask defiance that makes opening unsafe.[31] Trump used his lies and manipulation to brainwash supporters. As such, they are not entirely to blame for pro-death responses to the coronavirus. Like many other pro-death practices between 2016 and 2020, Trump's words serve as the source of those practices. Nevertheless, Trump supporters who continued to follow in Trump's pro-death ways after hearing the revelations from

---

31. Concha, "Woodward's Trump," paras. 2–12.

the Woodward tapes demonstrate that they love the lies of personal entitlement too much to care about the wellbeing of other people. So, how can we love if our daily lives and our political affiliations are filled with pro-death decisions? We cannot.

1.3.2.6 How Can We Love God if We Do Not Love Our Neighbor?

The Bible is full of statements that link loving God with loving humanity. So, I urge us all to use these considerations as a starting point to assess how well we love others. When we love God and love our neighbor, we know that our worship of God is true and complete. To help us move toward that perfected worship, we will transition into a liturgy.

> *Liturgy 4: Learning to Love*

1. Confess bondage to a loveless state as part of worship given to the American Dream instead of to God. I will assist in this confession by reproducing a part of Lutheran liturgy that deals with repentance:[32]

   > We confess that we are in bondage to sin and cannot free ourselves. We have sinned against you in thought, word, and deed by what we have done and by what we have left undone. We have not loved you with our whole heart; we have not loved our neighbors as ourselves. For the sake of your Son, Jesus Christ, have mercy on us. Forgive us, renew us, and lead us so that we might delight in your will and walk in your ways to the glory of your holy name, Amen.

2. Read the following Scripture passages. After each one, take time to journal your thoughts (if alone) or discuss how it relates to your group's context with one group member taking notes. Write down any ways you can receive God's forgiveness and renewal so as to turn away from a loveless state. Record specific ways you (individually or corporately) have shown love in the past that you have neglected more recently. Also write down anything that comes to your mind of how to choose love over convenience.

   - Deut 6:1–9
   - 1 Cor 13

---

32. Evangelical Lutheran Church in America, *Lutheran Book of Worship*, 56.

- Lev 19:17–18
- Matt 23:23
- Lev 19:33–34
- 1 John 4:20–21
- Mic 6:8

3. Use your journal or discussion notes to identify how you can follow the three directions Jesus gave to the Ephesian church: "Remember from where you have fallen, repent, and do the former works."
4. Invite the Holy Spirit to rid you of the culturally ingrained idolatry of convenience.

1.4 The Pale Green Horse

The first horseman is responsible for warfare, the second for bitter division, and the third for economic disparity. All of these evils can lead to types of death although not necessarily literal, physical deaths. Each one yields a different kind of death. Each one causes death by different means. Nevertheless, the result is always death. Therefore, the fourth horse represents the culmination of the work done by the first three. The pale green horse represents death itself. Since the name Death is ascribed to this horseman, we find a personification of all kinds of death in this symbol. Each of the methods he uses to kill relates to one of the first three horsemen. The first three horsemen are charged with causing death; the fourth horseman is charged with being death.

This shift suggests that we are now more in the realm of future *eschatology* than we were with the first three horsemen. Temporally, each *septet* moves from the present reality of the seven congregations toward Jesus's second coming. John's record of his vision might still have messages for the seven congregations within the latter portions, but those messages are far more evident in the earlier sections of each *septet*.

The significance of a character that embodies death is central to the overarching theme of Revelation. The book reveals Jesus as worthy of worship because of his sacrifice and resurrection that ensures a time when he will completely defeat death. As such, we should not think of this character named Death as Satan. Certainly, Satan and his demons play an important role in death in the present age. Nevertheless, the creation account of Genesis 1–2 implies that knowledge about death existed because humanity fell.

Again, Satan plays a role in that original death as evinced by the serpent, but the Bible never refers to Satan as an embodiment of death. Satan is an embodiment of sin and thus a cause of death and a promoter of death, yet Satan himself is not Death.

Scripture discusses many types of death: the physical cessation of existence, spiritual separation from God, an ending in the midst of one's life (i.e., the death to sin marking a new life,), and eternal death. Since the pale green horseman is death, he must represent the world's greatest enemy. Satan is only the enemy of God and God's people. Death (except for the positive implication listed above in parentheses) is the enemy that comes for all people in all areas of life. Jesus is the Resurrection and the Life. Although we experience all these negative forms of death, we can be assured that the world's greatest enemy will be defeated. The pale green horseman represents the realities of physical death, spiritual death, relational death, death of dreams or goals, etc. The list can go on almost infinitely, but we must not lose sight that the personification of death is listed fourth in this set of seven. This fact might sound inconsequential, but it actually offers significant hope. The pale green horse may indeed come for everybody in a multitude of forms, but it never has the final word. Since the text has transitioned into an *eschatological* setting, it is moving closer to the point when Death will be defeated.

2. DIVINE JUSTICE REVEALED (REV 6:9—7:17)

The unveiling of the first four seals all involved a devastating unleashing of evil on the world. The fifth and sixth seals highlight divine victory over those evils. John introduces a new group of characters here, who are marked by their faithfulness in persecution. Their faithfulness extends to the point of death.

2.1 The Cry of the Martyrs (Fifth Seal)

The characters introduced here cry out for vindication. Nearing the end of a *septet*, we know that the setting is closer to the end of the age than the content of the previous seals. This placement within the septet suggests that the group John sees represents all people throughout human history who have chosen faithfulness to God over life. They wait together until God's justice is fulfilled, the time when martyrdom will cease to exist. The words in their cry echoes the first martyrdom accounted in Scripture.

In the Gospels, Jesus pronounces judgment on a group of Pharisees that involves the promise of justice for all martyrs including Abel (Matt 23:34–36/Luke 11:49–51). God will right the wrongs done against them by punishing the guilty parties. When praising Abel's faith, the author of Hebrews writes, "although he died, he still speaks" (Heb 11:4b). Abel still speaks, because he did not live to experience the fruit of his sacrifice on earth. Abel's murder requires full vindication. As Abel still speaks after his death, so all martyrs cry out to God in the intermediary state (what we usually call heaven), longing for the time when God's justice will be complete.

2.1.1 The Cry of the Martyrs and the Congregation in Smyrna

Revelation 6:10 recounts the specific cry John heard from these martyrs. Smyrna's church would have related most intimately with the cry. In the prophecy to believers in Smyrna, God tells them that they will endure violent persecution in the near future (if they were not already experiencing it upon receiving John's Apocalypse). God instructs them to "be faithful unto death" (Rev 2:10). The cry of the martyrs assures the congregation expecting persecution that death is not the end of their faith. When they sacrifice their lives God, he will vindicate their deaths. Even though this cry presents a lament and a longing, Smyrna should have received it with hope, recognizing that God will reward all who are "faithful unto death." It would have reassured those in Smyrna that God will continuously judge those who persecute believers, even when he does not do so in the timing and manner they might desire.

2.1.2 The Cry of the Martyrs and Contemporary American Readers

I must note once again that the United States has no history or present habit of persecution against Christians. As such, the cry of the martyrs will not speak as directly to us as it would have to Christians in Smyrna. We might even feel uncomfortable with the idea of God's judgment, thinking that the martyrs sound vindictive. We rightly understand that the Bible depicts God's forgiveness. We tend to think wrongly, however, that all people must forgive their attackers and just move on with life regardless of any effort on the perpetrator's end. This idea is not faithful to the message of forgiveness we find in the Gospels. Our forgive and forget Christianity does not allow people to heal from wounds inflicted by others. It lets unrepentant sinners off the hook without needing to take the responsibility to change their behavior and to seek right relationships with their victims. American ideas about forgiveness tend to put the burden on the sinned-against, while all biblical commands put the burden on the sinner. To begin appreciating this truth, pay close attention to the order that Jesus presents for dealing with offenses amongst fellow believers in Matthew 18.

Because this idea is so contrary to what most of us have been taught, I recommend a book from the person who first opened my eyes to this neglected biblical truth. Leah Coulter is a professor of practical theology (she was my professor at the King's Seminary in Van Nuys, California). In her book *Rediscovering the Power of Repentance and Forgiveness*,[33] she puts the concept of forgiveness in the context of the Hebraic worldview out of which it was born. This worldview finds the idea of forgiveness without repentance impossible. Coulter then demonstrates how to practice what the Bible actually teaches about forgiveness and repentance in a way that allows people to heal. In cases when the offender refuses to repent, this teaching does not justify revenge or grudges; rather, it teaches sinned-against people to trust God to provide the justice they need. Most of Coulter's ministerial life has been dedicated to adult females who experienced sexual abuse in adolescence. Her book reflects this work but is broad enough to provide a biblical perspective on all needs for repentance and forgiveness. We cannot fully comprehend the cry of the martyrs without the renewed perception of justice that Coulter helps provide.

2.2 White Robes

2.2.1 *White Robes and the Seven Congregations*

The martyrs are told to continue waiting and to rest. John tells us that they are given "white robes" as they maintain their patience. The prophecies to the believers in Sardis and Laodicea also involved the images of "white robes." Members of Revelation's first audiences who were from Sardis or Laodicea would have paid special attention when that imagery was repeated.

Both prophecies use the symbol of "white garments" in the same way. People wearing white are contrasted with those wearing dirty garments. White represents purity. Those in "white garments" have been cleansed of their sins. Those in "soiled garments" have not. In both prophecies, the "white garments" are promises for the members of the two congregations who overcome in the face of the unique impurities present in each church.

Jesus mentioned no persecution in his rebukes of Sardis and Laodicea. The martyrs in Revelation 6, however, are given white robes as a result of

---

33. Coulter, *Repentance and Forgiveness*.

what they endured. The robes mark them as pure, because they remained loyal to God's own purity even in the face of death. The messages to Sardis and Laodicea, however, present congregations that did not have many people likely to express this kind of devotion to God. Thus, not many of them were pure like the martyrs. They were the ones most likely found in "soiled garments." The image of the "white robes" in Revelation 6 calls them to repentance. It encourages them to re-evaluate what they live for and what they would be willing to die for. The passage offers them the opportunity to trade their complacency for the willingness to join in the suffering and lamentation of those who have already been martyred. By this new attitude, they can learn to become "faithful unto death" like the believers in Smyrna were called to be. In that way, they would become pure and worthy to wear white robes, whether or not they became literal martyrs.

2.2.2 White Robes and Contemporary American Readers

The symbol of "white robes" exhorts hearers in Smyrna and Laodicea to embrace suffering, even to the point of death. It does not ask them to seek suffering. It demands, nevertheless, that they become willing to give up anything including their own lives to be counted among those whom God has made pure. In the United States, our circumstances are far more like those of Sardis and Laodicea than those of Smyrna. In a previous section, we discussed the common American idol of convenience. When we pursue comfort and convenience at the expense of others' lives, we wear the same "soiled garments" that most congregants in Smyrna and Laodicea did.

When we use the word "purity" in Christian settings in the United States, we tend to think only of sexual purity. Other portions of Revelation deal with that issue through images of white things, but the image of "white robes" challenges us to think outside of this box when we discuss purity. Sexual purity relates to what we do with our bodies. The purity involved in the "white robes" relates to what we do with our difficulties in life. The symbol forces us to ask ourselves if we embrace difficulties as a natural part of the Christian life that can even lead to martyrdom, which NT authors count as a source of rejoicing. Not many of us in the United States live like that.

We tend to act as if no suffering can yield rejoicing. Of course, many types of suffering come only from the fact that we live in a fallen, evil world and do not deserve rejoicing. Any suffering, however, that comes as the result of being faithful to the gospel is a type of suffering over which to rejoice, even if it has the potential to cause death. Instead of facing this reality, in the United States we are quick to shun all types of suffering. We think of suffering as something that we must avoid at any cost. When our highest priorities are our own comfort, convenience, and happiness, of course we view any difficulty as an evil to escape.

The message of the "white robes" for us, then, calls us to stop avoiding the things in life we find scary or uncomfortable. We must lay aside the idols of comfort, convenience, and happiness. Then, we must become willing to give back to God everything we have and everything we are, including our feelings about suffering. That new attitude toward suffering, whether it leads to actual distress or not, can make us pure and able to be counted among those willing to sacrifice their lives for the gospel message.

2.3 The Sixth Seal and Judgment

2.3.1 The Sixth Seal and the Negative Side of Judgment

We encountered many cosmic disturbances in Revelation prior to the sixth seal. All of them, however, connected to the theme of worship. On the surface, the cosmic disturbances of Revelation 6:12–17 do not relate to worship. They accompany destruction. It appears that these phenomena annihilate the world. The last three verses of Revelation 6, however, describe people seeking refuge, protection, and salvation. They need this help because of the destructive weather and celestial occurrences. The passage is very clear, however, that they seek help from the earth itself, not from its creator, sustainer, and healer. It explicitly states that the people are not hiding from the disasters; they are hiding from the Lamb. They refused to worship God.[34]

As the sixth element in a *septet*, this represents the last one prior to Jesus's second coming. People are hiding, because they know their destruction is imminent. Ancient Greco-Roman gods often represented earthly phenomena, both healthy and destructive. Zeus, for example, is connected with rain, wind, lightning, thunder, and meteorites.[35] People looking to the earth for refuge, then, probably means that they are seeking their gods to avoid the wrath of the one true God.

Therefore, we can assess that this passage does not refer to the destruction of the earth but to the destruction of idols. God's victory over Pharaoh at the Red Sea was preceded by the destruction of Egypt's gods. Likewise, the sixth seal confronts people with the futility of trusting in creation to hide them from God's wrath on the final day of the present age. Later portions of Revelation clarify that part of the earth will be destroyed prior to

---

34. Steinmann, "Tripartite Structure," 71.
35. Croy, "God by Any Other Name," 33.

Jesus's second coming. We must notice, though, that it is only part (i.e., "a third of the earth was burned up" in Revelation 8:7). Scripture never says that God will destroy the earth. In Genesis 9:11, God actually declares the opposite following the flood. He says he will never destroy the entire earth again. That does not necessarily mean that the earth will not come to an end. The sixth seal could culminate in the death of the earth, and the seventh seal could bring its resurrection along with the bodily resurrection of all people. We know for certain, however, that God himself will not be responsible for destroying what he created. If the earth comes to an end, it will be at the hands of humanity, not God.

Thus, in this passage, John indicates seeing a vision of a time in which God will destroy idolatry, not the earth. The people who seek refuge from the Lamb must do so because they know they have not received his salvation. Therefore, they are judged because they refused to worship the one true God. As such, the cosmic disturbances of Revelation 6 connect to worship just as much as the earlier ones. This passage merely reflects the opposite side of the matter. In earlier passages, the phenomena pointed toward a heavenly worship scene. Here, they point to the judgment against people who vehemently refuse to worship God and against the gods they worship in his place.

2.3.2 The Sixth Seal and the Positive Side of Judgment

Revelation 7 returns us to the earlier uses of cosmic disturbances. Chapter 6 depicted final judgment, so now John turns to the judgment of God's own people. That judgment is a joyful occasion. The first three verses deal with protecting God's people from the harm done to the earth as depicted in Revelation 6. In Revelation 7:4–9, John recounts seeing the ultimate result of God's salvation, first for the Jews in verses 4–8 and then for the gentiles in verse 9. Heavenly worship ensues for the rest of the chapter.

John interrupts the worship in order to recount a brief dialogue he had with his angelic mediator in Revelation 7:13–14. The angel explains to him that the people he sees worshiping here are "the people coming out of great distress." Many interpreters use this passage as the basis for their expectation of an *eschatological* time period that they refer to as the Great Tribulation. It is supposedly a time in which the earth experiences more trauma than it has ever known, because the Antichrist has arrived.

Two problems occur with this kind of teaching. First, the Greek phrase offers no credence to connect the people John sees to any particular time period. Secondly, the text merely says that these people have come "out of great distress." John, therefore, does not see people who have come out of the Great Tribulation; he sees people who have come out of great tribulation. A huge difference exists between these two ideas. Jesus promised his disciples and all who would ever follow him: "In this world, you will have tribulation, but be courageous; I have overcome the world" (John 16:33). In other words, all who follow Jesus in all time periods should experience tribulation. Because John records seeing Jews first and then gentiles without a clear temporal designation, he apparently refers to all people who have received the Messiah's sacrifice. "Coming out of great distress," then, points toward God's ultimate act of overcoming death. It gives us a picture of the resurrection of those who had been cleansed of their sins by Jesus's blood.

2.3.3 Hymnology of the Sixth Seal: A Call to the Seven Churches and to the US Church

The hymn that follows the victory demands Christ-followers to stop giving all these attributes away to the imperial cult. Once again, only God is worthy to receive this acclaim. The hymn summons the seven congregations to worship God alone. It condemns every attempt to give another what only God deserves. We must receive that same demand that the text placed on first-century churches.

When Brett Kavanaugh defended his Supreme Court nomination before Congress on September 5, 2018, Louisiana Senator John Kennedy asked him to discuss his favorite Federalist paper. Instead of answering the question as it was asked, he recited one passage after another, each with its appropriate chapter and verse citation. I watched the hearings as they occurred live, and I saw Kavanaugh's face, tone of voice, and entire demeanor change when he addressed this question. Before that moment, he consistently appeared focused to the point of panic, defending himself for no apparent reason (this happened a week before the first sexual assault allegation was placed against him). His facial expressions constantly communicated consternation and frustration. When he began reciting Federalist papers verbatim, however, he immediately and drastically changed. He demonstrated a meditative and serene presence as he quoted what made him comfortable. Kennedy (a senator from the same Republican Party responsible for nominating Kavanaugh) expressed frustration with the Supreme Court candidate for taking so long to answer. The senator quipped that he was not asking Kavanaugh to choose between his children, yet Kavanaugh reacted to a question about the Federalist papers with exactly that manner of seriousness.

Kavanaugh conveyed a deep devotion to and worship of merely human words that were written in the 1780s. He blessed those words through deeming them worthy of such elaborate repetition. He honored them by his unwillingness to choose one as he was asked to do. He upheld the whole canon as a sacred scripture and gave them spiritual authority in his life and over the nation. Kavanaugh is a practicing Catholic, so I am not intending to bring the genuineness of his Christian faith into question. Rather, I suggest that he appears guilty of *syncretism*, mixing religions in a way he might not even be aware of.

Kavanaugh's rapid change in temperament seemed to demonstrate the reception of strength through the repetition of the words he values so deeply. As such, he used them in the same way occult devotees perform hymnic incantations. Yet, he also used a blessing/curse formula for those who obey or disobey its contents similar to many OT texts. Kavanaugh declared the Federalist papers as the highest source of wisdom (at least for that time and in that setting). He bestowed upon those words a mystical type of wisdom. He evidently believes that such wisdom informs and shapes at least the body he addressed (a Senate committee) and the body he aspired to enter and eventually did enter (the Supreme Court). He seemed to exude a desire, nevertheless, that this spiritual authority he accredited to the Federalist papers extend to all Americans. He appeared to promote a type of evangelism; he wanted these words to go forth and spiritually transform the nation. As Kavanaugh praised, recited, and invoked the Federalist papers, it seems he communicated the basis on which one of his religions is founded. He gave the papers dominion over his life as a judge and as an American. Furthermore, he indicated that these two aspects of himself probably form his spiritual self-identity, not just his occupation. This example shows what nationalistic worship entails for one individual through a type of hymnology. Kavanaugh embodied such worship perfectly during the second day of his confirmation hearing.

3. THE SEVENTH SEAL (REV 8:1–5)

Since the final judgment and resurrection of the dead occur as part of the sixth seal, it appears that the fullness of God's will has been revealed. Nevertheless, one seal still remains unopened. The Lamb opens the final seal in Revelation 8:1. It functions literarily as a connector between two *septets*. On the one hand, the unveiling of the seventh seal contains a continuation of the eternal worship that first flowed out of the sixth seal in the previous chapter. It does so with its allusion to the OT sacrificial system via sacrificial silence and incense burned at the altar.[36] Revelation 8:5 concludes the passage with the specific cosmic disturbances that earlier in Revelation accompany heavenly worship scenes. On the other hand, the opening of the seventh seal introduces us to the next judgment *septet*. The seven angels have seven trumpets. After the seven seals, the text tells the results of the seven trumpets being blown. So, with the seventh seal, we find an ending of the first *septet* and a beginning of the second one.

Further Reading:

For warfare and judgment amongst the seven horsemen:
Keener, Craig S. *Revelation*. Grand Rapids: Zondervan, 2000. Pertinent pages 199–216.

For Revelation's criticism of Rome's economic disparity:
Kraybill, Nelson J. *Imperial Cult and Commerce in John's Apocalypse*. Sheffield, UK: Sheffield Academic, 1996.

For recurrences of themes as reminders to congregations of God's specific message for them:
Culy, Martin M. *The Book of Revelation: The Rest of the Story*. Eugene, OR: Pickwick, 2017.

For the connection between divine justice and human forgiveness/repentance:
Coulter, Leah. *Rediscovering the Power of Repentance and Forgiveness*. Atlanta: Ampelon, 2006.

---

36. Wick, "Silence in Heaven," 514.

Chapter 4

The Seven Trumpets (Rev 8:6—11:19)

8 ⁶ Then the seven angels who have the seven trumpets prepared to blow them. ⁷ So the first blew his trumpet, and hail came along with fire mixed with blood, and it was thrown to the earth, and a third of the earth was burned up, a third of the trees were burned up, and all the green grass was burned up. ⁸ Then the second angel blew his trumpet, and something like a large mountain burning with fire was thrown into the sea, and a third of the sea became blood, ⁹ so a third of the living sea creatures died, and a third of the ships were destroyed. ¹⁰ Then the third angel blew his trumpet, and a large star fell from heaven burning like a torch, and it fell upon a third of the rivers and on the springs of water, ¹¹ and the star was named Wormwood, since a third of the waters turned into wormwood, and many of the people died from the water that was made bitter. ¹² Then the fourth angel blew his trumpet, and a third of the sun was struck along with a third of the moon and a third of the stars with the result that a third of them was darkened, so day and likewise night; a third of its light could not shine. ¹³ Then I looked and heard an eagle flying in midair, saying in a loud voice, "Woe! Woe! Woe to those dwelling on the earth because of the remaining blasts of the trumpets from the three angels who are about to blow their trumpets."

9 ¹ Then the fifth angel blew his trumpet, and I saw a star that had fallen from heaven to earth, and the key to the pit of the abyss was given to him, ² and he opened the pit of the abyss, so smoke went up from the pit like the smoke of a great furnace, and the sun was darkened along with the air from the smoky pit. ³ Then locusts came out of the smoke to the earth, and authority was given to them like the authority that scorpions have over the earth. ⁴ Then it was told to them not to harm the grass of the earth, any green thing or any tree, but only the people who do not have the seal of God on their foreheads. ⁵ And authority was granted to them with the result that they not kill them, but will torment them for five months, and their torment will be like the torment of a scorpion when it stings a person. ⁶ And in these days, people will seek death but will certainly not find it; they will desire to die but death flees from them. ⁷ Now the forms of the locusts were like horses prepared for battle, on their heads was something like crowns similar to gold, their faces were like human faces, ⁸ they had heads of hair like women's hair, their feet were like those of lions, ⁹ they had chests like iron breastplates, the sound of their wings was like the sound of many chariot horses running into battle, ¹⁰ and they have tails and stingers like scorpions. Their authority is in their tails to harm people for five months. ¹¹ They have a king over them, namely the angel of the abyss, whose name in Hebrew is Abaddon, and in Greek, he has the name Apollyon. ¹² One woe has passed; behold, two woes are still to come after these things.

¹³ Then the sixth angel blew his trumpet, and I heard a sound from the four horns of the golden altar that is in the presence of God, ¹⁴ saying to the sixth angel who has the trumpet, "Release the four angels that are bound at the great river, the Euphrates." ¹⁵ So the four angels who had been prepared for the hour, the day, the month, and the year were released in order that they could kill a third of the people, ¹⁶ and the number of the troops of horsemen was 200,000; I heard their number. ¹⁷ Then I saw the horses and the ones seated on them in the vision in this manner: I saw them having red, blue, and yellow breastplates; the horses' heads were like lions' heads, and fire, smoke, and brimstone proceeded out of their mouths. ¹⁸ A third of the people were killed from these three plagues, from the fire, smoke, and brimstone proceeding out of their mouths. ¹⁹ Indeed, the authority of the horses is in their tails, because their tails are like snakes that have heads with the ability to harm by them. ²⁰ Then the rest of the people, who had neither died by these plagues nor repented from the works of their hands (that

is, they did not repent from worshiping demons or idols of gold, silver, bronze, stone, or wood which cannot see, hear, or walk) [21] also did not repent from their murders, their sorceries, their sexually immoral acts, or their thefts.

10 [1] Then I saw another mighty angel coming down from heaven wrapped in a cloud with a rainbow over his head; his face was like the sun, his feet were like fiery torches, [2] and he had a small scroll opened in his hand. He placed his right foot on the sea and his left foot on the ground, [3] and he cried out in a loud voice like a lion's roar, and when he cried out, seven thunders made their own sounds. Then, when the seven thunders sounded, I was about to write, but I heard a voice from heaven saying, "Seal up what the seven thunders said, and do not write the words." [5] Then the angel that I saw standing on the sea and on the ground raised his right hand toward heaven [6] and swore an oath to the one who lives forever and ever—the one who created heaven and all that is in it, the earth and all that is in it, and the sea and all that is in it—no more time exists, [7] but in the days of the sound of the seventh angel (when he is about to blow his trumpet), then the mystery of God will have been completed as God announced to his slaves, the prophets. [8] Then the voice that I heard from heaven spoke with me again and said, "Go and take the open scroll that is in the hand of the angel who stood on the sea and on the ground." [9] So I went to the angel and told him to give me the little scroll. Then he said to me, "Take and eat it, and it will make the stomach sour, but it will be sweet like honey in your mouth." [10] So I took the small scroll out of the angel's hand and ate it; indeed, it was as sweet as honey in my mouth, but when I swallowed it, my stomach was made sour. [11] Then he said to me, "It is necessary that you prophecy again concerning many peoples, nations, tongues, and kingdoms."

11 [1] Then a measuring rod like a staff was given to me; the one who gave it to me said: "Arise and measure God's temple along with the alter and places of prayer in it. [2] But leave out the courtyard outside the temple, and do not measure it, since it was given to the Gentiles, and they will trample the holy city for forty-two months, [3] but I will grant authority to my two witnesses, and they will prophecy for 1,260 days clothed in sackcloth. [4] These are the two olive trees and the two lampstands that stand before the Lord of the earth, [5] and if anyone wishes to harm them, fire proceeds out of their mouth, and it consumes their enemies. [6] These witnesses have authority to close heaven in order that no rain may fall during the days of their prophesying, and they have authority over the waters so as to turn them into

blood and to strike the earth with every kind of plague whenever they want. ⁷ Then, whenever they finish their testimony, the beast that comes up from the abyss will wage war with them, conquer them, and kill them. ⁸ Then their bodies will be left on the street of the great city, which is prophetically called Sodom and Egypt, where their Lord was crucified. ⁹ Then some from among the peoples, tribes, tongues, and nations see their bodies for three and a half days, but they do not allow their bodies to be placed in a tomb. ¹⁰ And all who dwell on the earth rejoice on account of them, celebrate, and send each other gift, because these two prophets tormented the people who dwell on the earth."

¹¹ Then after the three and a half days, the spirit of life from God entered into them, they stood on their feet, and great fear fell on the people who saw them. ¹² They heard a loud voice from heaven saying to them, "Come up here," so they went up to heaven in a cloud as their enemies watched them. ¹³ Also in that hour, a great earthquake occurred, a tenth of the city fell, 7,000 people were killed, and the rest became fearful and gave glory to the God of heaven. ¹⁴ The second woe has come; behold, the third woe is coming soon.

¹⁵ Then the seventh angel blew his trumpet, and loud voices shouted in heaven, saying, "The kingdom of the world has become the kingdom of our Lord and of his Messiah, and he will reign forever and ever." ¹⁶ Then the twenty-four elders who sit on their thrones before God fell on their faces and worshiped God, ¹⁷ saying, "We give thanks to you, O Lord God, the Almighty, who is and who was, because you have taken your great power and established your reign." ¹⁸ Then the nations were enraged, and your wrath came along with the time to judge the dead people and to give reward to your slaves—namely to the prophets, saints, and all who fear your name, both small and great—and to destroy the destroyers of the earth. ¹⁹ Then God's temple which is in heaven was opened, and the ark of his covenant became visible in his temple; then thunders, rumblings, lightnings, an earthquake, and a great hailstorm occurred.

1. THE FIRST SIX TRUMPETS: PLAGUES (REV 8:5—9:21)

The seven seals and the seven trumpets both present pictures of God's judgment. The seals deal more with the concept of judgment itself. That is, they detail the destructive evil of the world that demands divine justice as the only way of healing the world. They lay the blame for such necessity on human sin. Humans destroy the world, not God. As such, there are dimensions to the judgments represented by the seven seals that coincide both with the present age and with Jesus's second coming. The trumpets, however, convey a far more future-oriented message.[1]

Even as they point to the future, the trumpet imagery reflects both Israel's history and the present Greco-Roman world of John's day. Though the plagues against Egypt from Exodus serve as a stronger background for the seven bowls than they do for the trumpets, any language of plagues in the NT should remind us of Egypt. Like the judgments against Egypt, the seven bowls include destructive changes to bodies of water, hail, fire, locusts, darkness, and death.[2] Also similar to Egypt, the goal of the judgment is to call for the repentance of those who oppress God's people and who refuse to turn to God for salvation. As Pharaoh continued in stubbornness and refused to repent, the plagues worsened until a time when no more room for repentance existed. The imagery of the sixth trumpet foretells a time when God will execute his judgment mixed with his mercy, just as he does throughout the present age. At a certain time in the future, however, when sinners continue to refuse to repent, a point will come when God's judgment destroys them. So, the seals clarify that humans are responsible for destruction that comes to the world, not God. Likewise, the trumpets clarify that God will never destroy the whole world (just as he promised after the Genesis flood), even though his judgments might include destruction to parts of the world.

The plagues of Egypt consist of one source for the background of the seven seals. The other source is Greco-Roman plague myths. For example, Greco-Roman religious traditions assumed that hail aroused the gods[3] and represented chaos and hopelessness.[4] One of the purposes of the plagues against Egypt was to destroy Egypt's gods (Exod 12:12). The language in the seven bowls, then, reflect a plan to destroy the gods of the Greco-Roman world.

Egypt had its own set of deities, distinct from the gods of Rome. Those deities, nevertheless, share similar origins related to worshiping what is created rather than worshiping the Creator. As such, most world religions and all cults from all time periods are guilty of similar idolatry as the Egyptian and Greco-Roman pagans. The judgment that this passage points toward,

---

1. Mounce, *Revelation*, 176–77.
2. Koester, *Revelation*, 445–46.
3. Cicero, *Nat. d.* 2.5.14.
4. Artemidorus, *Onirocritica* 2.8–9.

then, does not require that people worship replicas of either the Egyptian or Roman gods. It assumes, nevertheless, that pagan worship (which entails worshiping aspects of creation) will exist in all time periods of world history before the second coming. Therefore, the plagues of the seven trumpets indicate God's eventual end to all gods of the earth from all periods of time, making the trumpets more future-oriented than the seals.

1.1 The Fifth Trumpet: Locusts

The devastation that the first four trumpets caused should be self-explanatory based on what we have already discussed. Therefore, I will let the introduction of this section suffice for the first four trumpets. Stars fall at the sounding of the fifth trumpet. Heavenly bodies fall in other portions of Revelation, but the fallen star of Revelation 9:1 cannot refer to a literal heavenly one like the others. It points, rather, to an angelic being. The other angel in this verse is an angel of God who opens the abyss (the same abyss into which Satan himself will eventually be thrown). Therefore, the star must refer to the fallen angel we know as Satan. The locusts that precede from the abyss, then, are not literal locusts like those that harassed Egypt; they are demonic beings temporarily released from bondage to inflict deep suffering on people who have not received Jesus as their Messiah. Throughout the OT, God used people who resisted him to judge others who continue too long in their own resistance. The concept is the same here, yet the locusts are not allowed to kill the people. So, even in this plague, room for repentance remains.

The phrase "one woe has passed" (Rev 9:12) indicates that the first five plagues have ended. As they come to a close, so does the offer for repentance to anyone who continually resists God in the face of the torment. The next plague, then, depicts the future moment in history when all opportunities for repentance will pass away.

1.2 The Sixth Trumpet: The Demonic Army

The angels standing at the Euphrates are characters introduced for the first time in Revelation 9:14. If we do not read it closely, we might be tempted to think that these four are among God's angels. The text, nevertheless, says that they are released from bondage like the locusts that came before them. Thus, they are also demonic beings. They carry out God's judgment like the locusts did earlier in Revelation 9 and like armies of God's enemies did often in the OT. This demonic army is released to kill the people who belong to Satan instead of to God (i.e., all who do not have God's mark on their forehead). Like the other trumpets' effects, the demonic army only kills a third of humanity, yet none who remain repent (9:20).

The number seven is the number of completion. Even though the seventh trumpet does not follow through with the deaths of those who remain, it does involve resurrection and other positive results of final judgment. Furthermore, the text indicates, "one woe has passed; behold, two woes are still to come" (9:12) and "the second woe has come" (11:14). The text never names the third woe. The first woe passes after the fifth trumpet, and the second woe passes after the sixth trumpet. Thus, when only one trumpet remains, only one woe remains. We know from elsewhere in Scripture that the final judgment against all unbelievers accompanies Jesus's second coming and restoration of the earth. The text never mentions when the third woe occurs, like it does for the first two; rather it moves abruptly to a joyous scene for the faithful. Thus, the third woe is an implicit part of the seventh trumpet in which sin and sinners are completely eradicated from the world. As such, the seven trumpets, just like the seven seals, culminate in Jesus's second coming, the general resurrection, and the final judgment.

2. INTERLUDE (REV 10:1—11:14)

2.1 Interlude Part 1: John's Prophetic Preparation

Although Revelation 10:7 makes mention of the seventh angel who has a trumpet to blow, Revelation 10 interrupts the flow between the sixth and seventh trumpets. It introduces us to yet another angel. This angel prepares John for two unveilings: 1) the blowing of the seventh trumpet in which "the mystery of God will have been completed" (Rev 10:7), and 2) something that was to remain mysterious to everyone but John, as the angel told him to keep it hidden and not to record it (10:4).

The angel prepares John to prophecy. The angel gives him a scroll to eat; this imagery echoes Ezekiel 2:8—3:3. Consuming the scroll prepared Ezekiel to deliver the difficult message of judgment God had commissioned him to convey. This concept of the scroll's bittersweet taste has been understood in three predominant ways throughout interpretive history. Although most choose one over the other two, I do not find any of these interpretations mutually exclusive. In fact, I believe they are all correct. First, some suggest that the sweet taste represents salvation and the bitter taste represents condemnation. Both realities are present in the contents of the scroll. Second, he prophetic calling involves the sweetness of possessing God's words for

God's people alongside the bitter inevitability that at least some will reject both the message and its messenger. Since we find the passage near the end of a judgment *septet*, we will shortly see the ultimate consequences of responding to God's words or rejecting them. Finally, others understand the scroll as a comment on the Christian life, sweet because of salvation and bitter because of the suffering Christians should expect to endure.[5] This *septet* presents divine vindication against false gods, against the people who worship those gods, and against those who oppress the people who belong to the true God. Therefore, all three interpretations fit.

2.2 Interlude Part 2: The End-Time Church

2.2.1 *John's Measuring Assignment*

Revelation 10 ends with a depiction of John's prophetic ministry. Revelation 11 begins with a call for John to measure, which is itself an extension of one form of prophetic ministry. Throughout the OT, the concept of a measuring line (especially in 1 Kgs 21:13; Isa 28:16–17; 34:11; 41:13; Jer 31:38–40; Lam 2:18; Job 38:5; Amos 7:7–9; Zech 1:16) related to prophecies of divine judgment and the desolation of those found wanting within that judgment.[6] John has just received a specific prophetic mission, and this passage is part of a judicial *septet*. Therefore, we can be certain that this passage's OT background is found in prophetic passages of judgment and not in any OT passage that conducts measurement solely for accurate dimensions.

Many OT passages discuss measuring for the sake of measuring within the context of the Jerusalem temple. Since John's measurements connect to OT prophecy and judgment, however, we must not look for direct correlation between Revelation 11's imagery and the temple. The "outer court" of the OT temple was for gentiles to worship *YHWH*. It was not as holy as the inner court, but it was still a holy place. If John intended to indicate a trampling of holy ground, however, the context of divine judgment would make God the one causing the trampling that destroys a place dedicated to him. We cannot possibly make any sense out of that, so it is much better to understand this measuring as a prophetic depiction of judgment, not a picture of any God-ordained sanctuary.

---

5. Koester, *Revelation*, 482–83. Koester outlines these three streams of thought with greater detail than I have outlined. He prefers the last option to the others. Since Revelation contains such a plurality of imagery, I suggest not deciding between these three. They all reflect the literary context of the text and the historical Christian beliefs regarding salvation, prophecy, and the Christian life.

6. Jauhiainen, "Measuring of the Sanctuary," 515.

2.2.2 Identity and Mission of The Two Witnesses

We have seen earlier how lampstands in Revelation point to the heavenly throne room. That throne room transcends time throughout John's Apocalypse. In this case at the end of a *septet*, nevertheless, John indicates he writes of a decidedly future aspect of the heavenly throne room. He does so by his reference to "olive trees" and "lampstands" within an entirely future context. Both of those symbols point more specifically to Christian witness. Revelation 11, therefore, presents a picture of evangelism in the last generation of the current age. The "two witnesses," then, probably represent the entirety of the church in that time period.[7]

The two witnesses play a role in the "second woe." They perform miracles that produce plagues just like Moses and Aaron.[8] God is the one exacting judgment, but he allows his people a role within it. Therefore, although the *eschatological* church will be involved in God's judgment, the text does not give license for people of any era to seek their own vengeance or to resort to violence. Since the text likens the *ecclesiological* role in the "second woe" to Moses and Aaron, it appears that the church will be a conduit through which plagues flow. This role can occur in a passive sense without God's people even knowing they are involved in judgment.

2.2.3 Persecution of the Two Witnesses

2.2.3.1 A Global Death Party

The context of Revelation 11:10 demonstrates that the deaths of God's people become the causes of global joy. Three future-tense verbs explain different aspects of that joy. First, the celebrants will proclaim their gladness and specify the deaths of the two witnesses as the reason for their exultation. Secondly, they will act out their gladness. I will call this act a global death party. One manifestation of this celebration will be sending gifts. John most likely would have used a verb that means "to give" if he merely meant a gift exchange, like most English translations treat this verb. By saying that they will "send each other gifts," on the other hand, he suggests that a mediator must take these presents from one person and place to another.[9] By this verb choice, John further communicates the universal reaction to the deaths.

---

7. Cf. Stevenson, *Power and Place*, 258–60.
8. Cf. Wong, "Two Witnesses," 347.
9. Bauer et al., *Greek-English Lexicon*, 795.

Isaiah 5:8–23 presents a similar situation in which people disregard the works of God, treating their own behavior as if it is morally good while God's is evil. They mistreat others for their own benefit and fail to recognize that God judges them for their inequity. They justify themselves as they "call evil good and good evil" (Isa 5:20). Revelation 11:10 foretells a moment at the very end of the age when calling what is evil good and calling what is good evil is a universal norm. The verse correlates with Daniel 8:1–14, which discusses a vision about a similar future time when humanity will be at its worst prior to God's restoration of all things: "And the host was given over along with the regular burnt offering because of transgression as it cast truth to the ground but continued succeeding in what it did" (Dan 8:12b).

Prior to Revelation 11:10, the vessels of God chosen to carry out judgment are named "two witnesses." Prophecy is part of their ministry, but the text predominantly identifies them as witnesses. This accreditation transitions in verse 10, when the text names them "prophets." People will rejoice over their deaths because of the torment they inflicted. But why will the ministry of the two witnesses yield distress? If we understand who God is throughout the totality of the Bible, we certainly cannot assume that they will harm people merely because God tells them to do so. In fact, if we understand the "two witnesses" as a literary reflection of Moses and Aaron as I suggested above, then the witnesses do not actually cause the harm. Rather, God's wrath inflicts the torment as a result of his righteous judgment.

God has called these two characters to be both witnesses (people who testify to the goodness of God in the midst of a dark world) and prophets (people who speak directly into the situations of their listeners). As prophets, they speak truth. Truth contradicts the ways of people who call evil good and good evil. These prophets remain faithful to God, which means they also remain faithful to the message God has given them to speak. Revelation does not provide a verbatim account of the message these prophets speak, but the context elucidates that it confronts the "inhabitants of the earth" with truth that they do not like. They would rather think of the two witnesses as the sources of their torment than take responsibility for their own sin, the real reason God must unleash wrath. Their rejoicing, celebrating, and gift-sending demonstrate their self-justification. They believe that everything that has happened to them must be the martyrs' fault; it surely cannot be their own. Nevertheless, the "inhabitants of the earth" are to blame. They have perverted justice and refused God's loving reign over their lives. The martyrs reflect God's goodness and justice.

Since we are nearing the end of a *recapitulation* in the text, we know that the final judgment is at hand. The witnesses die but experience resurrection. The "lampstand" language and *eschatological* context work together to indicate that the witnesses represent all believers at the end of the present age. This resurrection demonstrates full justification. The passage gives us a dramatic contrast between self-justification and real, divine justification. The former finds itself entitled to define morality on its own terms. The latter subjects itself to true love and goodness as demonstrated by God and his Messiah through sacrifice, suffering, and death.

2.2.3.2 Death Parties and the Seven Congregations of Asia Minor

Even though this passage foretells future events, the way in which Revelation communicates those events would have been meaningful to the congregations John addresses. Power is a central concept to Revelation 11. By calling what is evil good and what is good evil, the "inhabitants of the earth" will partner with the beast to exert power that attempts to destroy the earth. God's power ultimately overtakes the evil power through his love and justice. All seven congregations daily experienced earthly powers that tried to define good and evil in ways that brought about injustice and violence. Members of those congregations should have all known that this imperial power did not align with God's power. As the two witnesses express their prophetic power by speaking the truth, so John wanted his audiences to know that they can only experience the power of God when they are open to truth: when they rightly name what is good and what is evil, actively pursuing what they know to be good.[10]

The two witnesses exemplify "the fearless character of prophets from all time periods."[11] Telling of a future scenario in which all people celebrate the deaths of people who are faithful to God encourages John's first audiences to follow the example of these future witnesses. They would accomplish that by 1) trusting in God's empowerment toward fearless lives in the face of any enemy; 2) recognizing the gift of prophecy wherever it is present in their congregation and seeking to always hear "what the Spirit says to the churches" far beyond what they receive from John's Apocalypse; 3) loving truth and speaking truth in the midst of lies; and 4) committing to do what is good and to shun what is evil when others try to confuse them by calling evil good and good evil. We cannot find any records of what I am calling death parties from the Roman Empire in the first century CE. Nevertheless, whenever anyone "calls evil good and good evil," they speak with the same motivations that create these death parties in Revelation 11:10.

10. de Villiers, "Die kerk," 3.
11. de Villiers, "Die kerk," 4. Quote is my English translation of the Afrikaans article.

The celebration in the text develops out of a desire to continue in lifestyles that resist God's goodness and justice. The Roman Empire spiritualized much of its injustice, justifying its oppression of people to appease gods. Ancient Romans considered deadly gladiator fights entertainment. Many accepted the exposure of unwanted infants to the elements and likely death as humane. They found monotheism immoral; they actually referred to Jews and Christians as atheists, because to them not having multiple gods equaled having no god. In other words, ancient Romans were masters at calling what is good evil and what is evil good.[12] The seven congregations would probably not be as surprised as we might be that humanity could be so corrupt as to rejoice over the complete eradication of Jesus's followers from the earth. They should have taken this as motivation to keep receiving the divine empowerment available. The message should have encouraged them to endure whatever might come their way in the near future and to be constantly committed to speaking truth and to treating others well.

2.2.3.3 Death Parties and Current US Christianity

Like the ancient Roman Empire, we find nothing in our culture that parallels the actions of "the inhabitants of the earth" in Revelation 11:10. Just like the Roman Empire, nevertheless, we can be masters of calling evil good and calling good evil. Sadly, one of the most common places to find this error in the United States today is amongst some churches and church leaders. When people intertwine politics and religion too tightly like the ancient Romans did, they become convinced that they are right, even if their views of what is right blatantly contradict how Scripture says we are to live.

Franklin Graham called for a national day of prayer for Donald Trump that was held on Sunday, June 2, 2019. A day in which congregations commit together to pray for their nation's leadership should be a sacred time that all Christians in the country embrace as a spiritual duty, not a political one. Nevertheless, Graham's announcement made it clear that his motives were more political than spiritual. He promoted prayers that seek the prosperity of Trump's presidency and that protect Trump from his "enemies" (i.e., the Democrats). Graham's declaration suggests that Trump's presidency is God's will and that anyone who resists Trump's policies or personal traits actually resists God. His call for prayer never included the word "repentance." He never even hinted at the possibility that American congregations should pray for our leader to lead justly, wisely, or humbly. Rather, he implied that we must blindly accept everything Trump says and does as okay because

---

12. Jeffers, *Greco-Roman World*, 89–109.

Trump is God's chosen vessel.[13] Furthermore, Graham proved the truth in the words once spoken by his father Billy Graham. In a 1981 interview with *Parade*, B. Graham discussed a conversation he had with Jerry Falwell over plans similar to F. Graham's politically-inspired call to prayer. B. Graham said about Falwell:

> I told him to preach the Gospel. I want to preserve the purity of the Gospel and the freedom of religion in America. I don't want to see religious bigotry in any form. Liberals organized in the '60s, and conservatives certainly have a right to organize in the '80s, but it would disturb me if there was a wedding between the religious fundamentalists and the political right. The hard right has no interest in religion except to manipulate it.[14]

F. Graham's call to prayer included the very manipulation his father warned against when religion and politics overlap too much. This overlap has yielded religious *syncretism*, insisting that to be a Christian means not only to support Trump but also to call what is evil good and to call what is good evil. Like Roman gladiator fights, many Trump supporters find entertainment value in Trump's words and actions that harm so deeply that they cause death (usually figuratively, but occasionally literally). If supporting Trump is a prerequisite of Christianity, then we must accept boasts about sexual assault as a normal act for someone who accomplishes God's will.[15] We must embrace the separation of legally asylum-seeking parents from their children at the United States/Mexico border as an appropriate way to protect "law and order."[16] We must also forget that Trump's "law and order" language invokes racist stereotypes embedded in our culture and that his "law and order" policies are not saving lives but ruining them.[17] We must deny any hypocrisy in establishing law and order via means that were illegal prior to his then-attorney general's passage of the "zero tolerance policy." We cannot accept that the "zero tolerance policy" created massive chaos that has lasted far longer than the policy itself.[18] We must believe Trump when

---

13. The declaration was posted on F. Graham's deceased father's website, billygraham.org. It was removed after the event, but the transcript of the call to prayer can be found on third-party sources through a search engine.

14. Williams, "Regan's Religious Right," 135.

15. Video from a 2005 episode of *Access Hollywood* including Trump's boastful claim to "grab women by the p****" published by the *Washington Post*. See Fahrenthold, "Trump Recorded."

16. See "Inside President Donald J. Trump's First Year."

17. Nunberg, "Trump's Call."

18. Jervis, "Zero Tolerance," paras. 4–7.

he demonizes groups of people (e.g., when he said that most Mexicans are "rapists, murderers, and criminals," that most Muslims are terrorists, that the mainstream fact-seeking media is "the enemy of the people," etc.).[19] We must either submit to him or excuse him when he promotes violence against those he considers his enemies, like when he told "Second Amendment people" to do something about Hillary Clinton if she won the presidency.[20] We must call what is evil good. We must call what is good evil. And we must live our own lives according to these twisted views of reality that contradict Scripture. Thus, we must become recreated in the image of Trump. We must pay no heed to the wise words of B. Graham or the Mayflower Compact.

Many Christians try to excuse their Trump support by asking, "If God can accomplish his will through a donkey and the pagan Cyrus, why can't he do so through Trump?" Of course, God can. Just in American history, God has probably used every flawed and unbelieving president in some way or another. However, no previous president of the last century placed himself so firmly against the teachings of the Bible and against its principles of truth, love, and justice as Trump has. He did so as a candidate in 2016, so everyone who voted for him could know exactly what kind of president we would get: 1) a self-obsessed man-child who cares only about his image as a winner and not about the people he claims to serve, 2) a president who will stoke fears, racism, and violence when he believes it will help him politically, 3) and a leader who will take no responsibility for actions like the *Access Hollywood* tape that almost anyone else would try to distance himself from rather than justifying it as "locker room talk" and later claiming that he never said it, after everyone in the country had heard the tape.[21]

Therefore, I answered the typical question with another question: Why can't God use a different flawed candidate? Everyone else on the ballot in 2016 tried to demonstrate what kind of president he/she would be. All are human, so of course all would be flawed leaders. Except for Trump, all other candidates running for one of the two prominent parties made it clear in words and actions that they would do their best to benefit the country. As such, they placed themselves in submission to the US people, recognizing that they would—at least to some degree—try to work for us. This characteristic even applies to Hilary Clinton, whom Trump's own justice department cleared of corruption related to alleged national security breaches and an alleged Benghazi coverup. Trump's justice department exonerated her of

---

19. Marcieca, "Field Guide," paras. 1–35; Korte and Gomez, "Undocumented Immigrants," paras. 1–10; Michael Gryboski, "Evangelical Leaders Reject," paras. 12–20.

20. Corasaniti and Haberman, "Donald Trump Suggests," paras. 1–4.

21. Nelson, "From 'Locker Room Talk,'" paras. 1–18.

all such counts between October 2019 and January 2020.[22] To the contrary of the other candidates, Trump has demonstrated no interest whatsoever in anything related to submission, humility, or service.

Cyrus and the donkey both submitted themselves to be used by God despite their limitations and lack of knowledge that they were submitting themselves to God. All 2016 US presidential candidates other than Trump demonstrated some basic human decency that they would try to submit to. These forms of submission could have put any of them in a position worth comparing to Cyrus or the donkey. Trump, on the other hand, has submitted only to his own personal desires. God certainly has made good things come out of Trump's evil. Without some sort of sacrifice on Trump's part, however, we should not believe his common assertion that he is good for Evangelicals. We should also avoid listening to the *influo* (see chapter 1, section 3.2.3) of church leaders who suggest that Trump's presidency is the will of God. Such a belief skews the biblical truth of God's sovereignty, treating God as if he chooses presidents directly. We live in a democracy, not a theocracy. Therefore, the American people vote to choose their leaders.

God does not choose presidents, but he might judge the American people for their choice. I believe God has been judging the country's decision to elect an unrepentant, morally bankrupt billionaire celebrity who acts more like a religious cult leader than a president. More significantly, I believe God has been judging the church in the United States for its increasing submission to nationalism and specifically for its capitulation to Trumpism. I think that throughout the time I wrote this book (between the 2016 and 2020 presidential elections), God has been judging the United States and the church in it for all the sins that Trumpism demands. God would judge his church in order to lead us to repentance, since our nationalism and Trumpism are idolatrous distractions that prevent us from participating in the Great Commission.

How exactly has God been judging the United States, and especially God's people in the United States? Throughout Scripture, a pattern exists in which God judges those who claim to follow him by giving them exactly what they think they want. We find the most vivid example of this pattern in 1 Samuel 8–15, beginning with ancient Israel's plea for a king. When they wanted government their own way instead of the theocratic system *YHWH* ordained, God gave them King Saul. Saul practiced witchcraft and pursued his eventual successor with the constant threat of violence. Yet, the text is clear that God directly chose and anointed this man, fully aware of the

---

22. Haddad, "Hilary Clinton Cleared," paras. 1–10; Barrett and Zapotosky, "Investigation Winds Down," paras. 1–4.

harm he posed to God's people. The future King David could not even do anything about it when his life was in danger, because he understood Saul as God's anointed. Because Israel grumbled and complained about their lot in life, they became unwilling to recognize and accept the gifts of God. They wanted their own way. They wanted their own leader, no matter how contrary that leader might be to the actual will of *YHWH*. God gave them what they thought they wanted, not what he desired for them. Although God does not directly choose leaders in democracies (and hence, no president should ever be considered God's anointed), God certainly responds and acts within the choices made by people who chose their leaders.

Trump's election demonstrated the nation's desire for self-interest over the values of truth, love, and justice. The United States knowingly elected a corrupt, childish, thin-skinned businessman who unabashedly follows the playbooks of religious cult leaders and dictators as its president (see appendix 4 for connections between Trump and such leaders). Therefore, God has not spared the country from any of the consequences of that decision. Trump's emotional outbursts have dramatically changed the way the country's government works and how many of the people in the country act. God has allowed all the incivility and self-centered hatred associated with Trumpism to run rampant in the culture and possibly even to sabotage future leaders of both parties who will hopefully be better equipped for the job. Effects of COVID-19 have been far different in the United States than in other nations, because other nations do not possess the same divisiveness over basic facts. The choices of some to listen to Trump instead of truth has paved the way for a long punishment, affecting the nation's economy and other institutions long after Trump's presidency concludes. Those decisions have heightened the divisions that already existed and reflect divine judgment as God gives the nation exactly what it thinks it wants.

As American Christians, we can and should ask God for help with how to vote, regarding who will be most likely to partner with aspects of God's will for the world. By submitting only to his own desires, Trump surrenders not to decency or to the American people, but to sin and death. Sin and death never reflect God's will. As such, God's people should recognize that supporting anyone who stands so firmly against what we know about God's will is actually a form of resisting God's will. In other words, anyone who believes God told them to vote for Trump probably heard the voice of some other source of *inflo* and listened to that voice instead of the Holy Spirit. That confusion related to *influo* is both a cause of the judgment against God's people and a reflection of the judgment itself. As God gave the country exactly what it thought it wanted, so God's people who thought they heard from God will remain in a state of confusion until they repent and abandon the idolatrous cult of Trumpism completely.

When Christians pray for Trump, our prayers need to be based on truth, love, and justice. Since we have a president who has made himself the enemy of these three concepts, we are remiss and should not bother praying for him at all if we do not ask God to lead him to repentance. The day of prayer that F. Graham promoted was an event in which Christians (or at least those claiming to be such) refused to admit truth that would require such repentance. As such, the event called what is evil good, it called what is good evil, and it "cast down the truth to the ground." It may not have included a death party like Revelation 11:10, but it justified many wrongful deaths. For example, F. Graham's politicized call to prayer excused Trump's involvement in 1) the deaths of children in terrible conditions at border facilities that Trump's policies paved the way for,[23] 2) the aftermath of Khashoggi's murder,[24] 3) and countless deaths from natural disasters, breathing disorders, and cancers that could have been prevented if Trump had not denied the realities of climate change.[25] As segments of the church in the United States overlook Trump's pro-death offenses while aligning themselves with supposedly pro-life Republican politics, they call what is good evil and what is evil good. They might not be celebrating deaths, but they are certainly not standing against death when it is in their power to do so. Sadly, these Christians might be paving the way toward the global death party of Revelation 11:10.

3. THE SEVENTH TRUMPET (REV 11:15-19)

The first six trumpets all involved destruction. The interlude introduces us to the "two witnesses." If we accept that they represent the entire worldwide church at the end of the present age, we recognize the general resurrection in that interlude. The death parties end abruptly when the two witnesses experience resurrection. The end of the celebration coincides with the final judgment, while the resurrection of the two witnesses presents the hope of all believers: resurrection from the dead when Jesus returns. Thus, as the seventh angel blows the seventh trumpet, judgment finds its completion. The seventh trumpet's blast results in worship. The connection between the seventh trumpet and the first six trumpets ensures that the passages

---

23. Rappleye and Seville, "24 Immigrants Have Died," paras. 4–6.
24. Smith and Gubash, "Saudi Arabia Sentences 5," paras. 4–12.
25. Andrews, "Death and Climate Change," para. 1, section 2.5, figures 1–4.

surrounding the seventh trumpet unveil the primary aspects of this messianic kingdom as justice and victory.

Trumpets throughout Scripture and *extrabiblical* literature from antiquity often connect to the inauguration of a new king (e.g. 1 Kgs 1:35; 2 Kgs 9:13). The seventh trumpet announces such an event.[26] This portion of the text, therefore, reveals Jesus as the anticipated messianic king. God has rid the world of all sin and death. He has gathered his people in a renewed, healed, perfected earth that will be our home forever.[27] Such a radical divine act indeed deserves the worship that the seventh trumpet initiates.

3.1 The Anticipated Messianic Kingdom and the Seven Congregations of Asia Minor

The trumpets have all pointed toward the end of the current age. The message behind them, however, still called its first recipients to action. As the seventh trumpet yields worship over the culmination of God's kingdom on the earth, so it encourages its hearers toward anticipation of that kingdom, no matter how far off it might be. It calls them to embrace *eschatological tension*.[28] Thus, like the other worship scenes in Revelation, the text invites congregants to join in this heavenly worship.

3.2 The Anticipated Messianic Kingdom and Current American Readers

Just as the seventh trumpet calls Revelation's initial audiences to join in the heavenly worship, it does the same for all who read it after John's day. George Fredric Handel's oratorio *Messiah* includes a performance of this passage, known as the "Hallelujah Chorus." Through listening to the words of that movement of the oratorio, we can join the heavenly worshipers. We unite with those in heaven as they await the time when we will experience together the fullness of God's resurrection power and begin to participate in the fullness of his kingdom on earth. That expectation must drive our worship and our witness, making known that God has so much more planned for us and for all of his creation than we can imagine while bound to this sinful age marked by death and decay. For that reason, we will transition to a liturgy that involves only reciting the words of the angel to accept the

---

26. Keener, *Revelation*, 304–5.
27. Smalley, *Revelation*, 255.
28. Fee, *Revelation*, 157.

announcement of the Messiah's second arrival to earth to make all things new, including us.

Liturgy 5: Unity of God's Dwelling Place and the Earth

1. Recite the words of the angelic announcement from Revelation 11:15: "The kingdom of the world has become the kingdom of our Lord and of his Messiah, and he will reign forever and ever."
2. Find a recording of Handel's "Halleluiah Chorus" from *Messiah*. As you listen to that recording and the words you have just proclaimed, imagine what the earth will be like when this moment occurs.

Further Reading:

For John's OT sources for Revelation's plagues:
Reddish, Mitchell. *Revelation*. Macon, GA: Smyth & Helwys, 2005. Pertinent pages: 121–23; 163–73.

For John as a prophet:
Aune, David. *Revelation*. Dallas: Word, 1997. Pertinent pages: liii–lvi.

For an interesting (though I believe flawed) argument that the two witnesses call all audiences to care for the environment:
Johnson, Elizabeth A. *Ask the Beasts: Darwin and the God of Love*. London: Bloomsbury Continuum, 2015.

Chapter 5

The Seven Bowls

Judgment from Jesus's First Coming to His Second Coming (Rev 12–19)

12 ¹ Then a great sign appeared in heaven: A woman was clothed with the sun. Also, the moon was under her feet, and a crown containing twelve stars was on her head; ² she was pregnant, cried out having birth pains, and was tormented in labor. ³ Then another sign appeared in heaven: Behold, a great fiery red dragon had seven heads, ten horns, and seven diadems on its heads; ⁴ its tail pulled down a third of the stars of heaven and cast them to the earth. Then the dragon was standing in the presence of the woman when she was about to give birth so that whenever she gave birth, he could devour her child. ⁵ Then she bore a male child who will shepherd all nations with an iron rod. Then the child was taken away to God and to his throne, ⁶ and the woman fled to the wilderness, where she has a place prepared by God in order that they nourish her there for 1,260 days.

⁷ Then a war occurred in heaven; Michael waged war along with his angels against the dragon. The dragon also waged war along with his angels, ⁸ but he did not prevail, and no place was found for them. ⁹ Then the great dragon (namely the ancient serpent who is called the devil and Satan, the deceiver of the whole world) was cast out. He was thrown to the earth; his

angels with him were also cast out. ¹⁰ Then I heard a loud voice in heaven saying, "Salvation, power, the kingdom of our God, and the dominion of his Messiah have now come, because the accuser of our brothers and sisters—who accuses them before our God day and night—has been cast out." ¹¹ Indeed, they conquered him by the blood of the Lamb and by the word of their testimony; furthermore, they did not love life to the point of death. ¹² Because of this, the heavens and what dwells in them must rejoice. Woe to you earth and sea, because the devil has come down to you having great wrath, knowing that he has little time left.

¹³ Then once the dragon saw that he was cast to the earth, he pursued the woman who gave birth to the boy. ¹⁴ But the two wings of a great eagle were given to the woman so that she could fly to the wilderness, to her place where she is nourished for time, times, and half a time from the presence of the serpent. ¹⁵ Then the serpent issued water like a river from its mouth from behind the woman so as to make her drown. ¹⁶ But the earth helped the woman as the earth opened its mouth and destroyed the river that the dragon issued from its mouth. ¹⁷ So the dragon was angry at the woman and came to wage war against the rest of her children, namely the people who keep God's commandments and possess the testimony of Jesus. ¹⁸ Then it stood on the mouth of the sea.

13 ¹ Then I saw a beast coming up out the sea, having ten horns, seven heads, ten diadems on its horns, and blasphemous names on his heads. ² Now the beast that I saw was like a leopard, its feet were like that of a bear, and its mouth was like the mouth of a lion. And the dragon gave to it from its own authority, throne, and great dominion. ³ Now one of its heads looked as if it had been wounded unto death, but its deadly wound was healed. So the whole world was amazed after the beast's healing; ⁴ they worshiped the dragon because it had given authority to the beast, and they worshiped the beast, saying: "Who is like the beast, and who is able to wage war against it?" ⁵ Then a mouth was given to it speaking pompous and blasphemous words, and authority was granted to it to work for 42 months. ⁶ So, it opened its mouth to speak blasphemies against God so as to slander his name and his dwelling place, that is those who dwell in the heavens. ⁷ Then it was granted to the beast to wage war against the holy ones and to conquer them; authority was given to it over every tribe, people, tongue, and nation. ⁸ So, all the inhabitants of earth—anyone whose name had not been written from the foundation of the earth in the book of life belonging to

the Lamb who was slain—worshiped it. [9] Whoever has a pair of ears must hear. [10] If anyone is taken into captivity, into captivity he goes. If anyone is to be killed by the sword, let him be killed by the sword. This is the faithful endurance of the saints.

[11] Then I saw another beast ascending out of the ground; it had two horns like a lamb, and it was speaking like the dragon, [12] and it exercises all the authority of the first beast in behalf of it, and it controls the earth, that is its inhabitants, in order that they will worship the first beast whose deadly would was healed. [13] It also performs great signs; namely, it made fire to come down from heaven to the earth in the presence of the people, [14] and it deceives those who dwell on the earth by the signs that were appointed to it to perform in behalf of the beast, telling those who dwell on the earth to make an image for the beast who has the wound from the sword but returned to life.

[15] And authority was given to it to give breath to the image of the beast in order that the image of the beast also may even speak and act so that whoever would not worship the image of the beast would be put to death. [16] So, it controls all people (the small and great ones, the rich and poor ones, the free ones and the slaves) with the result that they give them a mark on each one's right hand or forehead [17] in order that no one who does not have the mark—that is the beast's name or the number of his name—can buy or sell. [18] Here is wisdom: Let the one who has understanding calculate the beast's number, since the number belongs to a human, and his number is 666.

14 [1] Then I looked and behold, the Lamb stood on Mount Zion, and 144,000 men having his name and his Father's name written on their foreheads stood with him. [2] I also heard a sound from heaven like the sound of many waters and like the sound of loud thunder, and the sound that I heard was like harpists playing their harps. [3] They sang something like a new song before the throne, before the four living creatures, and before the elders, and no one was able to learn the song except for the 144,000, that is, the people who had been redeemed from the earth. [4] These men are those who have not become defiled with women, for they are virgins; they are the ones who follow the Lamb wherever he goes. They have been redeemed from humankind, the first fruits for God and the Lamb, [5] and nothing false has been found in their mouth. They are pure.

[6] Then I saw another angel flying in midair, having an eternal message of good news to proclaim to the ones who dwell on the earth (to every nation, tribe, tongue, and people), [7] saying in a loud voice: "Fear God, and give him glory, because the hour of

his judgment has come. So, worship him who made heaven, the earth, the sea, and the springs of water." [8] Then another angel—a second one—followed, saying, "It fell! Babylon the great, who made all nations drink from the wine of the lust of her fornication fell." [9] Then another angel—a third one—followed them and said in a loud voice: "If anyone worships the beast and its image and takes the mark on his forehead or on his right hand, [10] then he will drink from the wine of God's anger, which has been mixed to full strength in the cup of his wrath, and they will be tormented with fire and brimstone before the holy angels and before the Lamb. [11] Now the smoke of their torment goes up forever. And as for those who worship the beast and its image, whoever takes the mark of its name, they have no rest day or night. [12] Here is the endurance of the holy ones: those who observe God's commandments and the faithfulness of Jesus." [13] Then I heard a voice from heaven saying, "Write: Blessed are the dead people who die in the Lord from now on. 'Yes,' says the Spirit, because they will rest from their labors; certainly, their works accompany them."

[14] Then I looked and behold a white cloud, and on the cloud one like the son of a human was seated, having a golden crown on his head and a sharp sickle in his right hand. [15] Then another angel came out of the temple and cried out in a loud voice to the one seated on the cloud: "Send out your sickle and reap, since the hour to reap has come, as the harvest of the earth has been dried out." [16] Then the one seated on the cloud swung his sickle on the earth, so the earth was reaped. [17] Then another angel came out of the temple that is in heaven, also having a sharp sickle. [18] Then another angel came from the altar; he had authority over the fire, and he called out with a loud voice to the one who has the sharp sickle and said, "Send out your sharp sickle and harvest the grapes from the earth's vine, since its grapes have ripened." [19] Then the angel swung his sickle on the earth, and he harvested the earth's vine and threw the fruit into the winepress of the wrath of the great God. [20] Then the winepress was trampled outside the city, and blood issued from the winepress as far as a horse's bridle: 16,000 stadia [about 1,800 miles]

15 [1] Then I saw another great and amazing sign in heaven: seven angels having the seven final plagues, by which the wrath of God was completed. [2] Then I saw something like a sea of glass mixed with fire, and I saw those who conquered the beast, its image, and the number of its name standing at the glassy sea having God's harps, [3] and they sing the song of Moses, God's slave, and the song of the Lamb: "Your works are great and

amazing, Lord God Almighty; your ways are just and true, king of the nations. ⁴ Who will not fear you, Lord, and glorify your name? Because you alone are holy, indeed all nations will come and bow before you, since your just deeds have been revealed."

⁵ Then after these things, I saw the temple of the tent of witness opened in heaven, ⁶ and the seven angels having the seven plagues came out of the temple clothed in clean, bright linen and girded around their chests with golden sashes. ⁷ Then one of the four living creatures gave the seven angels seven golden bowls full of the wrath of the God who lives forever and ever. ⁸ Now the temple was filled with smoke from the glory of God and from his power, so no one was able to enter into the temple until the seven plagues of the seven angels were complete.

16 ¹ Then I heard a loud voice from the temple, saying to the seven angels: "Go and pour out the seven bowls of God's wrath against the world." ² So, the first angel went and poured his bowl onto the earth; as a result, a severe painful sore came upon the people who have the mark of the beast and who worship its image. ³ Then the second angel poured his bowl into the sea, and it became blood, like that of a corpse, and every living thing that is in the sea died. ⁴ Then the third angel poured out his bowl into the rivers and springs of water, and it became blood.

⁵ Then I heard the angel of the waters saying, "Just are you, who is and who was, the holy one, because you judged these people, ⁶ since they shed the blood of the holy ones and the prophets, and you have given them blood to drink; it is fitting." ⁷ Then I heard a voice from the altar saying, "Yes Lord God Almighty, true and just are your judgments."

⁸ Then the fourth angel poured out his bowl on the sun, and it was assigned to him to burn people with fire. ⁹ So the people were burned up by the great heat, but they blasphemed the name of God—who has authority over these plagues—and they did not repent so as to give him glory. ¹⁰ Then the fifth angel poured out his bowl at the beast's throne, and its kingdom was made dark, and they gnawed their tongues because of the pain, ¹¹ but they blasphemed the name of the Lord of heaven because of their afflictions and because of their sores, and they did not repent of their deeds. ¹² Then the sixth angel poured out his bowl on the great river, namely the Euphrates, and its water was dried up in order to prepare the way for the kings of the east.

¹³ Then I saw three unclean spirits like frogs proceeding out of the mouth of the dragon, out of the mouth of the beast, and out of the mouth of the false prophet. ¹⁴ Now, they are demonic spirits performing signs that go forth toward the kings of the

whole world in order to gather them for battle on the great day of God Almighty.

[15] ("Behold, I am coming like a thief. Blessed is the one who keeps alert and guards his clothes, lest he walk around naked when people can see his shame.") [16] Then they gathered at the place that is called Harmagedon in Hebrew.

[17] Then the seventh angel poured out his bowl into the atmosphere, and a loud voice came out of the temple from the throne, saying, "Come." [18] Then lightnings, rumblings, and thunder came; a great earthquake also came, the like of which had not come since the time when humanity appeared on the earth. This is how devastating the great earthquake is. [19] Now the great city was broken into three parts, and the cities of the gentiles fell, and the great Babylon was remembered before God in order to give her the cup of the wine of God's wrath from which to drink.

[20] Then every island fled, no mountain was found, [21] and a great hailstorm came down from heaven on people, each hail stone weighing a talent [an amount of weight that cannot be clearly discerned today]. So, the people blasphemed God, because of the plague of the hail, for the plague against Babylon was so severe.

17 [1] Then, one of the seven angels having the seven bowls came and spoke with me. He said, "Come here; I will show you the judgment of the great prostitute who is seated on many waters. [2] The kings of the earth fornicate with her, and the people who dwell on the earth have been made drunk by the wine of her fornication." [3] Then he carried me away by the Spirit to the wilderness, and I saw a woman seated on a scarlet beast, full of blasphemous names, having seven heads and seven horns. [4] Now the woman was clothed in purple and scarlet and was adorned with gold, precious stone, and pearls, having a golden cup full of detestable things and the impurity of her fornication in her right hand, [5] and on her forehead, a name was inscribed. It is a mystery: "Babylon the Great, mother of the prostitutes and of the detestable people of the earth." [6] Then I saw the woman drunk from the blood of the saints and from the blood of the witnesses of Jesus, and I was astonished at the great marvel as I saw her. [7] Then the angel said to me, "Why are you astonished? I will tell you the mystery of the woman and of the beast that has seven heads and seven horns that carries her. [8] The beast that you saw was and is not. But he is about to come out of the abyss; then, he goes away to destruction, and those who dwell on the earth—whose names are not written in the book of life

from the foundation of world—will be amazed as they see the beast, because he was and is not and is coming. [9] This matter requires a mind that has wisdom: The seven heads are seven mountains where the woman is seated. Also, they are seven kings,[10] of whom five fell, one is still alive, and the other has not yet come, but when he comes, he must remain a short time. [11] As for the beast who was and is not, it is itself an eighth yet part of the seven, and it goes into destruction, [12] and the ten horns that you saw are ten kings who have not yet received a kingdom; nevertheless, they are to receive authority as kings along with the beast for one hour. [13] These kings have one purpose: they will hand over their power and authority to the beast. [14] They will wage war against the Lamb, but the Lamb will overcome them, because he is the Lord of lords and the King of kings, and the people with him are called, chosen, and faithful." [15] Then he said to me, "The waters that you saw, on which the prostitute is seated, are peoples, multitudes, nations, and tongues. [16] As for the ten horns and the beast that you saw, these people will hate the prostitute. They will make her desolate and naked, and they will eat her flesh and burn it with fire."

[17] Indeed, God has placed it into their hearts in order to accomplish his propose and to do it as one, namely, to give each one's kingdom to the beast until the time when God's words will be fulfilled. [18] Finally, the woman that you saw is the great city that has authority to reign over the kingdoms of the earth.

18 [1] After these things, I saw another angel coming down from heaven having much authority, and the earth was given light by his brightness, [2] and he cried out in a loud voice: "Fallen! Fallen is the great Babylon! Indeed, it became a dwelling place for demons, a prison for every unclean spirit, a prison for every unclean bird, and a prison for every unclean and disregarded animal, [3] because all nations have drunk from the wine of the wrath from her fornication, because the kings of the earth fornicated with her, and because the merchants of the earth became rich by the power of her luxury." [4] Then I heard another voice from heaven, saying, "Come out from her, my people, lest you take part in her sins, lest you take hold of her plagues, [5] because her sins have reached up to heaven, and God has remembered her wrongdoings. [6] Pay her as she has also paid, and double her recompense according to her deeds. Mix double strength for her in the cup from which she has mixed. [7] As much as she has glorified herself and lived in luxury, give to her that much torment and grief, because she says in her heart: 'I live as a queen. Behold, I am not a widow, nor am I ever in mourning.' [8] Because

of this, her plagues will take effect in one day—death, grief, famine, and she will be consumed by fire—because the Lord God who judges her is mighty."

⁹ Then the kings of the earth who fornicated and lived in luxury with her will weep and wail on account of her when they see the smoke from her burning, ¹⁰ standing from afar off because of fear of her torment, crying out: "Woe! Woe to the great city, Babylon, the mighty city, because in one hour your judgment came." ¹¹ Likewise, the merchants of the earth weep and mourn on account of her, because no one buys her cargo anymore, ¹² namely cargo consisting of gold, silver, precious stone, pearls, fine linen, purple, silk, scarlet, every kind of scented wood, all kinds of ivory products, precious wood, bronze, iron, marble, ¹³ cinnamon, cardamom, incense, ointment, frankincense, wine, oil, flour, wheat, flocks of domesticated animals, sheep, horses, carriages, and slaves—that is, human lives. ¹⁴ The fruit of your life's lust has gone away from you, and all the luxuries and splendorous things are lost to you, and you will never find them again. ¹⁵ These merchants who became rich because of her will stand from far away because of fear of her torments. They wept and mourned, ¹⁶ crying out: "Woe! Woe to the great city, clothed in fine linen, purple, and scarlet, and adorned with gold, precious stone, and pearl, ¹⁷ because in one hour, this wealth was ruined." Now, all shipmasters, all who go to the place of sailing, sailors, and anyone who works at the sea stood from afar, ¹⁸ and as they saw the smoke of her burning, they cried out: "What is like the great city?" ¹⁹ Then they threw dust on their heads, cried out, wept, and mourned. They said, "Woe! Woe to the great city, where people who have ships at sea became rich by her wealth, because in one day it was ruined."

²⁰ Rejoice over her, O heaven along with the saints, apostles, and prophets, because God judged her for your benefit. ²¹ Then a strong angel picked up a stone like a large millstone and threw it into the sea, saying, "The great city Babylon will be cast down in a violent rush, and it will never be found again, ²² the sound of harpists, skilled musicians, flutists, and trumpeters will never be heard in you again, all craftsmen of any trade will never be found in you again, the sound of the millstone will never be heard in you again, ²³ the light of a lamp will never shine on you again, and the sound of the bridegroom and the bride will never be heard in you again, because your merchants were the great people of the land and because all the nations were led astray by your sorcery, ²⁴ and by her, the blood of the prophets and saints

was found among all the people who have been slaughtered on the earth."

19 ¹ After these things, I heard a loud voice like the sound of a large crowd in heaven, saying: "Halleluiah! Salvation, glory, and power belong to our God, ² because his judgments are true and just, since he judged the great prostitute who was corrupting the earth with her fornication, for he avenged the blood of his slaves from her hand." ³ Then a second voice spoke: "Halleluiah! Now smoke goes up from her forever and ever." ⁴ Then the twenty-four elders and the four living creatures fell down and worshiped God who is seated on the throne. They said, "Amen, Halleluiah!" ⁵ Then a voice came from the throne, saying, "All his slaves and all who fear him, great and small: Praise our God!" ⁶ Then I heard the voice that sounded like a large crowd, like the sound similar to many waters, and like the sound similar to a strong thunder. It said, "Halleluiah, because the Lord our God, the Almighty took his reign. ⁷ Let us rejoice, exult, and give him glory, because the marriage of the Lamb has come, and his bride prepares herself." ⁸ Then, he granted for her the right to clothe herself in fine, bright, clean clothing. Now the fine clothing represents the righteous deeds of the saints. ⁹ Then he [John's angelic guide] said to me, "Write: Blessed are the people who have been invited to the wedding banquet of the Lamb." He also said to me, "These are the true words of God."

¹⁰ Then I fell before his feet to worship him. But he said to me, "See to it that you do not do that. I am your fellow slave along with your brothers who have the testimony of Jesus. Worship God! Indeed, the testimony of Jesus is the spirit of prophecy."

¹¹ Then I saw heaven opened, and behold a white horse, and the one seated on it is called faithful and true, and he judges and makes just war. ¹² His eyes were like a flame of fire, and many crowns were on his head; he had a name inscribed that nobody knows but him, ¹³ and he was wearing a robe dipped in blood, and his name was called the Word of God. ¹⁴ Then the troops that were in heaven clothed in fine, white, clean clothing followed him on the white horse. ¹⁵ A sharp sword proceeded out of his mouth in order that by it he could strike the nations, and he will shepherd them with an iron rod and trample the winepress of the furious wrath of God Almighty, ¹⁶ and he has a name inscribed on his clothing and on his thigh: "King of kings and Lord of lords."

¹⁷ Then I saw an angel standing in the sun and crying out in a loud voice, saying to all the birds that fly in the air: "Come here and gather to God's great feast ¹⁸ in order that you can eat

the flesh of kings, the flesh of tribunes, the flesh of horses and of their riders, and the flesh of all—free people and slaves, the small and the great."

[19] Then I saw the beast, the kings of the earth, and their troops gather to wage war against the one riding the horse and against his troops, [20] but the beast was captured; along with it was the false prophet who performed signs in its presence, by which he deceived the people who received the mark of the beast and who worshiped its image. The two were thrown alive into the lake of fire that burns with sulfur. [21] Then the rest were killed by the sword of the one riding on the horse that proceeded from his mouth, and all the birds were fed with their flesh.

1. THE WOMAN AND THE DRAGON (REV 12)

Revelation 11 closes the second *septet*. Without any overlap like we found between the first and second, Revelation 12 abruptly begins the third *septet*. This final *recapitulation* has the broadest scope, beginning with a creative retelling of the birth of the Messiah. Since it ends with Jesus's second coming, the general resurrection, and the final judgment like the first two *septets*, this scope encompasses the entirety of the church age. I taught an adult Sunday School class on the book of Revelation before beginning PhD work. As such, I taught that class many things based on ignorance. This passage marks one of my worst blunders. I assumed that the woman in the text must be the Virgin Mary, since she gives birth to the Messiah. This assumption, however, neglects to account for much of the literary background from which the symbols of Revelation derive.

The first verse of this passage gives us the first indicator that we should avoid my mistake. John refers to this part of his vision as a "sign." All of Revelation is filled with figurative language that we should not take literally. John takes that aspect of his writing even further when he labels each of the two stories in Revelation 12 as "a sign." The Greek word that translates to "sign" most often refers to a miraculous event in the NT. In *extrabiblical* texts, the same word most often refers to a constellation, god, or other aspect of Greek mythology. With a Jewish apocalyptic literary background in a Greco-Roman imperial location, John's symbols can come from many sources. This story links to Jesus's birth narratives and OT messianic prophecy only vaguely. It connects more directly to Greek mythological sources. These myths generally use the matriarchal symbol to point to a group of people rather than an individual. Scholars are generally unified that Revelation 12 should be understood in like manner without any correlation to Mary.[1]

If the woman is not Mary, how can she be giving birth to the Messiah? Some of the early church fathers hypothesized about this question. Victorinus saw her as all followers of the Messiah—both ancient Israel who awaited his coming and all who receive Jesus in the Christian age.[2] Other early interpreters recognized her twelve stars as imagery pointing to Jesus's twelve apostles.[3] Spiritually, ancient Israel begot the church age as ushered in by the Messiah Jesus. Israel ushered in the new era that Jesus brought about. Jesus was born into a Jewish family and raised with a Pharisaic worldview. In this way, Pharisaic Judaism gave birth to Jesus. (Please note: Pharisaic Judaism is one of many segments of ancient Israel. Jesus's teachings most closely aligned to those of the Pharisees, despite the specific Pharisees mentioned in the Gospels, whom the authors painted in a negative light. We must not think of the Pharisees of the Gospels as representative of all, or even a majority of Pharisees). The symbol of the pregnant woman, nevertheless, appears to demand a broader application. That is, we should not think she represents only first-century Pharisees who accepted Jesus as Messiah. Understanding the woman as a representation of all of God's people, then, allows the rest of the *septet* to flow more smoothly than it does under the assumption that she is Mary or a smaller group.[4]

Although we have spent some time discussing the identity of the woman, that identity is not the most important aspect of what John communicates through this symbol. What happens to her in the story is far more important than who or what she represents. She is granted rest and shares in the Messiah's victory.[5] This contrasts with the other woman who appears later in the story that this *septet* tells. In Revelation 17, Babylon, the great prostitute, suffers miserable defeat. Since Babylon represents the Roman Empire, we see the role that human governments play in spiritual warfare. Governments often partner with the demonic realm through attitudes of supremacy, entitlement, and corruption that harm people. We have already discussed how both the Roman Empire and the US government have cooperated with the demonic in all three of these ways. The pregnant woman's role in the story receives the opposite consequences as Babylon. Thus, her devotions and her lifestyle must likewise be opposed to the ways of the empire. When

---

1. E.g., Keener, *Revelation*, 313–15; Buisch, "Offspring," 396–98.
2. Victorinus, *Comm. Apoc.* 12.1–12.
3. Hippolytus, *Antichr.* 61.
4. Boring, *Revelation*, 152.
5. Collins, *Combat Myth*, 88.

we read the *septet's* whole story (chapters 12–19) under this framework, we see that its applicability to the seven congregations is exactly the same as how we should receive it today. We are still at war in the spiritual realm. If we genuinely follow Jesus, we join with all the people of the past and present to give birth to spiritual victory. If we give in to our culture's (and especially government's) ways that are opposed to the love, truth, and justice that Jesus embodies, we join the demonic realm in its destructive work.

So, it seems best to think of the pregnant woman as a representation of all of God's people throughout all time periods and as a contrast to the whore of Babylon who appears later. If we accept that interpretation and recognize the child as Jesus, then the warfare that follows flows easily out of those symbols. Revelation 12 begins the story of the spiritual warfare that Satan wages against God and God's people (the story that extends throughout the *septet*). The story of that warfare begins with Jesus's birth. It does not suggest that spiritual warfare did not exist prior to the Messiah's first coming. Rather, it is an appropriate starting point for a story told within a "revelation of Jesus the Messiah" (Rev 1:1).

2. THE BEASTS (REV 13)

Just as the symbol of good in this story—the pregnant woman—makes use of ancient mythology, the symbol of evil does the same. Each of the beasts John reports seeing in Revelation 13 has much in common with ancient chaos monsters. These monsters were central to many stories people told each other even before Greek mythology. The apocalyptic visions of Daniel 7 include images like Babylonian and Canaanite chaos monsters, one of which has a horn that probably represents Antiochus IV Epiphanes. Antiochus was the Seleucid king who prevented many aspects of Jewish worship and replaced the Jewish temple with a place of worship for Zeus in 167 BCE.[6] The Daniel vision has four beasts. Throughout Revelation 12–13, we find a "fiery red dragon" (12:3), a "beast coming up out of the sea" (13:1), "a beast ascending out of the ground" (13:11), and "the image of the beast" (13:14). Each of these monsters are characters in the narrative that the *septet* tells. As such, we see John's use of mythology aligning with and expanding Daniel's.[7] We noticed above that the final *septet* is the broadest one, dealing with various parts of the church age. Revelation 12 is about the birth of the church; we should not be surprised, then, to find that the next chapter

---

6. Koester, *Revelation*, 531.
7. Macumber, "Threat of Empire," 108.

relates the most directly to the seven congregations of Asia Minor than any chapter of Revelation since chapters 2–3.

2.1 The Beasts and the Seven Congregations

The seven prophetic messages warn both Pergamum and Thyatira against sexual immorality and eating foods sacrificed to idols. In Revelation 2:24, Jesus refers to these actions as "the depths of Satan" and connects them to someone named Jezebel. Jezebel alludes to the OT figure of the same name. Thyatira's Jezebel, however, could have been a living person or group of people at John's time and not merely a comparison to the OT figure. A new type of Jezebel probably surrounded the congregation at Thyatira and threatened to lead it down the paths of idolatry. Alongside the Nicolaitans and Balaam in other messages to the seven congregations, Jezebel is most likely a symbolic name given to represent the actual people who threatened the religious and sexual purity of each church. The character enhances the call of the whole book for each of the congregations to ensure that their lives are devoted entirely to God and not to the empire.[8]

That call for devotion is equally present in the midst of this dark vision of the final *septet*. The three monsters of Revelation 13 all follow the monster that represented Satan in the prior chapter. They represent realities of the Roman Empire that flow out of Satan's own monstrosities. John uses the images of these beasts inspired by Daniel's adaptations of ancient myths surrounding chaos monsters. John uses this technique as a way of referring to Roman imperial power as demonic. The beasts and the image of the beast in Revelation 13 appear to form a parody of the Trinity.[9] John, thus, accuses the whole empire of making itself a god.[10]

The mark of the beast most likely reflects the commonality of witchcraft in the ancient world. People took the mark as a response to seeing signs and wonders performed by the beast.[11] We see phrases like "signs and wonders" often in the NT, but until Revelation they usually point to works of God through Jesus or God's people. The beast's works consist of counterfeit acts that function similarly to the gifts of the Spirit, with which followers of the Messiah can be endowed. The difference between the gifts of the Spirit and the beast's witchcraft is that the gifts of the Spirit point people toward God and his Messiah. They direct people toward wonder, amazement, and

---

8. Macumber, "Threat of Empire," 109–10
9. Rissi, *Time and History*, 62, 69, 84.
10. Aune, *Revelation*, 735; Bauckham, *Theology*, 28.
11. Keener, *Revelation*, 351–52.

worship of the Almighty. The beast's magic also directs people toward worship, but it leads them toward the wrong object of worship. In this case, the "signs and wonders" lead people toward worshiping the emperor of Rome and the other Roman pagan gods.

The act of branding people with the "mark of the beast" echoes realities that occurred commonly as part of the emperor cult. Worshipers of various Greco-Roman gods would often tattoo the name of a god on their skin before offering sacrifices to that deity. During Domitian's reign, people could not enter legal courts without a sacrificial test that involved a seal. Most significantly, the Ephesian temple dedicated to Emperor Domitian was structured so as to make these other two types of brandings more common.[12] The "blasphemous names" mentioned in Revelation 13:1 probably refer to "lord and god" inscriptions that were imprinted on coins along with a picture of the emperor during Domitian's reign.[13] Those coins, then, suggest that no one could buy or sell without giving allegiance to the emperor who is treated like a god. As the story of the beast with "blasphemous names" develops, we are told that people cannot buy or sell without receiving "the mark of the beast." This scene describes vividly how the imperial cult spread throughout every aspect of Roman life; it encompassed the political, religious, social, and economic aspects of daily life.[14] So, those who received the "mark of the beast" represent people who willingly gave themselves to an economic system that was also an idolatrous religious institution. As such, whether he demanded worship or not, every Roman emperor was a god, even Domitian who was far kinder to Jews and Christians than earlier emperors.

Revelation 13 closes by identifying at least part of its imagery. Symbolic numbers existed everywhere in antiquity. Using various techniques of coded numeric language in the Greek, Hebrew, and Aramaic languages all yield the same results of the 666 riddle: Emperor Nero.[15] Beginning at the time of Nero's death in 68 CE, a myth began circulating of Nero's imminent return from death. That resurrection was not usually understood literally; rather, those passing along the stories expected that another emperor would rise up in Nero's power. Although they tended to assume that such a reincarnation would involve Nero's horrendous treatment against monotheists, such assumptions were not necessarily part of the myth. This myth is known as *Nero redivivus*.

---

12. Judge, "The Mark of the Beast," 159–60.
13. Collins, *Crisis and Catharsis*, 88–89; Reddish, *Revelation*, 250.
14. Friesen, *Imperial Cults*, 208.
15. Keener, *Revelation*, 354.

Revelation 13 presents a literary manifestation of *Nero redivivus*. The first beast represents Nero himself. The second beast is a different person or group, yet its evil flows out of the first beast's. As such, the second beast could refer to any emperor after Nero.[16] Domitian perpetuated Nero's evil of divine pretention. He may have otherwise been a decent leader, but his power nonetheless flowed out of his predecessors' authority, and his actions perpetuated their wrongdoings. Since this statement is true of all emperors, the second beast could represent either Domitian (as the emperor at the time of John's writing) or to the general imperial cult. Either way, the monstrous pseudo-trinity of Revelation 13 embodies the concept of humanity trying to be divine. Beyond its function as a riddle that we already discussed concerning 666, the number also has significance in Jewish numerology apart from the codes. The number six was understood as the number of humankind and as a parody of seven, the number of perfection. The number three was understood as the number of divinity. So, 666 connotes the number of a human trying to present him/herself as a perfected god, as Nero did.[17]

2.2 The Beasts and the Contemporary Church in the United States

Many modern interpreters erase the historical context we have just established from this passage. Assuming that it refers entirely to a future event, they apply a concept that appears nowhere in Revelation. Such interpreters presume that each beast must be connected to the Antichrist. An individual antichrist, however, never occurs clearly in Scripture. Whenever the word "antichrist" appears, it indicates either a concept or a broad group of people. First John 2:14–25 gives a literal treatment of the word. There, "antichrist" refers to anything or anyone that does not accept Jesus's identity as Messiah. Although that passage points toward a final antichrist connected to the "last hour" of this age, it does not clearly identify what that final antichrist is. From that passage, it could be a person, a nation, a demonic being, or an ideology. First John 4:3 reiterates this theme, adding only that all who do not confess Jesus have succumbed to an "antichrist spirit." The phrase "antichrist spirit" helps to show that the concept of antichrist transcends both a given time period and a specific identity. As such, it does not need to refer only to people. Second John 7–11 is the only time that the word "antichrist" can apply solely to humans. All people who do not accept Jesus's incarnation, according to this passage, are deceivers and antichrists. Does that mean that all antichrists must be human? Not necessarily. None

---

16. Caird, *Revelation*, 177.
17. Keener, *Revelation*, 354.

of these verses gives a way to identify how the other passages use the word. Thus, I offer a simple conceptual understanding of "antichrist" as anything (human or otherwise) that opposes Jesus's messianic identity.

The vagueness associated with these three verses does not connect well with the specificity of the beasts in Revelation. Certainly, these beasts deny that Jesus is Messiah and try to prevent belief in him. Each beast, however, has an identity found in the ancient world, whether an individual like Nero or the emperor cult as a whole. We cannot assume that "antichrist" ever refers to a single person, while the beasts certainly can. Interpreters who think that the first beast must be an end-times figure known as Antichrist seem to separate Revelation 13 from its historical background. Many such interpreters also do significant damage to the church. For example, between 2008 and 2016, I heard many Christians proclaim that President Obama was the Antichrist. I am certain that some American believers have also assumed that President Trump is the Antichrist, although I have never personally heard such claims. Many others have labeled other world leaders as the Antichrist. The choices of who to call the Antichrist almost always reflect the interpreter's political agenda. Thus, it is not true to Scripture but thoroughly intwined with the religion of American nationalism.

Revelation's beasts, on the other hand, are treated not only with specific identities but also with specific actions ascribed to them. Those actions make modern presumptions even more dangerous. When people separate this scene from the history of branding for Greek gods and coins that demand some level of *syncretism* in all monetary transactions, they reach some wild conclusions. Many assert the assumption that a one world order will arise in the end times that will kill anyone who does not worship the person that the beast represents. This idea births so much fear that people have been afraid of organizations like NATO that attempt to foster relationships of unity between nations. Others use the fear of a one world order to excuse violent practices at the United States/Mexico border. I have even encountered people who were afraid to sign up for Obamacare, because they believed that socialized healthcare was the mark of the beast, uniting the United States with Communist countries. The Bible and its history, however, can show us how ridiculous these fears are. The Bible gives very few clear hints about what events will lead to the end of the age. We know it will involve great tribulation (not necessarily a Great Tribulation) due to all the world's sin and decay. Also, we know there will be wars and natural disasters. Distress, war, and natural disasters are nothing new, however. Their consistency waxes and wanes throughout periods of history. Natural disasters are certainly more common at the present time due to climate change. No evidence, however, points toward any dramatic increase of all three common occurrences at the same time, which would need to happen if the Great Tribulation is real. It might be real, but I do not think anyone would know what to look for if it is. The Bible gives us these three signs of the end times, but they are all vague and part of normal human existence. The only reason believers should not be surprised when Jesus returns to the earth is that we believe he will come, whether he comes today, billions of years from now, or somewhere in between (1 Thess 5:1–2).

The churches discussed throughout the NT all seemed united in the belief that Jesus would return in their own day. Nevertheless, they worked hard to make certain that the gospel would be made known globally, thus allowing their legacy to last for millennia after them. Ancient people were much more comfortable with paradoxes and contradictions than we are. We must understand, therefore, that all biblical *eschatology* demands that we live in two contradicting realities that cannot both be accurate. We must live with the kind of urgency the first-century church possessed, because Jesus's return is imminent. We must also conduct the work of planning and organizing that the earliest church did to ensure that their lives could have purpose and spiritual impact long after their deaths. Therefore, we must fully believe that Jesus is coming back today. And we must fully believe that Jesus will not return for billions of years. We should be equally motivated by either possibility in order to make the most of the time we have for God's glory.

Although we must remain alert to stand against the fear caused by fallacies like the one world order, the scene of the beasts still has something to say for us today in the United States. The scene confronted the churches in Asia Minor with a difficult call: Do not compromise with the empire to give it your worship, even if it means you cannot use its coins and be part of its economy. Fortunately, in the United States, we have nothing close to a situation that threatens our livelihood for following Jesus. Although nationalistic symbols and honored people exist on our currency, our bills and coins do not explicitly deify them as Roman coinage did. The vague phrase "in God we trust" probably does not refer to the deistic entity who supposedly created and subsequently abandoned the world. Because deists do not believe in their god's continual presence in the created order, they cannot express trust in their god for anything other than making the visible cosmos. Since the currency's god is a singular being, it also does not likely refer to the polytheistic origins of the US government, founded on the worship of Libertas, the Roman goddess of freedom, and George Washington, the American god of democracy (see chapter 2, section 1.3.6.1 in this book). However, no evidence associates the phrase with YHWH either, so the original meaning of the phrase remains mysterious.

When the phrase "in God we trust" became a mandatory part of our currency in 1956, white American Christianity had its highest degree of power. Thus, white Christians from that time period are responsible for the Judeo-Christian clarification of the phrase, something that can be attributed to a combination of good intentions on the part of Christians and the entitlement at the center of the American religion, not to a genuine expression of the Judeo-Christian worldview. Nevertheless, because the words have not changed, many Americans can still define the god on the currency however they want. No deist, Christian, Jew, or Muslim can be accused of lying when saying, "I trust in God." Hindus, Buddhists, other polytheists, atheists, and agnostics, on the other hand, cannot lay claim to such a statement. As such, the images and inscriptions on our currency demand a vague monotheistic type of worship that betrays the nation's stated value for the freedom of religion. It only respects freedom of monotheistic religion.

Despite that betrayal, we live in an extremely religiously tolerant nation in which white, male Christians form the political majority. That reality, however, does not mean that we are invulnerable to compromise. The views regarding the one world order we just discussed actually make compromise inevitable. The fears they engender help us understand how a predominantly Christian country could vote for someone who promotes an "America first" ideology. Christian voters might not like the racism, xenophobia, and idolatry that the phrase alone can suggest (we have already been through many ways in which related policies have been built on those evils). They might think, however, that if he puts America first, Trump's isolationist policies will keep the United States exempt from any one world order if it develops. That isolationism, nevertheless, only paves the way for more fear. It promotes fear of immigrants, fear of people living in other countries, and fear of anything that stands against the fearful peoples' ideas of what it means to be American. This feeds into protecting a nationalistic identity of oneself as an American that we have already discussed as a form of idolatry. Further, the fears encourage people to excuse the actions of people that blatantly contradict God's ways of truth, love, and justice. Consuming fear (that is an ideology of fear, not just a natural feeling of being afraid) always opposes itself to love (1 John 4:8). Thus, we must be constantly on guard against theologizing of Revelation that promotes consuming fear and feeds into American exceptionalism, nationalistic idolatry, injustice, or anything that keeps us from loving God and our neighbors (i.e., all people God has created).

3. THE FALL OF BABYLON (REV 14:1-13)

In the introduction of this book, we talked about how prophecy is most often forthcoming. Prophecies solely for the seven congregations in Revelation 2–3 are either messages about the absolute or the imminently forthcoming. If Revelation 12 gives a creative retelling of the birth of Jesus and the beginning of the church age, while Revelation 13 directly reflects realities of the imperial cult that John's audience daily encountered, then chapter 14 tells "what must soon take place" (Rev 1:1). The singers lament Babylon's fall. We have already mentioned that throughout the Apocalypse, Babylon represents the Roman Empire. The empire completely ceased to exist five centuries after Revelation's composition, though its fall was a long process. Revelation 14, thus, transitions from past history to the world shortly after the writing of John's Apocalypse.

Revelation 14 reflects a general principle that also happened to be forthcoming: All empires die. Though the Roman Empire would not completely end for several centuries, the beginning of its fall was forthcoming. Under that framework, this prophecy does not even need to be specific about its time frame. If all empires die, then the prophecy's main purpose is to encourage believers in Asia Minor to remember that Rome's capability for destruction will come to an end, but God's kingdom will not. We must be careful, however, not to view this chapter as entirely dealing with the fall of the Roman Empire and the general truth that all empires die. The symbol of the 144,000 demands this caution. We first encountered this group of people in a decidedly *eschatological* portion of the first *septet*. In addition to its future setting, the characters in Revelation 7 referred solely to Jews. Revelation 14 identifies the 144,000 by their devotion to *YHWH* and their moral purity. John wrote, "they will rest from their toil" (Rev 14:13). Most often, scholars interpret this rest as the intermediate state for believers after death but before resurrection. Certainly, it carries this connotation and fits the context of Revelation's story. The word also conveys a uniquely Jewish connotation that strengthens the *eschatological* bond between this chapter and Revelation 7. Since the 144,000 "will rest from their toil," this imagery paints a Sabbath-like picture. Furthermore, the OT concept of resting from work is deeply tied to rest from Israel's enemies.[18] Babylon is clearly the enemy of the 144,000, and Babylon is Rome. Understandably, all of these images may feel overwhelming and contradictory, but it appears that in this part of the *septet*, the past, present, and future collide. The symbols, thus, carry temporal significance, but that significance is not found exclusively

---

18. Lee, "Rest and Victory," 350–57.

in the past, present, or future. Rather, these symbols find their temporal significance in all three sources equally.

3.1 The Fall of Babylon and the Congregations in Asia Minor

The passage promising the fall of the Roman Empire encourages members of the seven congregations toward endurance. They might have no idea when it will happen, but the text reinforces for them that any suffering caused by the empire will come to an end. Because they do not know when, they can receive the promise of rest as they await ultimate resurrection. The passage empowers them to wait well as it gives them the example of the 144,000 to follow. I do not intend to suggest that they must be virgins like the 144,000 but rather that they must follow their example by shunning idolatry and remaining sexually pure.

The virginity clause of Revelation 14:4 has puzzled biblical scholars for many years, appearing to some as though it belittles marriage. OT rituals often encouraged periods of abstinence, especially for priests. That abstinence was never permanent, however, as the Greek word that translates to "virgin" implies. Daniel C. Olson offers the only potential solution that I find plausible. Olson suggests that John makes an intentional allusion to the *extrabiblical* apocalypse *1 Enoch*. This early apocalypse would have been available at the time of John's writing. John was probably quite familiar with the material. His audiences might not have known any apocalypse other than Daniel, but they were surrounded by an apocalyptic worldview. That worldview would help them understand the reference even if they were completely unaware of *1 Enoch*. The audience must have at least been familiar with stories similar to the one being alluded to in order for John to have any persuasive impact on his hearers. *First Enoch* 6–9 tells of a situation of angelic beings impregnating human women (something common in ancient Jewish mythology). These angels were "defiled by the women." That phrase is the same one used with regards to the 144,000 in Revelation 14:4, although negated for the virgins. The negation shows that these characters are the polar opposite of Enoch's fallen angels. They are humans who maintain faith in God and are virgins in the sense that they do not experiment sexually outside of their God-ordained place in the world. In other words, they uphold the biblical ideal of monogyny. They are faithful to God and faithful to their spouses, highlighting the Bible's consistent linking of sexual immorality with idolatry, but this time from a positive point of view.[19]

---

19. Olson, "Not Defiled," 498–500.

3.2 The Fall of Babylon and Contemporary Christianity in the United States

If my proposal is correct that Revelation 14 combines past, present, and future connotations in its symbolism, then it is quite easy to apply the general principles found in this text. First, it reminds us that all empires eventually fall. We have already addressed similarities between the US governmental system and the Roman Empire despite the fact that the US is not a monarchy. This principle, likewise, applies much more broadly than to literal empires alone. In many ways, the United States fell November 9, 2016, when Donald Trump was elected president. Since that election, whether we approve of Trump's presidency or not, we must recognize that the country we knew before that date exists no longer. Trump promised that he would be a radical disrupter of everything that appeared to make the country work. In some cases, he rightly showed how the system was broken along with plans to break it even more to the point in which it might become irreparable. He has dismantled systems that had been set in place for decades. He has even redefined many aspects of what the country was founded on (see note for specifics).[20] Whether we are encouraged or unsettled by this extremism, we must recognize that the United States we once knew has fallen. Though this type of fall is nowhere near as drastic as the one the Roman Empire suffered, it nevertheless demonstrates the reality that the nations of the world can be upended at any time and by any source.

Second, the imagery calls us, along with all believers in all time periods, to spiritual and sexual purity. It encourages us to recognize the connection between our sexual behavior and our devotion to God. Throughout the OT, the connection is established, most explicitly in the book of Hosea. In the NT, however, Paul provides the most vivid explanation for this connection found in Scripture. He appears to have two points to make in his description

20. For a negative perspective of Trump's contribution to a type of fall of the nation, see Salmon, "Trump Has Done Irreversible Damage." For a positive perspective on the fall, see Dowd et al., "Donald Trump: The Great Disrupter." Please note that the latter source is written by a Trump policy advisor and two former Trump campaign officials. I cite the source to show that both sides recognize he has ended the United States as it had been known for all of its history. The authors, however, fill this article with "facts" that have been proved wrong by many reputable sources, so I by no means recommend looking to this article for a view of reality. Significantly, both articles I cite here are "opinion" articles. As part of this book's challenge toward critical thinking, I chose these two in order to demonstrate how not all opinions are equal. If opinions interpret facts, as the first article's author does, then they are worth considering in order to learn if we are convinced by the author's interpretation of facts. If they invent "facts," as the second article's authors do, then we must recognize the lies therein and give no credence to the source.

of the body as "the temple of the Holy Spirit" (1 Cor 6:19). Before discussing prostitution, Paul is addressing the whole church at Corinth, warning them against actions that are opposed to the kingdom of God. Although he switches modes to talk about an individual hypothetical man committing adultery with a prostitute, he maintains corporate language throughout the chapter. Very often, when we see the word "body" in the NT, it refers to the church, not to an individual's physical being. The statement about sinning outside of the body versus sinning against the body makes no sense when applied to one's own physical body. How could Paul say that only sexual immorality is against an individual's body? For example, gluttony is one of the vices that early church fathers included in the "seven deadly sins." Lifestyles of overindulgence in food are not likely to cause significant harm to others; they reflect sins against one's own physical body. Paul's warning in Galatians to not be drunk with wine but with the Holy Spirit alludes to the overindulgence in alcohol as a sin against one's physical body (Eph 5:18). So, what is Paul saying, then? Most sins committed directly against other people harm a limited number of people. Paul suggests, therefore, that sexual sin is a stain on the whole body of Christ, that it harms far more people than anyone committing it can ever know.

Paul's second point in this passage appears when he refers to every believer's individual body as the "temple of the Holy Spirit" (1 Cor 6:15). If individual bodies are members of Christ's body (1 Cor 6:15) and joining one's body to that of a prostitute harms the whole church, it is because of the equality the whole Bible makes between sex and marriage. We will discuss this in more detail in chapter 6 when we work through Revelation's attitudes toward sexuality, but for now it is sufficient to note that Paul says, "anyone who is united with a prostitute becomes one body with her" (1 Cor 6:16). Scripture consistently uses the language of two flesh becoming one for both marriage and sex, making the two concepts synonymous. As such, Paul uses the most dramatic example possible of prostitution to show the utter disgust of anyone part of the collective group that Revelation calls the Messiah's bride (19:19) succumbing to any type of sexual immorality. The whole passage clarifies that any sexual immorality is a sin against the church, but Paul uses prostitution to make his point as powerfully as possible. Likewise, Paul's second point regarding the synonymous nature of sex and marriage relates broadly to all sexual immorality as destructive to God-ordained relationships.

4. GOD'S WRATH (REV 14:14—18:24)

4.1 God's Wrath and One like the Son of a Human

After recounting a part of his vision that is timeless, John transitions into the final part of the septet, dealing entirely with the end of the age. The language John uses to discuss the end, however, still remains grounded in the daily experiences of Asia Minor. He records seeing the crowning of "one like the son of a human." We discussed the immense variety of uses for crowns in the ancient world in chapter 2, section 2.3.1. The crowned "one like the son of a human" bears much resemblance to Daniel's "one like the son of a human" (Dan 7:13). Daniel used this phrase as an apocalyptic and prophetic reference to the Messiah. The same appears to be the case with the victorious one in Revelation 14:14. Daniel uses the phrase within a royal context that is not shared with Revelation 14:14, unless the predominant purpose for crowning Revelation's "one like the son of a human" is to name him a king.[21]

Interestingly, the "one like the son of a human" carries out his duties after the order of an angel. Such a curiosity has led some scholars to propose that this "one like the son of a human," unlike Daniel's, must be another angel and not the Messiah.[22] The very nature of the designation, however, likens him to humanity, which in the context of the passage furthers the separation made between him and the other three characters (the angels). So, whichever designation we settle on, we have to wrestle with difficult language. Throughout Revelation, angels announce aspects of God's will being accomplished. Though they also command other characters to an action that fulfills God's will, the command can itself be a type of announcement. Jesus's second coming accompanies a trumpet in the second *septet*. According to the language of that passage, Jesus cannot come again without the blast of a trumpet. Does that give the trumpet player authority to command the Messiah to return to the earth? Since we have no indication that God the Father is the trumpet player, the answer must be no. In the same way, the angels in the end of Revelation 14 announce that the time for reaping has arrived. Indeed, they use language that appears to command the "one like the son of a human" to begin reaping. Their function in the text, however, seems to be to announce, not to command. Thus, the one already preordained by the Father to reap knows to begin reaping through the angelic decree.

---

21. Stevenson, "Golden Crown Imagery," 272.
22. Kiddle, *Revelation*, 285; Morris, *Revelation*, 184.

4.2 God's Wrath against the Beast

Babylon (aka Rome) was already defeated in Revelation 14. The beastly characters show up first in a part of the story that links clearly to the world in which the seven congregations lived. Then, the story conflates past, present, and future, still involving one of the same beasts. That beast shows up again in Revelation 15:1–4 in an entirely *eschatological* setting. The anticipated revival of a Nero-like leader can extend far beyond the ancient Roman Empire. Likewise, the symbol of Babylon will fall again before this *septet* concludes. Nero's acts of deception, violence, and anti-Judeo-Christian policies were not unique to Nero or to the Roman Empire. The carryover of the beast in the future-oriented part of the story coincides with the earlier demonic quality of the character. Just as John calls Roman rule demonic, so he suggests that demonic governmental systems with divine pretentions will last throughout the history of this age. Only at the end of the age will God obtain full victory over Satan. At that time, all demonic systems of the world will cease. The defeat of the beast, then, predicts that ultimate future when all sin and death will cease to exist on the earth, because God has defeated Satan and all who follow the evil one.

4.3 God's Wrath against the Followers of the Beast

In chapter 4, we noted that although the judgments of the seven trumpets possess similarities to the OT plagues against Egypt and its gods, the seven bowls parallel the Egyptian plagues almost perfectly. Like the plagues against Egypt, each one of the seven bowls attacks a particular god. The only difference is that these plagues allude to Greco-Roman deities rather than Egyptian, though some overlap exists. Although all seven plagues extend God's wrath to the people who took the beast's mark, only the first one places a direct parallel to the mark. Since the sores are leprous skin diseases, we can understand the judgment as also eradicating the gods who require branding for worship.

The second plague involves bodies of water turning into blood. Since the messages to the seven congregations involved warnings against eating food sacrificed to idols, the blood likely represents judgment against the idols to whom ancient Romans sacrificed. The third plague also involves blood, but the text is clearer here about the sin being judged. The people receiving the third plague are receiving it on account of their murderous actions against God's people. Thus, the plague judges the nationalistic god of Roman authority that was believed to hold even the life and death of all its constituents (not just the vilest of criminals) in its hands.[23]

The fourth plague correlates directly to judgment against the Greco-Roman sun god. The text tells us that the sun harmed people by scorching them with fire. Greek pagans used fire to offer sacrifices to their various gods. This judgment paints an ironic picture, as the sun (a part of God's creation that does not need to be judged) can no longer be worshiped when that god itself offers its followers as a sacrifice. Scriptures often tell us that the elements worship their Creator. This appears to be an example of just that. God judges the god of the sun by using the sun he created to end the worship of itself.[24] Similarly, the fifth plague is clearly directed against the deity known as the beast. Specifically, it judges the beast's throne or rule. So, this plague puts an end to the emperor cult. The text follows the same pattern for the sixth plague, as it mentions the Euphrates River as a god to be judged. From before the Roman Empire existed, kings beginning with Alexander the Great exerted dominion over bodies of water. As the Roman Empire grew, acquiring rivers was even more important than acquiring land, because it gave the impression of absolute control. Just as the Roman government assumed power over the life and death of all its constituents in some form or another, so it also presumed control over the same waters that God created and that Jesus commanded. No evidence demonstrates that the Euphrates was of particular importance to the Roman imperial system, but it was the first body of water that Alexander the Great attempted to exert authority over.[25] Thus, the judgment involving the Euphrates probably represents wrath against the gods of governmental authorities that express divine pretentions through declaring control over creation.

The final plague of the bowls also explains the idol that God judges. Once again, the symbolic use of Babylon in Revelation always points to Rome. The first six bowls all represent plagues against gods that ancient Romans worshiped, some relating to nature and some relating to the government. Parts of Rome fall with each of those six judgments. This time, the god of Rome itself is destroyed. We have already discussed how this final *septet* blurs the lines between past, present, and future. The other two septets both moved from the past to the future, while the bowls do not possess as clear of a chronology. The seventh bowl, until the end of Revelation 18, however, focusses entirely on Babylon/Rome and its fall. As mentioned before, it provides a picture for the seven congregations of "what must take

---

23. Várhelyi, *Religion of Senators*, 56.
24. Palladino, "Cult of Fire," 42.
25. Campbell, *Rivers*, 28, 369.

place in a short time." Therefore, like the earlier *septets*, the judgments end in the future, but not necessarily in the distant future like the other two. I say, "not necessarily," because the final judgment will condemn all false gods throughout all of human history. So, this judgment still blurs chronological lines, even though it is entirely future from John's perspective. It foretells both the imminent judgment that would come upon Rome and the final judgment.

Despite the temporal focus on John's day, the whole set of judgments continues the universal theme that all empires eventually fall. Just as God judged the wrong objects of worship through the plagues against Egypt in Exodus, so he did through the wrath represented by the bowls against Greco-Roman deities, including the imperial cult and the nationalistic governmental system of Rome. This teaches us something significant about God's judgment. God can and will judge false deities and their followers at any time without necessarily bringing a close to the age. As these symbols warned the seven congregations of Asia Minor to avoid compromising with the religious systems expressed through politics and social norms, so they warn us of exactly the same thing in the twenty-first-century United States.

5. ULTIMATE JUDGMENT (REV 19)

Revelation 19:1–6 continues to communicate the truth of God's judgment as something that occurs throughout history and is not limited to a single event at the close of the age. It also revisits the pattern early in the final *septet* to blur the lines between past, present, and future. The praise that occurs in this passage connects to God's judgment of Babylon/Rome. In verse 7, however, John introduces the concept of the wedding feast of the Lamb. At the end of Revelation, John explains the feast as an entirely *eschatological* event. So, the first six verses of the chapter provide a picture of the fullness of salvation that comes at the end of the age when God makes all things right and new. These verses also show that when God exacts judgment throughout the course of history on a smaller scale, he does so for the good of his faithful people. He commits these acts of wrath to make parts of the world right and new on a small scale as we await the fulness of the new heavens and new earth that Jesus will establish at his return. By verse 7, the introduction to the banquet places the text's references entirely in the future, where they remain throughout the rest of the *septet*.

During the plagues of the bowls, God commands other entities to execute his wrath. Therefore, we should take notice of the exceptional nature of the judgment in Revelation 19. Here, the one called "the Word of God" wearing "a robe dipped in blood" with the name "King of kings and Lord of lords" strikes the ungodly. In order to make all things right and new at the end of the age, God must rid the world of all sin and death. God charges his Messiah with that duty, by virtue of the Messiah's sacrificial death and resurrection. This action provides the ultimate fulfillment of a biblical promise that we often misunderstand as a command for people to avoid revenge. The phrase "vengeance and recompense belong to me" (Deut 32:25; referenced in Rom 12:19 and Heb 10:30) promises the world that its actions have consequences. For followers of the Messiah, Jesus's blood cleanses us of our sin and frees us from their eternal consequences. It also begins the process of sanctification so that we might begin producing fruit that will have positive current and eternal consequences.

Further Reading:

For "666" as a reference to Nero:
Lawrence, John M. "Nero Redivivus." *Fides et historia* 11 (1978) 54–66.

For a picture of the ancient coin that inscribes "lord and god" titles to Emperor Domitian:
Reddish, Mitchell G. *Revelation*. Macon, GA: Smyth & Helwys, 2005. Page 126.

For the Greco-Roman goddess who helps form the background of the whore of Babylon:
Schedtler, Justin Joseph. "Mother of Gods, Mother of Harlots: The Image of the Mother Goddess behind the Description of the 'Whore of Babylon' in Revelation 17." *NovTest* 59 (2017) 52–70.

Chapter 6

Jesus's Second Coming (Rev 20–22)

20 ¹ Then I saw an angel descending from heaven, holding in his hand the key to the abyss with a large chain. ² Then he seized the dragon (the ancient serpent, who is the devil, namely Satan); he bound him for 1,000 years, ³ threw him into the abyss, closed it, and sealed it above him, with the result that he could no longer deceive the nations until the thousand years were completed. After these things, it is necessary to release him for a short duration of time.

⁴ Then I saw thrones, and they sat on them, and the authority to judge was granted to them. I also saw the souls of the people who have been beheaded because of the testimony of Jesus and because of the word of God, who worshiped neither the beast nor its image, who did not receive the mark on their forehead or on their hand, and they lived and reigned with the Messiah for 1,000 years. ⁵ (The rest of the dead people did not come to life until the thousand years were completed.) This event is the first resurrection. ⁶ Blessed and holy is the one who has a portion in the first resurrection. The second death has no authority over such people, but they will be priests for God and for his Messiah, and they will reign with him for 1,000 years.

⁷ Then when the thousand years are completed, Satan will be released from his prison, ⁸ and he will go forth in order to

deceive the nations at the four corners of the earth, Gog and Magog, so as to assemble them for war. Concerning them, their number is like the sand of the sea. ⁹ Then they came up onto the whole extent of the earth and surrounded the camp of the saints and the beloved city. Then fire came down from heaven and consumed them, ¹⁰ and the devil who deceived them was thrown into the lake of fire and brimstone, where the beast and the false prophet also will be tormented day and night forever and ever.

¹¹ Then I saw a great white throne with one seated on it, from whose presence the earth and heaven fled, but no place was found for them. ¹² Then I saw the dead people, great and small, standing before the throne, and scrolls were opened. Then another scroll was opened, which is the book of life, and the dead people were judged based upon what is written in the scrolls, according to their works. ¹³ Then the sea gave up the dead people who were in it, and death and Hades gave up the dead people who were in them, and they were each judged according to their works.

¹⁴ Then death and Hades were thrown into the lake of fire. This is the second death, namely the lake of fire. ¹⁵ Now when anyone was not found written in the book of life, that one was cast into the lake of fire.

21 ¹ Then I saw a new heaven and a new earth, since the first heaven and the first earth had passed away, and the sea is no more. ² I also saw the holy city, the new Jerusalem, coming down out of heaven from God, prepared like a bride adorned for her groom, ³ and I heard a loud voice from the throne. It said: "Behold, the dwelling place of God is with humanity. So, he will dwell with them, they will people his people, and God himself will be with them. He will be their God. ⁴ He will wipe away every tear from their eyes, and death will exist no more. No grief, weeping, nor pain will exist anymore, since the former things have passed away."

⁵ Then the one seated on the throne said, "Behold, I make all things new. Write: 'These words are faithful and true.'" Then, he said to me, "These things are finished. I am the alpha and the omega, the first and the last. I will give water to the thirsty from the spring of the water of life as a gift. ⁷ The overcomer will inherit these things; I will be God to him, and he will be a son to me. ⁸ But as for cowards, unbelieving people, detestable people, murderers, sexually immoral people, idolaters, and all liars, their lot will be in the lake that burns with fire and brimstone. This is the second death."

⁹ Then one of the seven angels having the seven bowls that are full of the seven final plagues came, and he spoke with me. He said, "Come here. I will show you the bride, the wife of the Lamb." ¹⁰ Then he took me away in the spirit to a great and high mountain, and he showed me the holy city Jerusalem coming down out of heaven from God, ¹¹ possessing the glory of God. Its splendor was like a precious stone, like a clear-crystal jasper stone, ¹² having a great and high wall, twelve gates, twelve angels on the gates, and names inscribed, which are the names of the twelve tribes of the children of Israel: ¹³ three gates on the east, three gates on the north, three gates on the south, and three gates on the west. ¹⁴ Now the wall of the city had twelve foundations, and on them the twelve names of the twelve apostles of the Lamb were inscribed.

¹⁵ Now the one speaking with me was holding a golden measuring rod in order to measure the city, its gates, and its wall. ¹⁶ The city lies four-square (its length is the same as the width). So, he measured the city with his rod: 12,000 stadia [about 1,800 miles]. Its length, width, and height are equal. ¹⁷ Then he measured its wall: 144 cubits [the exact measure of a cubit is unknown, but 144 cubits is somewhere between four and five miles] according to human measurement, which is the measurement the angel used. ¹⁸ Now the structure of its wall is jasper, and the city is pure gold like pure crystal. ¹⁹ The foundations of the city wall are adorned with every kind of precious stone. The first foundation is jasper, the second sapphire, the third chalcedony, the fourth emerald, ²⁰ the fifth sardonyx, the sixth carnelian, the seventh chrysolite, the eight beryl, the ninth topaz, the tenth chrysoprase, the eleventh jacinth, the twelfth amethyst, ²¹ and the twelve gates are twelve pearls; each one of the gates was made from one pearl, and the city street was pure gold, transparent like glass.

²² I saw no temple in it [the city], since the Lord God Almighty is its temple, as is the Lamb. ²³ Likewise, the city has no need for the sun or moon to shine on it; indeed, the glory of God shone, and its light was the Lamb, ²⁴ and the nations walked by its light, and the kings of the earth bring their glory to it,²⁵ (its gates will never be shut by day, since night does not exist there), ²⁶ and they will bring the glory and honor of the nations to it. ²⁷ But nothing unclean nor anyone who practices what is detestable or false—if their names are not written in the Lamb's book of life—will ever enter into it.

22 ¹ Then he showed me the stream of living water, clear as crystal, coming out of the throne of God and of the Lamb. ² In

the middle of its street and around the stream was the tree of life, which produces twelve kinds of fruits, yielding its fruit according to each month. The leaves of the tree are for the healing of the nations. ³ So, every curse will be no more, but the throne of God and of the Lamb will be in it. Thus, his slaves will serve him ⁴ and see his face, and his name will be on their foreheads. ⁵ Night and day will be no more, and no one will have need of a lamp or sunlight, because the Lord God will shine on them, and he will reign forever and ever.

⁶ Then he said to me, "These words are faithful and true, and the Lord God of the spirits of the prophets sent his angel to show his slaves what must take place in a short time." ⁷ "Behold, I am coming soon. Blessed is the one who keeps the words of the prophecy of this scroll."

⁸ I John, am the one who heard and saw these things. So when I heard and saw, I fell in order to worship before the feet of the angel who showed me these things. ⁹ But he said to me, "See to it that you do not do that. I am a fellow slave of yours, your brothers among the prophets, and the people who keep the words of this scroll. Worship God!"

¹⁰ Then he said to me, "Do not seal the words of the prophecy of this scroll, since the time is near. ¹¹ Let the evildoer still do evil, the defiled one still be defiled, the just one still practice justice, and the holy one still be holy."

¹² "Behold, I am coming soon along with my recompense with me, judging each person according to what his work is. ¹³ I am the alpha and the omega, the first and the last, the beginning and the end. ¹⁴ Blessed are the people who wash their robes in order that their right will be to the tree of life and in order that they can enter into the city through the gates. ¹⁵ Outside are the dogs, sorcerers, sexually immoral people, murderers, idolaters, and all who practice a lie. ¹⁶ I Jesus, sent my angel to you to witness these things for the congregations. I am the root and descendent of David, the bright morning star."

¹⁷ Now the Spirit and the bride say, "Come," Also, let the one who hears say, "Come." And let the thirsty one—who desires to receive the water of life as a gift—come.

¹⁸ I testify to everyone who hears the words of the prophecy of this scroll: "If anyone adds to them, God will add the plagues recorded in this scroll upon him. ¹⁹ Likewise, if anyone takes away from the words of the scroll of this prophecy, God will take away his portion from the tree of life and the holy city that are written about in this scroll."

[20] The one who testifies to these things says, "Yes, I am coming quickly." Amen, come Lord Jesus. [21] The grace of the Lord Jesus be with all.

1. THE MILLENNIAL REIGN (REV 20:1-10)

Revelation 20 marks one of the most contentious portions in Scripture. No one from the earliest church fathers to current biblical scholars have ever been able to agree on what this passage's millennium is. Does it refer to a literal thousand-year period of time? Is the number of years symbolic but the event something real? Is the whole concept of a millennium a symbol or a real event? If it is an actual event, will it take place before or after Jesus's return to the earth? None of these questions are particularly relevant to this book. Portions of Revelation 20, however, are extremely significant for our purposes. Since the millennial reign is the primary focus of the chapter, however, I will begin this section with a critical thinking exercise. I will present a different scholar's argument for each of the five important interpretations without any of my own comments. You can learn the various explanations of the millennial passage through the summaries of each defense. As you do so, you will notice that one does not coincide at all with what we have already established about John's Apocalypse. The other four, however, can all fit, even though some specifics depart from what I have put forward. After the critical thinking exercise, I will offer minimal comments of my own on the millennium in order to transition us back to the goals of this book.

Critical Thinking Exercise 3: Millennial Reign

A. Historic Premillennialism[1]

Revelation follows a general chronological pattern, though not a literal one. Some symbols of Revelation should be taken literally. Others have literal and symbolic referents, while yet others are entirely symbolic. Likewise, all of God's promises to Israel in the OT have two layers of fulfillment, one for ancient Israel and one for the church consisting of both Jews and gentiles. The Bible gives no indication that the church should ever be viewed as a replacement of Israel as God's chosen people. Whatever they might have also meant to the seven churches, the beasts represent actual people of the

---

1. See Ladd, *Blessed Hope*.

future who will usher in a time of suffering like the world has not yet known. That Great Tribulation period will be marked by persecution of God's people—both Jew and gentile. It will culminate with a Rapture, through which saints will be spared as the wrath of God is poured out on the earth (though they will not escape the Great Tribulation). Jesus's second coming to the earth, then, establishes a temporary earthly reign during which time Satan is bound. God's people will return to the earth in resurrected bodies during this time period before the final judgment. Jesus's second coming, not escape from tribulation, is the blessed hope.

B. Dispensational Premillennialism[2]

The Book of Revelation is a portion and climax of the overarching theme of human history from creation to God's destruction of the world. John's Apocalypse gives the most detailed treatment of the last two dispensations of human history. Thus, most of it must be taken literally. The limits to this literal approach come only when dealing with animal characters. The beasts do not cause us to expect that animals will cause destruction in the last days. Rather, Revelation's main beast is a symbolic representation of the future, human Antichrist; the other beasts are the antichrist figures that must come prior to the Antichrist. Any portion of Revelation that is symbolic derives from the book of Daniel, in which those symbols are explained. They must refer to the same things, since we can only interpret Scripture through the use of other Scriptures. The fifth of the sixth dispensations is the age of grace, inaugurated with Jesus's crucifixion. Subdivisions of this dispensation include the apostolic age, after which God ceased to make the gifts of his Holy Spirit available to the church. During this fifth dispensation, various antichrists reign in terror, including Hitler. This age of grace will conclude when all living followers of Jesus are carried to heaven in the Rapture. Many people will remain on the earth; they will endure the Great Tribulation that Christians get to escape. After the Great Tribulation, once the age of grace has passed away, the earth will enter into the millennial period. Jesus will reign on the earth with the people who had been raptured and all who are left on the earth for a literal one thousand years. Because Israel and Christianity are completely separate entities, the millennial age will be the time in which God fulfills all his OT promises to Israel. The age of grace is mostly for the church, while the millennial reign is the time in which most, if not all, Jews who remain after the Great Tribulation will be saved. Satan will no longer be able to deceive Jews as he did throughout the age of grace.

2. See Pentecost, *Things to Come*.

After the millennial reign, all people—dead and alive—will be gathered for judgment. After that judgment, some will go to heaven and some will go to hell, while the earth will be left uninhabited for the rest of eternity. The two sources of *eschatological* hope are 1) the Rapture, through which believers escape the Great Tribulation, and 2) eternity in heaven.

C. Postmillennialism[3]

The end times began when Jesus established his kingdom on earth through his ministry, death, and resurrection. As he inaugurated his kingdom, his people were empowered with the Holy Spirit on the day of Pentecost (a fulfillment of the *eschatological* prophecy in Joel). In this age, Jesus's ministry continues through the gifts of the Holy Spirit. The age will culminate in Jesus's second coming. Revelation 20's millennium encompasses the whole of that age. Because the center of this ministry is the Great Commission, world evangelization is the purpose of this *eschatological* time period. A time in this age will come when almost all people of a certain generation will have received the gift of salvation. Peace and prosperity will exist among all nations. This general human commitment to love, truth, and justice will usher in Jesus's second coming. The general resurrection and final judgment will accompany the messianic appearance. Then, God's reign on the earth will be physical and eternal, as opposed to the previous millennial reign (the church age) that is spiritual and has an ending point. The postmillennial return of the Messiah fulfills all ancient Jewish hopes regarding *eschatology*, resurrection, covenant, and partnership with God. Aligned with Paul's language, it represents the fullness of God's will for the Jew first, and also for the gentile.

D. Augustinian Amillennialism[4]

The "first resurrection" of Revelation 20 refers to the regeneration of lives who receive the sacrifice of Jesus applied to them. It is only *eschatological* in the sense that it occurs continuously throughout the time between Jesus's two appearances, which the Bible calls "the end times." The whole era is a time of "great tribulation" that will likely continue to worsen (though not necessarily consistently) until Jesus returns. The phrase "first resurrection" implies that a second one must occur, though it is not mentioned in the text.

---

3. See Gentry, "Definition."
4. See Berry, "Highlighting the Link."

The general resurrection at the end of the age is that second resurrection. Similarly, the text associates the "second death" with the lake of fire, but it does not mention a first death. The first death is the general human reality that earthly life comes to an end. The "second death" is the eternal death connected to the final judgment for those who do not belong to God. The millennium of Revelation, then, represents the whole time period between Jesus's first and second advents (cf., postmillennialism).

E. Adjusted Amillennialism[5]

The "first resurrection" does not refer to an individual believer's salvation but to his/her death. The "first resurrection" and the implicit first death are the same event. At this event, a believer is united with God in an intermediate, disembodied state awaiting the general resurrection. The implicit second resurrection refers to general resurrection. *Eschatological* hope, then, comes from the promise of bodily resurrection, not from the intermediate, disembodied state in heaven.

Hoekema's view represents just one of several developments that have adjusted the Augustinian amillennial view in recent decades. These adjustments do not have large groups of proponents but are nevertheless important to give a full picture regarding the options available for interpreting the millennial reign. Some other marginalized thoughts include the idea that the millennium is over, having ended at some point in the first century CE, sometimes connected to the fall of Jerusalem in 70 CE.

1.1 Brief History of Interpretation of the Prominent Millennial Views

The viewpoint known as *chiliasm* appears to be the earliest millennial view held in the church. *Chiliasm* represents a fragmentary basis for what would become historic premillennialism. The church father Augustine first detailed an amillennial approach in the book *City of God*, which involved many beliefs about Israel and the church that many interpreters now consider inappropriate. The skeleton of his interpretation with attention to the "first resurrection" and "second death," however, became the most prominent way of reading Revelation 20 from the fifth century through the nineteenth century. Dispensational premillennialism became most prominent in the United Kingdom for a short period at the end of the nineteenth century. It

---

5. See Hoekema, *Bible and the Future*.

spread to the United States and dominated here for a large portion of the twentieth century but has never spread significantly beyond the two countries. Postmillennialism, similarly, enjoyed prominence in the West during the nineteenth century but has neither experienced a long history nor ever been a global majority. Currently, historic premillennialism is the widest held view in the church worldwide. The skeletal structure of Augustinian amillennialism, nevertheless, remains the most prominent view among biblical scholars universally.[6]

1.2 The Millennial Reign and the Binding of Satan

The text states that during the millennial era, however we understand it, Satan will be bound. As you read through each of the five interpretations outlined above, hopefully you noticed that only the premillennial ideas make Satan's bondage explicit. That surface, however, does not mean that the other *eschatological* viewpoints ignore what the text says about Satan's temporary inability to deceive the nations. When Jesus fasted and experienced his temptation in the wilderness, he was victorious over Satan. He diminished Satan's power and began the process of binding him. Satan was obviously present and continued tempting Jesus throughout Jesus's time on earth. Jesus's death and resurrection, however, further limited Satan's authority. The text of Revelation says that Satan was bound "in the abyss." As such, he exists in the netherworld. He himself may be bound, but he still has a demonic army that accomplishes his work of deception in his behalf. Therefore, the viewpoints that are not premillennial still account for Satan's binding in the abyss. It does not mean that Satan is powerless; it means that his power is reduced from what he possessed before the Messiah's first arrival and that others must do his bidding on the earth for him.[7]

We do not have to subscribe to one of the premillennial viewpoints to accept Satan's binding, but what about the release of Satan? Postmillennialists have such an optimistic view of the future that they seem to leave no room for a time period when Satan gets a final chance to personally deceive the nations. Because amillennial believers have a similar temporal emphasis as postmillennialists and are far more agnostic about future *eschatology* than millennialists, the same risk seems evident. That *eschatological* agnosticism, nevertheless, can actually fill in the blanks for both postmillennial and amillennial views of the release of Satan. Simply admitting that one does not know exactly how to understand this millennial issue opens

---

6. Kovacs and Rowland, *Revelation*, 200–219.
7. Waldron, *End Times Made Simple*, 187–88.

the door to accept many possibilities without requiring commitment to one. The Augustinian amillennial suggestion that Satan's bondage occurs during the time between Jesus's two advents does not necessitate that Satan be bound during the whole age. The willingness to remain uncertain about these matters helps amillennial proponents to avoid contradiction. They do not need to know which part of the age involves Satan's bondage and which part involves his release to deceive the nations for a final time. Finally, this agnosticism prevents the certainty found in dispensational premillennialism, a certainty that contradicts many portions of Scripture. So, I do not wish to promote one millennial view over the other, but rather I encourage willingness to find strengths in all possibilities except for dispensational premillennialism.

1.3 Millennial Thrones and Resurrection of the Beheaded Saints

1.3.1 Whose Thrones?

Most English translations try to make up for the Greek vagueness at the beginning of Revelation 20:4 by saying "those seated on them were given authority to judge." This manner of translation, of course, offers no help to answer who is seated on these thrones. This linguistic matter is important, because in the first clause of 20:4, the Greek word for "soul" is a direct object of the verb "saw." This implies that that John saw the souls of the beheaded separately from the thrones. Those on the thrones who are given judgment authority are not the same as those who were beheaded.

Earlier in Revelation, the elders sit on thrones. So, though we have no definitive answer, it seems most likely that John is again referring to the thrones of the twenty-four elders. The twenty-four elders possess authority connected to judgment elsewhere in the book, so this context helps to give a better idea that John is probably talking about them here.

1.3.2 Beheading

Martin Scorsese's 2015 movie *Silence* depicts Jesuit missionaries in Japan during the seventeenth century. A mass execution is shown; those who refused to renounce their faith in Jesus are condemned to death by beheading. The proceedings, led by a man known as the Inquisitor, all happen in the Japanese language. The two missionaries are kept in a cell with a window where they are forced to watch the proceedings. After the beheadings are done, the Inquisitor arranges to have the heads of the missionaries' converts rolled in the direction of the missionaries. He then screams in English in order that the missionaries will understand: "This is what happens to Christians!"

The book of Revelation agrees with the Inquisitor. John mentions martyrdom throughout the book, and although this is the only direct mention of beheading, the Roman Empire was known to have used various forms of execution, including beheadings during times of programmatic persecution against monotheists. Beheading is probably used at this juncture in the Apocalypse because of the context of resurrection. For John to see people who were not only dead but dismembered return to life and physical wholeness could not be more miraculous. However, we are not quite ready to talk about resurrection. John sees the "souls of the beheaded" and says that they are people who did not worship the beast or have the mark of the beast. Naturally, this means that they worshiped God.

These martyrs did not take the mark of the beast, but they still possess a mark symbolizing to whom they belong. Their beheading is that mark. Beheading, or any form of martyrdom, declares the fullness of one's devotion to God and refusal to worship anything other than God. Revelation reminds its audiences that being killed and dismembered often happens to those completely devoted to Jesus.

Revelation is not the only part of the NT that agrees with the Inquisitor of *Silence*. The Gospels recount the well-known beheading of John the Baptist. Although John the Baptist was a forerunner to the Messiah and thus not a Christian in any historically sound sense of the word, his ministry was to "prepare the way" for the Messiah. His beheading occurred because of his devotion to that call. Just as he baptized in order to lead people to repentance in preparation of Jesus's ministry, so his death occurred because he refused to compromise the righteousness that his calling entailed. Therefore, the accounts of John the Baptist agree with the Inquisitor that beheading is what happens to those devoted to God's Messiah. Acts 12:1–2 recounts the martyrdom of James by King Herod (most likely Herod Agrippa). The text uses the vague clause "by the sword," not specifying into what part of James's body the sword cut. History and legend, nevertheless, give strong evidence that his cause of death was beheading.[8]

Church history also agrees with the Inquisitor. Although *Silence* is based on a novel, its fictional narrative is grounded in the history surrounding the Jesuit missionaries who first introduced Christianity to Japan. Gruesome events like the one depicted in the film were not uncommon at that time in Japanese history. We have already discussed Nero's persecution in

---

8. Nixon, "Boenergess," 1354.

the middle of the first century of church history. Some of the murders Nero ordered included beheadings. Following is a list of a few other examples out of many throughout the last two thousand years:

Year (nation):	Description of Persecution Events that Included Beheadings:
258 (Roman Empire)	Emperor Valerian ordered execution by beheading for all clergy who would not offer sacrifices to pagan gods.[9]
Late 800s (Spain)	During a time of oppressive Muslim rule over Spain, Christian worship was technically legal, but many Christians were executed by beheading under baseless charges of blasphemy against Mohammed.[10]
1647 (India)	Missionary John de Britto was responsible for many conversions in India. One was a prince with many wives. When de Britto demanded that he divorce his wives, one wife turned to the King of Ramanathapuram for revenge. The king had de Britto beheaded and began a widespread assault against Christians and Christianity.[11]
1791–1888 (Korea)	Over ten thousand lay Catholics were killed for their acts of worship to God that denounced tenets of Confucianism.[12]
1773–1861 (Vietnam)	A long series of murders by beheading occurred whenever missionaries attempted to convert Tonkinese people of northern Vietnam during the almost-ninety-year period of violent persecution against Christians.[13]

This table represents only a small sample of the many instances throughout history of beheadings against those who follow Jesus. It includes a few of many victims who can be easily established as martyrs. In recent years, ISIL has committed many beheadings against Christians worldwide. ISIL terrorists, however, have never consistently made it explicit that they kill anyone because they are Christians or refuse to renounce their faith in the lordship of Jesus. In fact, the reason I choose ISIL rather than ISIS to identify the terror organization is because the L refers to the Levant. Their name alludes to a desire to violently take over the entire region, including Israel. Giving attention to the most accurate acronym, as former president Barak Obama

9. Frend, *Rise of Christianity*, 326.
10. Osuna, "Cordova," lines 20–51.
11. Woods, "John de Britto," lines 10–16.
12. "Martirologio," https://www.vatican.va/roman_curia/pontifical_academies/cult-martyrum/martiri/009.html. This document on the Vatican's website lists those who were killed for their faith among these Korean martyrs
13. *Vietnamese Martyrs* provides a database of Christian persecution in Vietnam, including this particularly horrendous period. View the database at https://sites.google.com/site/vietnamesemartyrs/home.

first did prominently in the United States, helped anti-terrorism officials bring attention to the terror organization's specific intentions to kill Jews. Of course, ISIL has killed more Muslims than Jews or Christians, but one of its original aims appears to be an eradication of Jews in the Levant. ISIL's beheadings of Christians represent a small portion of a larger program of hate and murder. Not all beheadings of Jews and Christians occur *because* the victims are Jewish or Christian. The martyrs mentioned in Revelation 20:4 are all killed *because* they follow Jesus. Furthermore, if you look at Wikipedia's depressingly long (but far from conclusive) list of people who have been beheaded, you will find that a vast majority have nothing to do with their faith. In fact, you will see that many of the perpetrators claimed to be Christian. Therefore, even though beheading is a mark of one's devotion to the Messiah for the saints mentioned in Revelation, for the victims of the Inquisitor, and for victims worldwide throughout church history who were specifically beheaded *because* of their faith in Jesus, beheading is not always a mark of the believer.

Just as beheading is not always a mark of the believer, it is not the only mark of believers, thank God! I noted earlier that John probably emphasizes beheading in this passage because of its resurrection context. Unfortunately, we are still not quite ready to talk about resurrection. The passage of the martyrs suggests that all martyrdom (deaths that occur *because* one chooses and continues to follow Jesus) is a mark of the believer. Fortunately, broader martyrdom is not the only mark of the believer either. The NT includes many ways in which genuine followers of Jesus can be recognized. We have the Holy Spirit dwelling within us. We have access to the supernatural gifts of the Holy Spirit. We are empowered by the Holy Spirit for good works, holy living, and overcoming temptation. Because God lives within us and because God is love, the ability to express real, sacrificial, and selfless love is the most significant and unifying mark of all believers. These examples are just a few of the more practical marks of the believer that can set our minds at ease, lest we think (like many people throughout history have, though not very many in recent history) that we must die as martyrs in order to be faithful servants of Jesus.

My reasoning for spending so much time on the likely vomit-inducing topic of beheading (and general martyrdom) is to show its commonality throughout history. No, it is not the only way to prove our devotion to Jesus. Nevertheless, we should be surprised at the lack of genuine persecution over devotion to Jesus around us. People experience violent oppression for their faith worldwide. Only in parts of the West have we assumed ourselves immune to it. We have made that assumption, because we have not experienced much of the real persecution that most of the world has. For this reason, many Christians in the United States have been deceived into believing they are persecuted. The reality, however, is that they are more likely expressing what marks them as an American (entitlement to rights that are not actually human rights) rather than what makes them Christian. At any time, this reality could change for us. Genuine persecution could hit very soon. In fact, as many people as there are who think they are being persecuted when they are not, I believe they could be paving the way for real, violent persecution in the United States. The victims of that real persecution would be Christians who choose to live according to the truth, love, and justice of Jesus instead of the "American way" that many other Christians are choosing. We must not take the minority status of un-persecuted Christians lightly as if it indicates some special favor with God. We could become subject to violent persecution at any time, and we must be ready to accept it as a mark of the believer.

1.4 Millennial Reign and the Enemies of God's People

1.4.1 *Gog and Magog as Symbolic Types*

The personal name Gog and the place name Magog have invited much speculation about the future, because the text links them to the *eschatological* battle of Armageddon (or Harmageddon, to more precisely transliterate the Greek name). Ezekiel's prophecy against Gog (Ezek 38–39) provides a prophetic promise of God's defeat of the leader named Gog, though no historical evidence points to the existence of such a person. Portions of Ezekiel, including chapters 38–39, are apocalyptic in nature. The OT book as a whole is a prophecy, not an apocalypse. Some of its prophecies, nevertheless, include the apocalyptic elements listed in the introduction of this book (including dualism, resurrection, and *eschatology*). Many OT prophecies are not meant to be taken literally; their fulfillments often occurred in layers that revealed the full impact of the message only as they were being fulfilled. As a micro-apocalypse in the midst of a prophetic book, Ezekiel 38 should be taken even less literally than the entirely prophetic portions of Ezekiel.

Most often, scholars suggest that the name Gog represented the arrogant King Nebuchadnezzar for Ezekiel.[14] God's defeat of Nebuchadnezzar is detailed in the book of Daniel, thus explaining the fulfillment of Ezekiel's prophecy against Gog. Although Magog does not appear until Revelation, the place name applicable to Nebuchadnezzar's reign would be Babylon. As such, we should instantly associate the use of Gog in Revelation with

14. Galambush, "Necessary Enemies," 255.

Revelation's own Babylon, namely Rome. As Gog most likely represents one of Israel's most fervent enemies, so Rome represents the most fervent enemy of the church in the first century CE. More importantly, Gog in Ezekiel and Babylon in Revelation both represent people who have made themselves enemies against God himself.

The Roman Empire was not consistent in its violent persecution against monotheists. It always took a stance in some way or another, however, to make itself the enemy of God and his people—both Jew and gentile. Since the latter half of Revelation 20 presents an unambiguously future setting, we must not view it solely as a prophetic message to the Christians in Asia Minor. It does not need to be a promise that God will defeat Rome, because so much of Revelation's earlier content has already made that promise. Furthermore, since the fall of Rome does not accompany Jesus's second coming as the battle at Harmageddon does, this passage must provide a much broader and more final message. Revelation 20 still gives a promise, nevertheless. Many portions of Revelation illustrate that God would defeat the Roman Empire, but Revelation 20 promises that in the fullness of time, God will have victory over all his enemies. Thus, we can understand the personal name (Gog) as representing any ruler that rises against God's people and the place name (Magog) as representing all the people who follow that ruler. The battle at Harmageddon promises that God will have the final say and that all violence and persecution on the earth will come to an end.

1.4.2 *Gog and Magog in US Politics*

If the battle at Harmageddon offers a promise of God's certain defeat of all his enemies, then the symbols of Gog and Magog do not necessarily point to a single future ruler and a single nation. To the contrary, though, just as the names have yielded much speculation about the future, they have also played significant roles in American warfare over recent decades. When Ronald Regan was governor of California (between 1967 and 1975), he cited the Ezekiel passage, claiming Communist Russia was beginning to fulfill that prophecy through its role in the Cold War.[15]

In 2007, Thomas Römer—a theology professor at the University of Lausanne in Switzerland—suggested that in 2003, President George W. Bush asked the president of France to aid the United States in the Iraq war. To that end, Bush allegedly claimed that he needed help because the United States was fighting a war that fulfilled the biblical prophecy of Gog and Magog. This was the first of several accusations of this sort coming against

---

15. Lee, "Enemies Within," 1–2.

Bush from different parts of Europe. Bush never denied this encounter, and it fits his tendency to comingle theological viewpoints with policymaking. The story, nevertheless, was covered far more in Europe than it was in the United States and did not develop until four years after the alleged event. Furthermore, no French authorities ever arose to say they heard Bush make this claim, so we should not be too quick to accept the veracity of these accusations.[16] They are important to mention, however, because they are part of a broader tendency that places US-centered interpretations of Scripture at the center of national political occurrences.

This tendency is dangerous in many ways, since it encourages the nationalistic idea that God uniquely favors the United States (as is suggested in the line "God shed his grace on thee" in the patriotic song "America the Beautiful"). It requires people to give inflated honor to the nation at the expense of the worship due only to God. More specifically, the assertion that Russian Communists or Middle Eastern terrorists represent Gog and Magog twists the promise that the passage presents. Instead of presenting the assurance of God's victory over his enemies, it presumes upon God's victory over America's enemies, something that Scripture never promises.

2. FINAL JUDGMENT AND NEW CREATION (REV 20:11—22:5)

2.1 Judgment

The concept of judgment is found consistently in Revelation. Only at the end of septets and in the final three chapter, however, does it refer to a situation entirely in the future. God is love, and God is just. God has never laxed on justice in order to demonstrate love, nor has he ever laxed on love in order to demonstrate justice. Throughout all of history, divine judgment has occurred and will continue to occur until the end of the age. We talked earlier about the OT tendency of nations rising against each other, sometimes even against Israel as a reflection of divine judgment. Certainly, this does not mean that any time a crisis occurs in the world, God must be exercising judgment. Within any crisis, however, because we live in a fallen world subject to pain and suffering, God might execute judgment against some of the people involved. We can rarely be certain when this is the case, though, so we must be exceedingly slow to offer such speculation.

We can be more certain, however, when we see evil institutions come to an end. The end of slavery in the United States was the end of an evil

---

16. Lee, "Enemies Within," 1–2.

institution with demonic roots. Not all slaveowners repented or died as a result of their abuse. The end of slavery, nevertheless, had dramatic negative consequences for former slaveowners; God was surely involved with the judgment against that institution. It does not mean, however, that his wrath against those perpetrators was complete. A final judgment awaits that will give the unrepentant participants in that evil system the punishment they have always deserved. It will also end all the evil that has continued to flow out of slavery. Because of slavery, systemic racism in all aspects and locations of US society developed. I desperately desire a time before Jesus's second coming that involves divine judgment that ends societal and ignorant racism. We have no scriptural guarantee that such will happen, however. As followers of Jesus, nevertheless, we have an obligation to do our part toward change within the contexts of our churches, interpersonal relationships, and individual gifts, talents, and interests. If that desired goal happens in our generation, we can know that God empowered his people toward love that partners with the judgment that rightfully belongs only to him.

The ultimate judgment, then, which is the subject of much of Revelation 20–22, is the prerequisite to God setting all things right and in their proper order. As we looked at the type of divine judgment that occurs throughout history, we can see how God's love and justice interact. He demonstrates his love for his people through the judgment and destruction of those who rise against them violently. In this age, though, that divine protection is a reality but not a guarantee. Only by the final judgment will God bring the fullness of his protection, healing, and covenant with his people to fruition. At the cross, Jesus conquered sin and death. Sin and death, nevertheless, still exist in the current world order. Final judgment is not only the punishment of sinners and the demonic realm. Final judgment is also the means by which God will rid the world entirely of sin and death.

Critical Thinking Exercise 4: Lake of Fire/Hell

When Jesus rids the world of all sin and death, what happens to the unbelievers? Many non-Christians in the United States wrongly believe that *all* Christians understand the passages of Scripture dealing with judgment as pointing toward eternal punishment of unbelievers. Some of the most vocal (and obnoxious) would-be evangelists like to talk about hell so much that they seem to believe fear will motivate people to follow Jesus, even though "perfect love casts out fear." We should not be surprised, then, that the concept of eternal punishment (at least the way some believers present it) turns people away from the gospel. This problem occurs in part because people in many Christian traditions tend to assume that the "lake of fire" and "hell" discuss eternal punishment without critically evaluating the literary and historical contexts of these themes when they are used in Scripture. It simply does not occur to such believers that genuine followers of Jesus might exist who do not accept these concepts as literal realities. Such believers do exist, and their stance is known as annihilationism.

The only statement I will offer personally on this topic is to caution against thinking you know what the Bible says about the end results of judgment before having introduced yourself to contrary ideas. Our cultural and denominational upbringings can give us a type of tunnel vision on this issue, so that we wrongly make devastating assumptions about people on the other side. Many of those who accept a traditionalist view of hell believe that it is an essential doctrine of Christianity (i.e., that anyone who does not accept it is not truly a Christian and will thus be subject to eternal punishment). Christians who do not accept eternal punishment tend to think that those who do are incapable of love, assuming they serve a god of fear and punishment, rather than the God who is love. Of course, neither of these stereotypes reflect truth. I hope that both of the articles I summarize here help to begin remedying these dangerous pigeonholes. As you read the summaries, I hope you gain understanding regarding the literary and historical background behind the concept of *Gehenna*. *Gehenna* is usually thought of as hell. It serves as the biblical background for Revelation's "lake of fire." I also want to note that my summary of the defense of the nontraditional view is significantly longer than that of the traditional view. This decision is based on the general burden of proof lying on the nontraditional view, because you are less likely to be familiar with it. I do not intend length to imply my personal leanings on the topic, which are admittedly uncertain.

A. "Lake of Fire" and "Hell" Do Not Refer to Eternal Punishment[17]

The traditional view of hell as eternal punishment finds its roots in Saint Augustine. To interact with Augustine's theological presupposition, we must ask two questions about the concept of eternal punishment, especially as related to the depiction of final judgment and resurrection in Revelation. First, how could a resurrected human body endure constant exposure to physical and emotional torment without eventually losing consciousness? Second, how could flames identical to earthly flames (the meaning of the biblical word *gehena*) fail to consume a person? The idea of eternal torment takes the biblical imagery of fire seriously and literally, but so does

17. See Pinnock, "Destruction of the Finally Impenitent."

the annihilationist view. Since the word *gehena* literally connotes the fire of a trash heap, such a fire could only provide a negative answer to each of the two questions posed above. Like the word *geheha*, the general description regarding the fate of the unsaved is "destruction." That word demands an end. The destructive fire can continue forever, as Revelation says it will, but once a person's body and soul are totally destroyed, their suffering can endure no longer. Revelation states that only the "beast" and the "false prophet" are subjected to eternal suffering. Those characters may represent individuals, but Revelation's imagery is too layered to assume that they cannot also represent satanic entities. The symbols will experience eternal torment, but that statement does not necessitate that humans must be subject to the same thing. The judgment against humans will be painful beyond our imagination. It will adequately reflect God's justice. Individual judgment will begin with torment in a disembodied state after the person's death [note: not every annihilationist believe this]. It will conclude with the "second death" that destroys the whole person. Their suffering does not need to be eternal, however, to prove that God is just. The results of the final judgment for humans "not recorded in the book of life" must come to an end in order to achieve "destruction." The spiritual beings expressed by at least one layer of the two symbolic characters do not logically require the same end or destruction.

B. Scriptures Testify to the Eternal Suffering of the Damned[18]

Proponents of annihilationism often use fire to justify their convictions about immortality. Fire, they say, purges, cleanses, and destroys and cannot continue to harm anything after it has been destroyed. This particular fire, however, "is not quenched" (Mark 9:44, 48). "Weeping and gnashing of teeth" (Matt 13:42) implies a far greater degree of suffering than annihilationist believers recognize. That suffering is typified by fire in Revelation's "lake of fire," in which it is said that the beast and the false prophet "will be tormented day and night forever and ever" (Rev 20:10). This same lake of fire is the "lot" (Rev 21:8) of individual sinners (Rev 20:15). These factors explain that all lost people at the time of the final judgment will be resurrected from the dead, only to be subjected to their new manner of existence where they will suffer endlessly. Their distress will be physical and emotional. It will reflect the just punishment for their crimes against God. The images of final judgment are not always consistent, referring to language including "outer darkness" and "fire" that cannot logically coexist. Since these

---

18. See Peterson, "Does the Bible Teach Annihilationism?"

are merely images intended to explain the inexplicable, however, they do not need to be consistent to be true representations of eternal punishment.

2.2 New Creation

In chapter 2, section 3.6, we discussed the problems of the Western view of *eschatological* hope as going to heaven when we die. At the end of Revelation, we get a beautiful picture of what our expectations should be. God makes all things new. He does not abandon his creation or let it be (or at least remain) destroyed. The text leaves room for a scenario in which it is possible that the world comes to an end, though it does not necessitate that kind of reading.

If the world comes to an end, then the heavens and the earth experience death. God's creation of a "new heaven and new earth" will be the resurrection of the same heaven and earth he first created. The resurrected world, however, will be void of all sin and decay. If the world does not come to an end, then God will make all things right on the earth by healing the world. That restoration, like a resurrection, would accompany final judgment to give God's people access to the world as he originally created it, free from all evil and mortality. Because the ultimate result is the same, it does not matter if we expect the world to end or not, but it is important to notice that the text leaves the possibility open without requiring it.

Either way, our *eschatological* hope is marked by a paradoxical continuity and discontinuity. The location is in the very same earth we currently inhabit. We know that world intimately. Without sin and death in it, however, it will be impossible to recognize. Likewise, we currently live by faith that God is with us and constantly active in the world he made. He lives in each of us. We may at times feel distanced from God, but we know that those feelings are not based on reality. Nevertheless, when God creates a new heaven and new earth, he will be its incarnate ruler. We can know God intimately now, but only in a spiritual sense. When we live in a world in which we can know the glory of God in a physical sense, that world will be unrecognizable.

2.2.1 *Wedding Banquet and the Invitation to New Creation*

John introduces us to the new creation using marital language similar to Paul's. Paul often refers to the church as "the bride of Christ." This final portion of John's vision provides a picture of the consummation of that marriage. To be clear, please note that I use the word "consummation" entirely in its sense of "completion," not suggesting any kind of sexual relationship between God and the church. Whenever the Bible addresses marriage between humans, however, it makes the concepts of marriage and sex synonymous. Although it would be completely inappropriate to think of our relationship with God in sexual terms, the imagery is certainly no mistake. The intimacy of whole persons involved in covenanted sexual relationships is the closest, albeit far-from-accurate, analogy to the relationship with God that God's people will enjoy. John was evidently incapable of communicating the God-human intimacy he saw at this point in his visionary experience, so he used the best analogy available.

I suggest that John had only one way to tell his audiences about the event that inaugurates the promised unity between God and humanity. That form of communication, the analogy to a wedding banquet, is sorely limited, but it is the best he could do. Certainly, he was authorized and empowered by God to write the accounts of what he saw, as most of my readers will probably agree. His words are divinely inspired. When seeing esoteric visions in an *ecstatic* state, however, we must expect that words cannot always convey what the writer desires to express. The scene of the wedding banquet is followed by the promise that at the time the event occurs, God will be with us. He will be ours. We will be his. Of course, these statements are all true now, but when Jesus appears physically, consummation of that relationship can occur. We will be united with God and with each other in a way we cannot begin to understand in this age.

2.2.2 *Those Excluded from New Creation*

John's Apocalypse contains multiple vice lists like the two in Revelation 20:11–22:5. These last two are the only ones that correlate directly to final judgment. The multiple lists overlap greatly in terminology, but the one in Revelation 21:8 also includes a few that do not appear elsewhere. For that reason and because of the grave nature of the context in which this list occurs, I have waited until now to define each item.

2.2.2.1 THE COWARDLY

Fear is a natural, God-given emotion that can produce either good or evil dependent on how we use it. Therefore, it should surprise us to see cowardly people listed among those who experience the second death. Many of us probably think of the Cowardly Lion who may not always use fear in a healthy manner but is neither dangerous nor evil. In fact, when he meets the

Wizard of Oz, he learns that he is not cowardly at all. The wizard tells him that he confuses courage with wisdom when his fearful inclination to run away from danger can be helpful. Many of us who read this vice list have the same confusion. Running away from danger is only cowardly if it puts other people in danger.

Ancient Greek historians used the same word that translates in our text to "the cowardly" to describe soldiers who recoiled in battle at the expense of others in their troops.[19] Their actions are treasonous. For such soldiers, their cowardice was punishable by death. In the context of final judgment, then, the word must refer to those people who have renounced their devotion to our Lord, foolishly believing they have a good reason to terminate their relationships with God. As Jesus explained in his parable of the sower, some will fall away when they are either confronted with persecution or wealth. They prioritize self-preservation or their treasures in the present age above their relationships with God (Mark 4:13–20/Matt 13:18–23/Luke 8:11–15). Fear always involves both danger and respect. People who turn away from Jesus determine that the beasts of the world pose a greater threat than the fate of those who turn from the Messiah. They also conclude that those beasts are worthy of more respect than the God who loves them. Such people are guilty of spiritual treason, forfeiting their relationships with God.

This type of cowardice is not a matter of giving into temptation, of habitual sin, or of being angry with God. Not even every person who claims to be a former Christian has committed spiritual treason. Some of these people might not actually be as distant from God as they believe. Rather, spiritual treason involves a conscious decision to stop following Jesus. Once an individual makes this decision, he/she begins carrying it out immediately and continues to do so relentlessly through the rest of his/her life. Luke's Gospel alludes to this process of degeneration through a discussion on Judas Iscariot (Luke 6:16). Hebrews 6:1–8 details the process. From the Hebrews passage, we know that not many commit this act. If we can be afraid that we might have fallen away from God, then we can be assured that we are not guilty of spiritual treason. The text of Revelation further clarifies this assurance by using the same language that ancients used to describe a soldier's choice to let the rest of his troop die in favor of preserving his own life.[20]

---

19. Polybius, *Hist.* 6.38.1–3; Josephus, *J.W.* 5.482–83.
20. Koester, *Revelation*, 800.

2.2.2.2 The Unbelieving and the Defiled

The second category of people in this vice list ("the unbelieving") is self-explanatory. The only thing that distinguishes it from the first category is the duration of an individual's unbelief. "The cowardly people" intentionally stop believing, whereas the "unbelieving" people habitually reject the Messiah and his sacrifice throughout their entire lifespans. They never surrender their lives to Jesus.

The word "defiled" often recalls OT ritualistic law. In such a context, some defilement results from sin, but some can derive from sickness, menstrual periods, or many other situations in life. To be defiled in the OT is to be ceremonially unclean; it does not necessarily point to immorality. The Greek word used here, however, in no way relates to either ritual or natural life occurrences that no one can control. Rather, the Greek word points to a complete defilement; it refers to things or people that are opposed to what is holy.[21] The "cowardly people" and the "unbelieving people" certainly resist God's holiness. So, what makes "the defiled" a unique category?

Revelation's beast corrupts absolutely. The beast represents many aspects of the Roman imperial cult. Worshiping the emperor defiles in part. Worshiping any of the various gods that the cults upheld defiles in part. Giving one's entire self to an object of worship other than the triune God defiles completely.[22] We have discussed in great detail the ways in which American culture calls people to worship nationalistic entities. The difference between complete and partial defilement suggested here points toward the great lengths of God's patience. In our context of American nationalism, I consistently stress that a way of repentance exists. People who come to recognize that they have given into such *syncretism* were likely unaware of it before their awakening. They fell prey to cultural brainwashing. Turning away from false beliefs, idols, and wrong priorities and running to God's "throne of grace" (Heb 4:16) ensures that God will cleanse us of these defilements. If it is possible to be purified, then we have surely not become completely defiled. If, however, a person becomes aware of the ways in which he/she has been corrupted and chooses the defilement over purity, he/she then risks becoming completely defiled and making a similar decision as that of "the cowardly people."

---

21. Bauer et al., *Greek-English Lexicon*, 172.
22. MacLeod, "Seventh 'Last Thing,'" 450.

2.2.2.3 The Murderers

The first three types of people in the vice list are broad categories that pertain to how one responds to God's offer of forgiveness. The remainder of the list associates people with specific deeds. This factor is the most important thing to realize about lists like this. When vice lists appear to link deeds with consequences, they do not communicate that everyone who has committed the given deeds will be liable to the prescribed punishment. A group of people is identified by their practice of the behavior, while the Bible clarifies that people who belong to Jesus are identified by that relationship, not by any sin. Therefore, the list's inclusion of "the murderers" does not suggest that everyone who has ever intentionally and unnecessarily taken another person's life will experience the lake of fire. The same holds true for each grouping that follows "the murderers."[23]

The apostle Paul refers to himself as a person formerly guilty of murder. His reception of divine forgiveness means that God no longer views him as a murderer but as a saint. Paul recounts this change in most of his letters. The other behaviors in this vice list lend themselves more easily to the possibility of stumbling or backsliding after experiencing God's forgiveness. In other words, someone who was once known as a liar may find it difficult to break that habit and still struggle with it after becoming a Christian. Murder, when taken literally, should not have the same kind of pull.

Nevertheless, Jesus's expansion of murder went far beyond the premeditated, avoidable killing that the word literally entails. "You have heard that it was said from those of ancient times, 'Do not murder,' and 'Whoever does murder will be liable to judgment.' But I say that whoever is angry with his/her brother/sister will be liable to judgment" (Matt 5:21–22). When the Bible uses vice lists, it intends to make a generalization for something much larger than the words in the list suggest.[24] As such, we should understand "the murderers" in line with Jesus's statement about the heart behind murder so as to include anyone who uses anger in a destructive manner.

A murderer in this context is foremost a person whom God identifies as a murderer, regardless of any specific attitudes or actions. Therefore, if someone sins against another person out of anger and regrets it, that person is clearly not in danger of being classified as one of "the murderers." The conviction that follows the action is a gift from God, as the Holy Spirit urges believers toward repentance. The people that this vice list refers to have seared their consciences to the point that they justify their actions and can

---

23. López, "Study of Pauline Passages," 301–16.
24. McEleney, "Vice Lists," 208–9.

no longer feel remorse when they use anger inappropriately, even in cases of literal murder.

2.2.2.4 The Sexually Immoral People

Who are the "sexually immoral people"? Many segments of the church in America today would answer this question by saying anyone who willfully commits a sex act outside of marriage as God defines it: between one man and one woman. Two biblical problems arise with this dogma. First, the Bible simply does not define marriage. It never circulated with a dictionary, so we should not expect it to define any word. What the Bible does say about marriage, however, leads to the second problem. Biblical marriages are not always between one man and one woman. Most men named in the OT had multiple wives. The NT writers tend more towards a value of monogamy as did the Greco-Roman culture that surrounded them. Nevertheless, no NT passage condemns the practice of polygamy. When Paul instructs Titus regarding the appointment of elders, he states that elders should be married only once (Titus 1:5–6). This speaks in no way to the rest of the believers in that congregation. As such, Paul suggests that monogamous marriage is an ideal, not a command. If the first church leaders encountered people with such a culturally ingrained lifestyle, Paul's message implies that they should embrace those with multiple wives and not judge them. No evidence exists, however, to demonstrate any significant presence of polygamy in NT cultures. As such, Paul suggests that the church should promote the ideal of monogamy for anybody who does not already have multiple spouses.[25]

The OT accounts of polygamous relationships demonstrate how prone such lifestyles can become to strife and inequality. Similar problems, however, exist commonly in twenty-first-century households with one husband and one wife. Paul's instruction implies that, despite any limitations and likely problems with polygamy, nobody would fit into Revelation's "sexually immoral" category for having multiple spouses. Many missionaries learn this lesson when people from cultures that embrace polygamy receive Jesus's salvation. Missionaries must determine whether to encourage people to divorce all but one spouse or to welcome the whole family into fellowship as Paul and Titus likely would have if they ever encountered that issue.[26]

Although the Bible does not define marriage, it includes enough information to help us determine who these "sexually immoral people" are and who they are not. Another part of the American church's tendency towards

---

25. Mann, "Polygamy," 21.
26. Falaye, "Polygamy and Christianity," 22–23.

understanding sexual immorality is to call premarital sex a sin. This tendency goes back far before the United States's existence and was once more universal than it is today. It may not reach back as far as the time in which the NT was written, however. We cannot know this for certain in part because the Bible does not define marriage, cultures do.

The cultures represented in both biblical testaments tend toward definitions of marriage that revolve around familial financial agreements. Neither love nor sex enters the equation of wedding preparation. While marriage and slavery are distinct in antiquity, both involve the sense of human property. Slaves were the property of their owners, and wives were the property of their husbands. Because of the diversity of families in ancient cultures (especially Hellenistic cultures), this was hardly ever as harsh as it sounds to modern ears. Although neither marital relations nor master-slave relations had any pretense of equality, neither was commonly marked by abuse or control over the people considered to be property.[27] The Bible, nevertheless, offers a vision of marriage and sex that was completely countercultural. While never defining the word "marriage," every portion of Scripture that discusses the topic uses the concepts of marriage and sex interchangeably. Both are described as the act of becoming one, emphasizing unity and equality.

The OT stories of Ruth and Song of Solomon both imply sexual relations may have occurred prior to a wedding ceremony. Twenty-first-century Americans are tempted to call that situation premarital sex. Scripture treats both relationships (Ruth and Boaz and the couple in the Song of Solomon) as ideal marriages consisting of love, equity, and sexual intercourse. We cannot know for certain whether either couple waited until after a ceremony to consummate their marriages, yet both stories use language that makes it safer to guess that they did not. The Bible has nothing to say about premarital sex because of its interchangeable use of the concepts. The Bible's consistent message is not that sex before a wedding ceremony is wrong, but that sex without lifelong commitment simultaneously makes and breaks a covenant. In other words, when a couple has sex for the first time, their marriage begins. For this reason, I suggest changing the language we use from "premarital sex" to "non-marital sex," since we can clearly determine that non-marital sex (sex outside of a lifelong covenant relationship) is sinful.

While the OT only implies this covenantal pattern of marriage through its stories, the NT greatly illuminates it. Paul clearly states that sex outside of a marital covenant marks a type of fornication (see 1 Cor 7:7). Though we cannot determine whether or not he believed that a ceremony must initiate

---

27. Swain, *Economy, Family, and Society*, 151–63.

that covenant, his Jewish background and OT knowledge suggest he probably did not. Further, each of the birth narratives in the Gospels imply many cultural irregularities about the betrothal of Mary and Joseph. The couple's lack of sexual consummation prior to Jesus's birth (i.e., prior to a ceremony) could be one of those countercultural aspects of their relationship.

United States culture has followed the lead of many centuries of global church history in one aspect of its definition of marriage. We consider marriage to be a lifelong commitment that is first offered verbally at a wedding ceremony. Our wedding ceremonies emphasize the exchange of rings. Diamonds signify the indestructible nature of a committed romance founded on genuine love and faithfulness. Granted, some Americans take that commitment much more seriously than others, paving the way for a wide variety in marital health and likelihood of divorce in the country. Despite how it plays out in individual relationships, however, it is nearly impossible to find a lifelong American whose definition of marriage would be anything other than a commitment made at a wedding ceremony. Because of this cultural definition, we actually have it easy in determining whether or not what we call premarital sex is a sin. Scripture clarifies that sex outside of a lifelong marital commitment is sinful, and our culture defines marriage as a lifelong commitment made through wedding vows. Therefore, under the current cultural norms in which we live, we do not need to be countercultural to be true to the Bible's teachings on sex as OT Jews (and probably the earliest NT believers) would have been. In our culture, to say that sex prior to the wedding ceremony is wrong parallels the biblical principle that sex is a covenant, so anything that breaks that covenant is sinful. To live this principle out, however, we must be exceedingly countercultural. We live in a time and place inundated with sexual imagery in almost every possible setting. To maintain sexual purity in such an environment requires that we not normalize or legitimize non-marital sex.

We also must be careful to recognize that Christians with different cultural backgrounds than ours (including some living in the United States) may define marriage differently than we do. Maraline E. Tukker, a practical theologian in South Africa, writes about this topic to the Africana culture (citizens of South Africa with a Dutch background). Tukker suggests that Africana Christians tend to define marriage as a process with the wedding ceremony as an important part of that process but not necessarily its initiation. This process is similar to the view most likely promoted in the OT. Africana Christians, then, might be able to practice sexual behavior within a lifelong marital covenant that does not look exactly the same as it does for us with regards to the ceremony. This caution demands that we uphold the biblical equity afforded to sex and marriage. We cannot automatically assume that a non-American is sexually immoral for being in a spiritually and sexually covenanted relationship (a marriage) without a ceremony.[28]

Next, we must consider divorce. If anything that breaks a marital covenant is sin, then logically we should avoid divorce at any cost. Unfortunately, that ideal does not always work in a fallen world subject to the evils of spousal abuse, infidelity, and a number of other issues that can toxify a relationship beyond healing. Of course, nobody wants divorce, including God, but does it inherently break a covenant and thus yield sin? The Bible's teachings about divorce are clear but often misunderstood. Most English translations of Malachi 2:16–17 read, "'I hate divorce,' says the LORD." This translation misses several aspects of the grammar found in the Hebrew and Greek texts.

First, the Hebrew verb in the *Masoretic Text* is third person, not first. In the Greek *Septuagint*, the verb is replaced with a participle. Therefore, the passage reads, "he hates divorce," in Hebrew and either "hating divorce" or "out of hatred, he divorces" in Greek. The common translation, "I hate divorce" does not reflect either language at all. The previous context involves a man (generally speaking, any man) acting unjustly toward "the wife of his youth." This most likely refers to the first woman a man married, assuming polygamy as the cultural norm. The rest of the verse is notoriously difficult to understand, which is why translations attempt to smooth out the confusion by saying God hates divorce. Yet, the text does not actually say that. A literal translation of the *Masoretic Text*, as nonsensical as this will sound, is "'Because he hates and dismisses,' says *YHWH*, the God of Israel, 'violence indeed covers his garments.'" Similarly, a literal reading of the passage in the *Septuagint* says, "'but if out of hatred, you send away,' says the Lord God of Israel, 'ungodliness will cover your thoughts,' says the Lord God Almighty."

The context clarifies that the masculine pronoun refers to the hypothetical man and that the one "dismissed" is the "wife of his youth." While it might be impossible to grasp exactly what this passage means, we can compare it to the law about divorce in Deuteronomy 24:1–4. That law seems, at least on the surface, to permit divorce, but it places all the burden on the husband. The whole law is conditional; the condition is if a man divorces a wife. If a man divorces his wife, according to that law, he defiles her. It is his sin, not hers. Malachi seems to be making a similar point as the Deuteronomic law: a man's decision to divorce his wife out of spite causes her deep harm, as an act of violence or abuse, and it is his fault, not hers.[29]

---

28. Tukker, "Sexuality and Spirituality," 1–8.
29. Lizorkin-Eyzenberg, "Does God Hate Divorce?," 1.

When Jesus gave his supposed condemnation of divorce (Matt 5:31–32; 19:1–10; Mark 10:2–12; Luke 16:18), he likewise addressed Jewish men. He was saying to each of them, "Do not dismiss your wife." Indeed, infidelity is the only reason provided to legitimate divorce. Infidelity can be expressed by extramarital sex, physical abuse, emotional abuse, or neglect. For Jesus to say "do not dismiss your wife" means very simply to love her. Anything apart from love is infidelity. In our culture today, marital structures are not the same, so the burden may not always be on the husband as it was in both the OT and the NT. A woman in today's world can just as easily hate her husband and so dismiss him. If a spouse has been legitimately discarded, in most cases, it will take a long time to prayerfully analyze the situation and to receive genuine peace from the Holy Spirit that divorce is necessary. If divorce is necessary, then the person who leaves his/her spouse out of a genuine need can in no way be considered among the "sexually immoral people."

Only in Mark's Gospel do we find an instance of gender reversal in Jesus's teaching. "If she divorces her husband and marries another, she commits adultery" (Mark 10:12). This suggests the possibility (albeit unlikelihood) of a woman unnecessarily divorcing her husband in Jesus's time. The context of Jesus's teaching about divorce as recorded in all the *Synoptic Gospels* (John's Gospel never addresses the issue) implies careless dismissal. Such action was almost exclusively male in that culture, since women were generally dependent on their husbands for their livelihood. A man divorcing his husband robbed her of most of her ability to live. As such, it is more akin to abuse and neglect in the modern world than literal divorce, making it difficult to apply the teachings of remarriage today. If our emphasis as the church of God, however, is to help couples avoid divorce wherever possible and healthy, then we can trust victims of divorce to make their own decisions informed by the Holy Spirit regarding whether or not to remarry. Such victims did not break covenant; their marriages ended because their spouse broke the covenant. They are certainly not among the "sexually immoral people" of the Revelation 21 vice list because of divorce or remarriage.

So far, I have attempted to establish that the "sexually immoral people" subject to the lake of fire consist of those who willingly and unrepentantly give themselves sexually outside of a lifelong covenant relationship. This line of reasoning does not align perfectly with the American church idea that sexual morality is only possible between one man and one woman after a wedding ceremony. We have discussed that alignment problem with regards to polygamy, so-called premarital sex, and remarriage after divorce. Now, we must attend to the part of the paradigm that assumes only heterosexual behavior can be moral. I lived most of my life assuming that the biblical word that translates to "homosexual" in English meant the same thing in its original context that the word means to us. The more I learn of biblical languages and biblical history, however, I have had to reconcile with the fact that this assumption is false. My beliefs on the topic are changing and developing constantly. Although I will present facts and an interpretation of those facts, I am still wrestling with this matter in my own mind and spirit. My primary goal for this discussion is to invite you to do the same. Therefore, I encourage you to read the rest of this section with an open mind about what the Bible says and to consult sources that evaluate the same facts I work with but reach different conclusions. For the second part of that encouragement, I recommend two interviews with N. T. Wright.[30]

Both Wright and I agree that the Bible never directly condemns all homosexual behavior. Wright assesses facts regarding the broader culture of the time periods in which the OT and NT were written. In doing so, he concludes that a wide gamut of sexual expression (including that which paralleled gay marriage) existed in antiquity. If Wright is correct, then it is possible (though not necessary) to understand the word "homosexual" as having broader application than its immediate scriptural context. On the other hand, if no mainstream recognition of open, committed homosexual relationships existed in antiquity, then we absolutely cannot take anything from the biblical references to homosexual sins outside of the narrow literary contexts in which they exist.

Several biblical texts use a word that translates to "homosexual," and they all condemn the behavior. That word, however, means something much different to us than it did in its original usage. Many records of homosexual behavior exist from antiquity, but they generally reflect actions of rape, pedophilia, and prostitution, not relationships. Thus, we should not expect to find a word for relational homosexuality in their vocabulary. The Greek word translated "homosexual," then, must have meant something different to those who first received the words of Scripture than the English word "homosexual" means to us. The same is true for OT stories and laws that condemn homosexual behavior.

A few ancient Roman playwrights wrote satires that included wedding banquets between two men. Those stories, however, always involved mistaken identities or some other situation that highlighted how ridiculous the culture viewed the idea of a committed homosexual relationship. Some scholars have tried to suggest that ancient Romans expressed homosexual relationships openly because of Emperor Nero's pseudo-marriage

---

30. See https://www.youtube.com/watch?v=xKxvOMOmHeI and https://www.youtube.com/watch?v=YpQHGPGejKs&t=20s.

to the slave boy Sporus. This situation, however, probably resulted from grief after the death of Nero's wife. He apparently saw a resemblance of her in Sporus and had the boy castrated in an attempt to treat him as a wife, though they never made formal or legal arrangements. Furthermore, Nero was the most unstable of all Roman emperors, so this episode most likely resulted from his insanity and abusive tendencies rather than sexual orientation. His attachment to Sporus could not have been a marriage, according to either the biblical vision of marriage or the ancient Roman culture's definition of marriage. Rather, it was an act of sexual abuse. As an act of abuse, it tells us nothing about ancient attitudes towards homosexual relationships.[31]

Plato's *Symposium* (fourth century BCE) places high value on sex between middle-aged men and adolescent boys. The key word to Plato's discussion is *eros* (sexual gratification). He describes the act as the greatest possible pleasure of the senses for the middle-aged man. He focuses on the action with self-centered motivation for the older man, without any relational motives behind the sex. This attitude implies abusive tendencies that victimize adolescents. Furthermore, overarching Platonic philosophy values celibacy over sensual pleasure. As such, Plato would have viewed same-sex activities as merely a means to gain momentary pleasure.[32] It may be tempting to take some of the language of *Symposium* in isolation and thus assume that Plato depicts open, permanent relationships as Wright suggests in the interviews I recommended. Plato's central philosophical doctrine, however, suggests that the homoerotic behavior in *Symposium* never involved lifelong commitment or even relationship. Also, in Plato's last book, he referred to heterosexual intercourse as natural and homosexual intercourse as unnatural.[33] Therefore, it remains impossible to even know what one philosopher thought of the topic. Did he change his mind, or did he refer to a different type of homosexual behavior in *Symposium* than he did in *The Laws*? We simply cannot know the answer to these questions, probably because no openly gay relationships existed at Plato's time.

In addition to Plato's *Symposium*, Wright uses the myth of Achilles and Patroclus as an ancient example of faithful homosexual partnerships. These male characters from Homer's *Iliad* had an unquestionably committed, lifelong relationship. Just as the word *eros* is key to understanding what Plato referred to when he wrote about homosexuality, so the word *philos*

---

31. Fontaine, "Gay Marriage in Ancient Rome," lines 1–126.
32. Gerson, "Platonic Reading," 47.
33. Plato, *Leg.* 5.10–11.

(brotherly love) is the key for Achilles and Patroclus. The word suggests that Homer never intended any sexual implications between these characters.

Both the Hebrew OT and the Greek NT include stories and teachings that condemn and warn against sexual behaviors that moderns are tempted to call homosexual relationships. Yet, since no ancient cultures clearly exhibit knowledge of openly committed same-sex partnerships, these biblical passages must refer to something else. Biblical scholar Robert K. Gnuse addresses the relevant passages of this nature in his article "Seven Gay Texts: Biblical Passages Used to Condemn Homosexuality." He convincingly concludes that every one of these texts refers to either rape or prostitution. Each of these actions can be homoerotic, yet both prevent any possibility of romantic relationship. Furthermore, they also constitute aspects of Babylonian or Greco-Roman cult worship. Both the OT and NT make strong links between sexual immorality and idolatry, so Revelation's vice lists likely involve that same correlation. In the following table, I briefly outline each one of Gnuse's conclusions.[34]

Gen 9:20–27	Ham rapes Noah.
Gen 19:1–11	This story parallels Judg 19:15–28 almost perfectly according to Gnuse. Only the number of people changes. The stories may represent two different versions of a single situation that was rendered slightly differently over time through Jewish oral tradition. Both accounts include rape, so the genders involved in the sexual activity do not matter in order to determine that these plans are vile.
Lev 18:22	The homosexual injunction is placed between two laws about the worship of Canaanite deities. Child sacrifices and bestiality both existed in Canaanite cults. The same is true for prostitution, including same-sex prostitution. The three, thus, form a cluster of prohibitions against evil deeds done as worship to pagan deities. Specification of men lying with other men merely reflects the commonality of homoerotic cult prostitution, not of committed same-sex relationships.

34. Gnuse, "Seven Gay Texts," 68–87.

Lev 20:13	Like the previous one, this law also exists as part of a cluster. Unlike the last one, this cluster is entirely sexually oriented. The prohibitions that surround it relate to incestual intercourse that may or may not be consensual. Although they might be consensual, one person is thought to be dominant in the behavior while the other is passive. Jewish norms understood the man's role in sex as dominant (that is, initiating; it does not excuse demanding or violent sexual behavior), and the woman's as passive (meaning she must not deny her husband sex for selfish reasons, not suggesting that she allows him to treat her disrespectfully). Just as no man should subject a family member to that submissive role, so no man should take a submissive role. This injunction would preclude any type of homosexual behavior for those bound to this law, but because nothing of this nature can be found repeated in the NT, followers of Jesus would not be bound to it.
1 Cor 6:9–10; 1 Tim 1:10	Usually translated "sodomites," "male prostitutes," or "homosexuals," the most literal rendering of the word in each of these NT vice lists is "soft people" or "passive ones." The type of submission discussed above with regards to Hebrew culture was not part of the Greco-Roman culture Paul wrote to. Paul would more likely have in mind situations in which men made themselves appear like women in order to prostitute themselves to men.
Rom 1:26–27	Verse 26 begins with the phrase "for this reason." So, when we get to the part about men with men and women with women, we must ask "for what reason?" The reason established in verse 26 is idolatry. The homosexual behavior Paul refers to must be cultic, not relational.

Each element of Gnuse's article clarifies a significant aspect of the literary context in which the word "homosexual" appears throughout the Bible. The only argument I would make against any of his conclusions is his close link between the Genesis 19 and Judges 19 stories (or story). He correctly points out that the Genesis account remained a common story retold and revised throughout Israelite history until the close of the *Second Temple era*. I argued earlier that Revelation 14:4 alludes to the specific retelling of that legend found in *1 Enoch* 6–9. Genesis 19, *1 Enoch* 6–9, and countless other renderings of this Jewish oral tradition all involve angelic beings raping humans. The story in Judges, however, clearly refers to human males who want to rape other males, making it distinct from the Genesis story. Gnuse is correct that if both stories were about humans, then the genders would not matter, since the sexual activity is unquestionably sinful, whether heterosexual or homosexual. Since the Genesis account, however, appears to be about angels raping humans, we must remember that no Scripture assigns gender to angels. Masculine pronouns and names help provide clarity for human readers. They do not give warrant, though, to understand biblical angels as male beings. The sin, then, is not homosexual rape but rather rape that requires created beings to abandon their God-ordained role in the created order.

Although I find that distinction important, the Genesis and Judges accounts share a unified theme that is likely to puzzle and unsettle modern readers. We should be caught off guard by each righteous person's strange sacrificial attitude. Both of the righteous men express willingness to offer virgin daughters in place of the intended victims. Many interpreters assume that these stories suggest that homosexual activity (consensual or otherwise) is a graver sin than a man raping a woman. To the contrary, the proposed sacrifices in the passages reflect the extreme societal importance for Israel on welcoming the stranger into their midst. Each man apparently believed it was godlier to make a type of sacrifice involving his own child/children than to allow foreigners to endure abuse. The sins of Sodom—mentioned many times throughout Scripture in reference to the Genesis passage—consist of rape and general social injustice.[35] The emphasis on radical hospitality to the foreigner suggests that we should use both of these stories as examples to correct our attitudes on modern-day immigration, not to condemn LGBT lifestyles.

Having looked at these examples, we can wisely conclude that the Bible does not directly condemn all homosexual behavior. If the biblical idea of homosexuality is confined to rape and cultic prostitution, how should we interact with modern ideas about homosexuality that extend far beyond incontrovertibly harmful deeds? Unlike the ancient world, we live in a culture that experiences many people attempting to live out lifelong commitments with partners of the same gender. This existed before any country legalized gay marriage. Much of Christianity, however, has maintained that such marriage is sinful and not true marriage because of what we think the Bible says about homosexuality.

If the Bible says nothing about what we call "homosexuality," then such people cannot be those who are identified as "sexually immoral" in the vice list. It means that we should not expect that sexual preference or same-sex marriage excludes anyone from the kingdom of God or is punishable by the lake of fire. It also means that the Bible cannot say whether or not gay unions might be legitimate marriages if they are built on covenant and not diluted by casual or experimental sex. Many of us have probably judged all

---

35. Lasine, "Guest and Host," 39–41.

LGBT actions as sinful. Yet, if the Bible does not address these matters, we must rethink our judgments of what we have unswervingly called sinful.

On the other hand, we must not assume that the behavior is moral simply because the Bible does not call it immoral. When we read literature as old as the books of the Bible, we must realize that candid and permanent homosexual relationships are relatively recent sociological phenomena. Therefore, we have no historical precedence to know how to apply what the Bible teaches about sex and marriage to LGBT lifestyles [Please note: Throughout this section, although I use the common initialism, I predominantly work with its first three sexual orientations (lesbian, gay, and bisexual). Revelation's vice list deals with sexual activity, not gender identity, so I keep my scope within that same realm. Thus, I will not comment on the morality associated with the desire to change one's gender. That authorial decision, however, does not diminish the Christian calling to love transgender people.].

Since we cannot look to the Bible to answer this particular question of morality, we should probably change the question. Of course, we know that the Bible's foremost mandate for interactions with other people is love. If we could determine conclusively that all homosexual behavior is wrong, then we could easily demonstrate love by trying to help people out of those lifestyles. Conversion therapy might be a viable option to help people in that direction if it were not for the likely connection between conversion therapy and suicide. If we could determine conclusively that same-sex unions can be legitimate marriages when they fit the marital criteria we have already discussed, then we could easily demonstrate love by encouraging church-blessed weddings for those committed to biblical marriages. However, since we cannot grasp a clear way forward based on Scripture, it is difficult for us to learn what it entails to love members of the LGBT community as God has called us to do. The question of how to love people who identify as LGBT should be the dominant part of our discussion on the topic as Christians, rather than whether or not the behaviors are acceptable.

The next question we can ask as we try to discern how to love LGBT people is whether or not the lifestyle is natural. People who maintain the nature argument against homosexual behavior often recite the cliché, "The parts don't fit." Yet logically, in order for sex to work pleasurably, the parts would have to fit and feel natural to those enjoying it. The argument is too simplistic and narrow to take seriously. As far as I am aware, however, no branch of medical science has provided clear insight into whether or not homosexual behavior is natural and healthy.

For many years, the American Psychiatric Association (APA) considered the alternative lifestyles represented by each letter in the LGBT acronym to be mental health disorders. The organization labeled all homosexual thoughts, identities, and behaviors as distinct illnesses, alongside desires or plans to change one's gender. They removed all homosexual and bisexual classifications in 1973. In 2013, they replaced their assessment of transgender inclinations as disordered thinking with a clinical definition of gender dysphoria, an individual's belief that he/she should be a member of the opposite gender. As of 2013, the APA recommends treatment of this disorder with chemical and surgical therapies that help gender dysphoria patients transition to the gender with which they identify. The APA, nevertheless, has not provided (at least as far as I am aware) their methods for reaching either their unhealthy or their healthy conclusions. They are usually rigorous in presenting data to defend their choices in updating their Diagnostic and Statistical Manual (DSM).[36] Without such data, however, we are left in the same conundrum as we were asking whether or not the Bible says that all homosexual actions are sinful. If we knew for certain that all aspects of LGBT identity are sourced in either an organic illness or in traumas such as childhood abuse or neglect, we would know how to love such people. That love would involve encouraging them to receive medical and psychiatric care and to provide a healing environment for them to work through past trauma psychologically and spiritually. If we knew for certain, on the other hand, that same-sex attractions result from a natural diversion in how some people develop, then we would love them by teaching them the values of biblical marriage expressed above. We would fully embrace their potential contributions in any aspect of church life. We would recognize that people can have bisexual attractions without acting on them, maintaining commitment to the person they marry.

This conundrum means that we are forced to become comfortable with what we cannot know. We must recognize that our ideas, no matter how firmly we hold onto them, could be disproved at any time. As such, no Christian likely has a good grasp on how we should understand LGBT concepts, including LGBT believers. Nevertheless, I think we have made it a much bigger problem than it needs to be. All believers have the source of all wisdom living and working inside of them. When communities share that power and pray together, seeking God's wisdom for how an individual congregation should love LGBT people without risking moral compromise, the Holy Spirit will provide an answer. Because it is not a matter addressed in Scripture, however, we should not expect that the Spirit's answer will be the same for every congregation. The Holy Spirit will direct each congregation how to both love LGBT people and to maintain purity within its own unique context.

---

36. Drescher, "Out of DSM," 565–75.

My proposed solution might not sound like a solution at all. It suggests that some congregations (or denominations) will find LGBT ordination acceptable, while others will not and that these differences are fine (at least until we have more conclusive data available). It also finds room for disagreement regarding whether or not an individual church will perform gay weddings and whether they will promote monogyny or celibacy amongst its LGBT members. Nevertheless, we should draw a line when it comes to a political prohibition of gay marriage. If a congregation or its pastor(s) believes the Spirit is leading them against performing gay marriages, its LGBT congregants can still get legally married elsewhere. If they do not have that ability, then, based on what we have already discussed about marriage and sex, the church in America is doing them a grave disservice. It actually encourages gay Christians to excuse living in sin.

Some segments of the church have taken strong stances against political motions to legalize gay marriage. At best, these Christians operate on wrong notions regarding what the Bible teaches. At worst, they carry out those biases militantly and claim a right to discriminate against LGBT people. They discriminate by denying people jobs and services or refusing to sign legally binding marital documents. They make these decisions in the name of religious freedom. Several states have passed so-called religious freedom bills that allow such discrimination to avoid interfering with peoples' religious sentiments. If our religious sentiments are based on the Bible, however, we cannot demand rights that potentially harm other people. In other words, these attitudes among some American Christians do not have anything to do with religious liberties. They have everything to do with American exceptionalism and entitlement. These Christians want the US government to work the way they think the Bible says it should. As such, the religious liberty policies they support not only harm LGBT people, but they also deeply harm the church. By not upholding the separation between church and state that the country's Constitution demands, Americans have yet another opportunity to find false justification through political leaders and other nationalistic forms of worship, instead of through the blood of Jesus. These religious liberty laws help to deepen the immoral and idolatrous relationship between some parts of the church in the United States and right-wing politics.[37]

---

37. Gourley, "Religious Liberty." Gourley wisely and compassionately addresses the issue of Christian hypocrisy as expressed through religious liberty laws. Nevertheless, his biblical arguments tend to be shallow, resorting to OT laws that discuss executing sexually immoral people without working through the exegesis or history of who these sexually immoral people are. He also creates such a large distinction between OT and NT morality that his argument might border on anti-Semitism. Nevertheless, I cite this

To conclude the section on "the sexually immoral people," I simply want to reiterate the limitations of the common American definition of marriage: the union of one man and one woman. The Bible does not define marriage as such believers claim it does. Rather, it is full of polygamous people, and it never condemns their sexual behaviors within multiple marriages. The Bible describes both marriage and sex as not only a union, but a covenanted, life-long union. It presents marriage and sex as the same thing. It offers no insight regarding whether or not a gay union can be a biblical marriage. Through these considerations, we must determine that "the sexually immoral people" subject to the "lake of fire" represent unrepentant people known to God for their non-marital sexual idolatry, as opposed to the people that God calls his saints.

2.2.2.5 The Sorcerers

The Greek word *pharmakos*, often translated "sorcerer," conveys multiple related meanings. In addition to referring to one who practices witchcraft, it can also point to a person who makes poisons to harm or kill others, and the noun can also connote the ancient Greek concept of scapegoating.[38] This scapegoating does not refer to the scapegoat of the OT which a worshiper offers to God in place of something more valuable that he/she cannot afford (the lamb sacrificed in Isaac's place is an example of such a scapegoat).[39] The Greek concept stands much closer to the current idea of wrongfully blaming another person for something that allows the accuser to avoid taking responsibility for his/her own actual wrongdoing. More precisely, the Greek practice related to both witchcraft and poisonings (the other connotations of the word). Many Romans worshiped Hecate, the Greek goddess of vengeance. They expressed devotion to Hecate through black magic intended to redress perceived wrongs and through concocting deadly poisons in order to attain their desired retribution. Whichever way Hecate's worshipers chose to seek vengeance, the actions were known as scapegoats.[40]

If John used the word "sorcerers" only to convey making poisons, it would overlap with "the murderers" on this same vice list. Likewise, if he meant the word only in terms of "sorcery," it would overlap with "the idolaters." Although Hecate-inspired scapegoating can involve either murder or

---

article because of its value regarding how Christians can harm people deeply by politically promoting discrimination in the name of religious liberty.

38. Bredin, "*Pharmakos*," 105–12.
39. Girard, "Ancient Trail," 14.
40. Bredin, "*Pharmakos*," 105.

sorcery, it suggests more about vengeance than it does about the specific ways in which vengeance can be carried out. As such, for John to name "the sorcerers" with this connotation alludes to the promise in Deuteronomy 32:25. *YHWH* says, "Vengeance and recompense belong to me. I will repay." Two NT authors repeat this statement (Rom 12:19; Heb 10:30). All of Revelation deals with God making everything new and right for the world he created. God gets vengeance both in the present age and ultimately at the final judgment. God's vengeance promises that all will be well for those who follow him. It also provides warning regarding the judgment accompanying the Messiah's second coming for those who refuse to follow him in the present age. To take matters into our own hands and try exacting revenge against others parallels the ancient Greek action of scapegoating. This practice is not the mere harboring of ill-will related to people who have harmed us, people whom we may find it difficult or even impossible to forgive. To classify as Hecate-inspired scapegoating, it must extend significantly further than one's inner thoughts and feelings. It manifests itself in specific actions that deny God's right to be God through his mercy and just judgment. Any action built on the determination to get back at someone for a perceived wrong takes a stance opposed to mercy and justice and thus prevents God from demonstrating those characteristics to the recipient of retaliation. Through such actions, a person makes a scapegoat claiming him/herself to have a better grasp on justice than God. It is to say, "Vengeance belongs to me, not God." Attempting to take the place of God is indeed an act of sorcery.

Various voodoo traditions practiced throughout the world provide perfect examples of Hecate-inspired scapegoating. Voodoo practitioners seek retribution through curses, potions, or dolls intended to make the recipient suffer or die. Such vengeful exercises obviously entail witchcraft, poisoning, or both. Nevertheless, we do not have to subject ourselves to measures that would seem foolish to most of us to be guilty of Hecate-like scapegoating. At the time of writing, we could find a perfect example of such behavior in the White House. The Trump administration has consistently practiced scapegoating that involves both witchcraft and murderous intentions that are nowhere near as obvious as they are in voodoo practices.

President Trump could be called the scapegoat maker-in-chief. Any attempt to control another person's private thoughts constitutes an act of witchcraft.[41] Trump's war against the media intends to manipulate American people (and perhaps the whole world) so as to think about him and his enemies the way he wants them to. We have seen rallies in which people believe the obvious lies he spreads. Many of these people make it their

---

41. Cohan, "Problem of Witchcraft," 803.

goal to spread Trump's message to the uninitiated as if the falsehood is an important sociological or even spiritual truth.[42] Such evangelistic efforts rarely consist solely of extolling Trump's virtues but are usually dominated by ways of attacking Democrats, mainstream media professionals, legally asylum-seeking migrants, Muslims, humanitarian activists, intellectuals, undocumented immigrants who have overstayed their visas to no fault of their own, or anyone else Trump has blatantly described as his enemy. This type of behavior demonstrates that Trump has brainwashed a portion of the population. By stoking their fears and perceived needs, he has given them a delusion that by viewing the world as he wants them to, they can exercise Trump's power of winning. They join his victory by helping him get revenge against his enemies. This fits within a general definition of witchcraft that aligns with what Scripture says against the practice.[43]

The murderous intentions related to Trump's behavior as president may not be direct. Nevertheless, when we take seriously the scriptural connection between words, life, and, death, we can determine him guilty of this kind of scapegoating as well. "Death and life are in the power of the tongue, and those who love it will eat of its fruit" (Prov 18:21). Almost every time Trump stands before an audience or uses his Twitter account, he speaks death. He attacks anyone he is angry with and accuses them of saying something worse about him. The facts, however, always point these childish contentions squarely on him. He acts as if his words do not matter when he claims he has not said the things plenty of video footage has caught him saying. He blames others to avoid taking responsibility for his own reckless actions, just like the modern concept of scapegoating.[44] He has placed blame on legally asylum-seeking migrants, wrongly accusing them of bringing drugs into the United States and of human trafficking because of their role in caravans. While criminals may exist in these caravans, Trump's policies have partnered with his words to bring death to the majority who are in great need and of no threat to the United States. Prior to Trump (regardless of the political party in the White House), border patrol agents and immigration lawyers assessed asylum claims to help ensure criminals were not allowed in the country. Those with legitimate needs would be granted sanctuary in this country. By reversing these policies and priorities, Trump has spoken death and enacted death.[45] Many children have endured abuse,

---

42. See *Politifact* personality profile for Donald Trump at https://www.politifact.com/personalities/donald-trump/.
43. Musopole, "Witchcraft Terminology," 348.
44. Gibson, "Gaslighting," paras. 5, 15–18.
45. Argen, "If Our Countries Were Safe," paras. 1–12.

lack of health care, malnutrition, and insufficient clothing. Some have died in detention centers because of these practices. Trump has spoken death over innocent people, both figuratively and literally. He has done so to such a degree that some members of the medical community suggest that his words and actions have even negatively affected the physical and emotional health of children who are American citizens.[46] Trump's same penchant for anti-immigrant words paved the way for the family separation policies enacted by former Attorney General Jeff Sessions. At least three deaths of children are known to have resulted from his "zero tolerance" policy. Many detention centers documented suicides among parents who had their children taken from them. Through these policies, Trump has "eaten the fruits" of the reality that his words can literally enact death.[47]

Pastor and anti-abortion activist Rob Schenck pointed out the deadly effects of Trump's words in his insightful article "Trump's Rhetoric Is Inciting Violence, Just Like Mine Did." In this article, Schenck confesses and takes full responsibility for the ways his words against abortion providers became fuel for people with violent intentions. Schenck's words paved the way for the murder of a doctor that Schenck had previously called out militantly at an anti-abortion rally. As he confesses his own past of violent rhetoric (albeit accidental on Schenck's part; I will be far more charitable to Schenck than he is to himself in the article), he writes the following about Trump's intentional and unambiguous choice of words:

> President Donald Trump has called Mexicans rapists and killers. He's warned that people coming across the southern border are "bringing drugs." He has claimed that Mexican officials are "cunning, and they send bad ones over because they don't want to pay for them." And he has tweeted, "We cannot allow all of these people to invade our country." By saying these things, Trump dehumanizes and vilifies his subjects and leaves them fair game for a depraved mass shooter like the one in El Paso who killed 22 people, injured even more and traumatized an entire community.[48]

The investigation that followed the El Paso shooting gave full credence to Schenck's suspicions. It revealed that the perpetrator, Patrick Wood Crusius, targeted Hispanic people at the Walmart he attacked. Crusius claimed to be responding to a "Hispanic invasion of Texas," blatantly reflecting Trump's oft-repeated warnings about an "invasion of illegals." The investigation

---

46. Cervantes and Walker, "Trump's Immigration Orders," 2–6.
47. Lind, "People Are Dying," paras. 1–18.
48. Schenck, "Trump's Rhetoric," paras. 1–5.

discovered that Crusius carried out his crime as a member of a right-wing terror organization whose plans were generally motivated by the words of Trump.[49]

"You have heard that it was said from those of ancient times, 'Do not murder,' and 'Whoever does murder will be liable to judgment.' But I say that whoever is angry with his/her brother/sister will be liable to judgment" (Matt 5:21–22). Matthew applies brother/sister language to Jesus's words, clarifying that Jesus referred to believers upon saying this. As such, this passage cannot apply well to a man who has expressed the belief that he has never done anything for which he would need to receive God's forgiveness. Trump may call himself a Christian, as he seemed to do out of anger when Pope Francis suggested that he might not be a Christian.[50] If he truly believes that he has no vulnerability to sin, however ("Why do I have to repent or ask for forgiveness if I'm not making mistakes? I work hard. I'm an honorable person"),[51] he simply cannot be. In the midst of Jesus's statement to his followers in Matthew 5:2–22, nevertheless, we find a general principle that applies regardless of Trump's spiritual state.

That principle communicates that when anger is not constrained or aligned with God's own righteous indignation, it can cause murderous desires. Trump may not exhibit these longings *per se*, but he does express vengeance through desires to end peoples' careers and through his highest value of winning.[52] Winning for Trump is not merely a successful endeavor; it is a victory at the expense of another that gives him a sense of retribution over those he wrongfully thinks have harmed him. Every attempt to win for Trump requires a new batch of scapegoats. In the process of making scapegoats, he incites the anger of others through words that contribute to physical violence. His words, thus, are a form of brainwashing, forming scapegoats that make him guilty of the type of "sorcery" to which John refers.

Trump's Hecate-inspired scapegoating aligns his behavior not only with ancient Greco-Roman pagan worship, but also with the violence spread

---

49. In response to an Associated Press article titled, "Trump Words Linked to More Hate Crimes? Some Experts Think So?" Snopes conducted fact-checking to answer the title's question as "yes." The organization confirms the connection between Trump's words and actual murders in four isolated attacks, including the one in El Paso, each one occurring at a different time in Trump's presidency. It also uses the dramatic rise in right-wing politically motivated hate crimes as evidence that can further link many hate crimes to Trump's words. See "Trump Words Linked to More Hate Crime?"

50. Yardley, "Pope Francis," paras. 1–3.

51. Nothstine, "Repent or Ask Forgiveness," paras. 5–11.

52. Benen, "Driven by Vengeance," paras. 1–4.

by dictators throughout world history. All leaders who have commanded horrendous persecutions and ethnic cleansings needed to convince a large number of people that the given targets were indeed enemies. Trump uses "enemy" language consistently for a host of people groups, against whom he wants to pit his followers. Comparisons between Hitler and Trump have certainly been overstated and overused during Trump's presidency. Nevertheless, multiple people with first-hand knowledge of Hitler or the Nazi party have made these comparisons. At the time of writing, Ben Ferencz was 100 years old, the last surviving Nuremberg prosecutor. In 2018, he gave an interview with the United Nations Commissioner for Human Rights, Zeid Ra'ad Al Hussein. Ferencz referred to the Trump administration's family separations as one of the greatest "crimes against humanity" currently being perpetrated.[53] As a Nuremberg prosecutor, Ferencz would likely be among the last people to use the phrase "crimes against humanity" lightly. He recognized that as Trump used his words and fueled fears to control how people viewed immigrants (and many other people groups), Trump followed Hitler's tactics against the Jews (and all other non-Arians). If enough people believe the dictator's lies, the brainwashed people will be willing to enact the dictator's terroristic desires. Also notable, Eva Schloss possesses more firsthand experience with Hitler's evils than Ferencz. She is an Auschwitz survivor and Anne Frank's stepsister. As Schloss watched the events of Trump's campaign unfold in 2015 and 2016, she wrote a warning to the US coinciding with 2016's Holocaust Memorial Day. In that warning, she stated that Trump "is acting like Hitler." She recognized the *influo* (see chapter 1, section 3.2.3) of an autarch and the beginning stages of tyranny. Because of that *influo*, she showed that she would not be nearly as surprised by Trump's eventual electoral victory as most Americans were.[54]

Trump has followed the beginning stages of the world's most violent leaders in ways beyond the family separation policy. By declaring the mainstream media "the enemy of the people," he seeks to control what the country believes about him. Whenever he calls a fact about him "fake news," many believe him. Most of the time he decries "fake news," the same people have access to Trump's own words and actions that prove the supposed "fake news" to be correct. Many of Trump's supporters have been lulled into believing what comes out of their cult leader's mouth instead of what they see with their own eyes and hear with their own ears. So, all autocratic leaders brainwash and commit acts of witchcraft in the beginning stages

---

53. Watch the portion of the interview I referenced at Sampathkumar, "Last Surviving Prosecutor." For more of Ferencz's insights regarding Trump's autocratic tendencies, visit his website: https://benferencz.org/.

54. Schloss, "Anne Frank's Stepsister," paras. 1–8.

of their tyranny (e.g., Nero claimed that Christians were responsible for a destructive fire and thus needed to be destroyed). During Trump's first term as president, he was so consumed with maintaining power for a second term that no full-scale tyranny or ethnic cleansing seemed imminent. If the American people allow him to serve a second term, however, we should not be surprised if he initiates violence that appears similar to any other tyrannical ruler. He has followed in their footsteps and given special considerations to the desires of modern-day tyrants including Vladimir Putin and Kim Jong-un, while turning the United States's allies into foes.[55]

Trump's witchcraft has appeared increasingly obvious throughout his term. In order to hold on to his power and avoid criminal prosecution for tax crimes, he railed against mail-in voting. He successfully convinced his followers that absentee voting is acceptable, but mail-in voting will yield voter fraud. In practice, however, no distinction exists between absentee ballots and mailed ballots. Any differences between the two are entirely terminological differences, not practical ones. In other words, expansion of mail-in voting to meet the needs created by the coronavirus can only increase turnout of legal voters. It cannot yield the voter fraud that Trump insists is inevitable.[56] Trump appointed Postmaster General Louis deJoy at the center of his fight against expanded mail-in voting. In all likelihood, he did so because he knew deJoy would instigate all manner of chaos in the United States Postal Service (as he did) to give the appearance that the USPS cannot handle ballots. Federal judges banned the specific requests for chaos that Trump had asked of deJoy. Based on the knowledge that no evidence exists for increased voter fraud through mailed ballots, these judges have thus far been successful in preventing this manifestation of Trump's witchcraft.[57]

Throughout his reelection campaign, Trump was thoroughly aware that he was performing worse in the polls than in 2016. Although he often said he did not believe the polls, his actions showed that he believed them completely. He took some of the most desperate actions possible in his attempt to maintain power. Along with those already outlined in the last paragraph, Trump refused a peaceful transition of power in the event that Joe Biden wins the election. Trump hinted at the possibility of violent mobs of his followers conducting armed and aggressive protests.[58] If he loses, he will certainly use the constitutionally provided loopholes of state electors

---

55. Bazzle, "Trump Praised Dictators," paras. 4–45.
56. Rayome and Conner, "Mail-in Voting" *CNET* (Sept. 3, 2020), paras. 3–9.
57. Lau and Nelson, "Empty Trucks, Falsified Records," paras. 1–7.
58. Porter, "Trump's Refusal to Commit," paras. 1–29.

and the Supreme Court in an attempt to convince those entities of election fraud. Further, because of his lies about mail-in voting, Trump's supporters will most likely do all their voting on election day. The extreme amounts of absentee ballots will probably not be counted until after November 3. Thus, Trump will probably appear to have a landslide on election night that will shrink dramatically in the day(s) that follow. That apparent landslide will exist before a majority of the votes have been counted and will not indicate whether or not he actually won reelection. Trump will surely attempt to use this anomaly to his advantage with both state electors and the Supreme Court, if indeed the scenario plays out as expected. Trump seems highly unlikely to reap any benefits from these attempts to hold on to power if he loses the election.[59] Nevertheless, his penchant for sorcery means he carries a great deal of *influo* in some of the least-expected places. It played a role in how he became president in the first place. If he maintains his power for another term, the *influo* of Hecate-inspired witchcraft will certainly be one of the factors to explain his second term, whether or not the results are contested. Remember, his policy discussions and actions between 2015 and 2020 almost always centered around revenge against his predecessor, Barak Obama, not actual policy.

Further, Trump's desperation has much higher personal stakes than any other incumbent president has faced in recent elections. At the end of September 2020, the New York Times published the findings of their investigation into Trump's tax history. They presented actual tax documents that had not been altered. They covered all their bases to ensure that Trump's typical "fake news" cries would be the fakest news of the day (as they usually are). The documents demonstrate extravagant and illegal tax deductions for limos and hair treatment, among many other flagrant tax violations. The documents do not support the image Trump has always tried to display of himself. They do not help his case that he is a self-made billionaire who always worked hard to achieve his positions in life. Rather, these tax records support the testimony of Trump's former fixer Michael Cohen. For good reason, none of us knew if we should believe Cohen's portrayal of Trump as an inept businessman with no scruples, who could not keep himself from bankruptcy. Cohen has developed as much of a reputation for being a liar as Trump has. Nevertheless, the New York Times produced incontrovertible documents that told us Cohen's testimony was trustworthy.[60]

These tax documents illustrate much more about Trump than merely his financial and business failings. They help us unlock the methods behind

---

59. Halper et al., "What if Trump Loses," paras. 1–20.
60. McIntire et al., "Tax Records," paras. 1–88.

his sorcery. We have already discussed how he speaks death and enacts death out of vengeful attitudes. The tax records help us recognize that he accomplished this Hecate-like scapegoating by death speech that reveals something about himself. His favorite insults include "failure," "loser," "weak," and "low IQ individual." The truth about his own business dealings and financial cheating show who he apparently believes the biggest failure is, who the worst loser is, who the weakest one is, and who the stupidest person is. He went to great lengths to cover up both his crimes and his self-perception. He levels those insults on others as he brainwashes his people to help him feel better about himself. If he uses sorcery to convince others that he is not a "failure," a "loser," a "weakling," or a "low IQ individual," then he might have a better chance of seeing himself in a more positive light. If he is as good of a sorcerer as he occasionally appears to be, it might even help him avoid the legal ruin that would otherwise await him on the other side of an electoral defeat (or even keep his presidency illegitimately) if he loses. But above all, Trump seems to use Hecate-inspired witchcraft to protect himself from his own insecurity.

2.2.2.6 Idolaters and All Liars

We have discussed idolatry thoroughly throughout this book both with regards to the Roman Empire of the first century CE and to our own twenty-first-century American culture. So, we need not rehash any of that material here. Likewise, the list finishes with a self-explanatory designation. To conclude the vice list, I want to remind you that these last two categories have the same limits as the previous three. "Idolaters" in this context do not refer to people who have unintentionally fallen prey to acts of worship to a god other than *YHWH* through cultural influence or more malicious forms of brainwashing. Similarly, "all liars" do not point to everyone who has habitually spoken untruths. "Idolaters" are those people whom God recognizes as worshipers of false gods, as opposed to those whom he recognizes as his children. "All liars" are the people whom God recognizes as controlled by their lies, as opposed to those whom he recognizes as his saints.

2.3 New Creation and The Holy City

Revelation 21 begins with discussion of the New Jerusalem. Then the text transitions into the vice list, discussing the people who will not experience the newly created order that this city embodies. After the vice list, the text returns to the holy city with a grand description of it. Ezekiel 40–48 also envisages a new world order in which all wrongs are made right and the entirety of the earth experiences healing. Some of the other portions of the OT written the latest (especially Daniel) discuss the resurrection of saints as the trademark of this new creation and holy city. The *extrabiblical* apocalypse *1 Enoch* consists of five distinct books, each of which was probably written between the time of Daniel (middle of the second century BCE) and the beginning of the first century CE. *First Enoch* also includes a renewed earth where the righteous live with God for eternity following the general resurrection and final judgment. These are just a few examples of literature that shows us that resurrection and a restoration of the earth, including a renewed Jerusalem, was a common Jewish expectation. Jews expressed this anticipation even before Jesus's resurrection. The NT clearly adapts this early Jewish *eschatology*, in many places using Jesus's resurrection as proof that a resurrection for all people awaits.[61]

Wright's book *The Resurrection of the Son of God* traces the history of beliefs in resurrection and new creation between the times in which Daniel and Revelation were written. Also, Wright traces ideas of the immortality of the soul (i.e., the idea that no human life ends) and an intermediate state between death and resurrection. He points out that ancients expressed beliefs about the afterlife (*Scheol* for those of a Jewish background and *Hades* for those of a Greco-Roman pagan background). The Jewish worldview of apocalypticism that dominated the early church at the time in which all of the NT was written, however, did not emphasize the afterlife. Scriptures provide a vague expectation of afterlife, but neither an eternal afterlife nor an afterlife from which anyone should derive significant *eschatological* hope. Rather, the Jewish apocalyptic worldview reflected in Scripture emphasizes what Wright refers to as "life after life after death."[62] In other words, heaven—where we go when we die—is temporary, and we know very little about it except what Paul says in relation to his own eventual death: "To be absent in body is to be present with the Messiah." The holy city of Revelation 21 is clearly eternal. Furthermore, resurrected people inhabit the holy city, not disembodied souls existing in an otherworldly dimension surrounded by the presence of God. Since this New Jerusalem is for whole people (body, soul, and spirit), it cannot be the same type of post-death existence that Paul discusses. As the earth is made right, every human on God's side of eternal judgment is restored to the state of humanity that God originally intended before sin entered the world. That restoration includes new and eternal life given to formerly dead bodies.

---

61. Beale, *John's Use*, 16.
62. Wright, *Resurrection*, 31, 86, 108–23, 130, 199–201, 215.

2.3.1 The Holy City and the Churches in Asia Minor

The imagery of a perfected holy city, and specifically a renewed Jerusalem, would have carried a clear message to the congregations that John addressed. The city Jerusalem was the epicenter of all religious activity in ancient Judaism. The temple was the religious center of Jerusalem, just as Jerusalem was the religious center of Israel. As such, Jerusalem was known as the holy city and was treated as sacrosanct. The destruction of the temple in 70 CE, however, caused dramatic change in how people perceived the city. Jerusalem was not Jerusalem without its temple, and Judaism would never be the same again. By the time Revelation was written, even though the city of Jerusalem still existed, the Judeo-Christian world understood the need for a new Jerusalem, a new holy city.

As we have discussed earlier, the book of Revelation is thoroughly Jewish in its language and imagery. The New Jerusalem and discussion of temple imagery later in Revelation 21–22 makes this character of the Apocalypse abundantly clear. It is also, nevertheless, a thoroughly Greco-Roman document, filled with pictures of the everyday realities that surrounded the Christians John addressed. Because of these factors, we must recognize that John's initial seven audiences were a mixed group of Jewish and gentile believers. They lived nowhere near the literal Jerusalem, so this imagery not only points them toward the future fulfillment of a New Jerusalem but also provides direction for their own present situation. At the end of Revelation 21, we learn that the New Jerusalem has no need of a temple because of God's constant presence (presumably physical presence manifest in Jesus).

The OT directions for the temple involve the holiest place that was reserved for priests, an inner court where Jews offered sacrifices, and an outer court for gentiles. Since the temple had been destroyed, John appears to use this picture of the future to direct his audiences toward what it looks like to worship God in a post-temple world under a new covenant. The Gospels and writings of Paul clarify that Jew-gentile divisions are not to exist. The destruction of the temple was a great devastation that caused immense trauma for Jews (both Messianic and those who still lived under the Old Covenant) and for gentile Christians. John's instructions do not downplay the significance of that horrible event. They do, however, illustrate the truth that God uses the worst experiences of life to teach his people, to draw people nearer to him, and to build his kingdom on earth. By alluding to the destruction of the temple in reference to a future New Jerusalem without a temple, John suggests how the audiences can find the sacred space they need in a post-temple age. They find it not through a building, but through their Jewish-gentile unity under the spiritual reign of *Yeshua* in this age.[63]

Recently, scholars have begun to note some architectural features of the New Jerusalem that provide further connection to the earliest hearers of John's Apocalypse. By the time they began hearing about the New Jerusalem, the concept of a lavish wedding banquet would have been in their minds from the imagery shortly before this part of the text. The adornments of this city have more in common with upper-class houses in Asia Minor than they do with any known portion of ancient Jerusalem, including the temple.[64] While discussion of the New Jerusalem likely pointed early audiences toward directions for the present, the adornments of the holy city pointed toward the future. The imagery sends a similar message as Jesus's command to accumulate treasures in heaven, where they are stored until the fruits can be reaped at the time of the general resurrection. The New Jerusalem provides a picture of the *eschatological* hope they can find in a reversal of fortunes. If they focus their lives on partnering with God to build his kingdom on earth, they will be rewarded in a resurrected life. John appears to intentionally portray that life to look like what some audience members might be afraid they are missing in the current age. Thus, he calls them to sacrifice comforts of the current age through receiving the promise that a time will come when all God's people share in the riches and glory of his physical presence.

2.3.2 *The New Jerusalem and Current Application to the Church in the United States*

The concepts we just considered in the context of first-century Christianity in Asia Minor apply quite easily to our own cultural context. We have already talked about how other portions of the Apocalypse call us to global Christian unity. The picture of the New Jerusalem can further motivate us toward that goal. Our cities in the United States are large and diverse. They consist of people from "every tongue, tribe, and nation." That description of cities I just provided is the same description many portions of the NT offer in their pictures of the kingdom of God. The pursuit of a holy city for us, then, is the call to fellowship and to disciple-making, so that the kingdom of God in our communities can look as diverse as our communities themselves. I used the word "look" because the kingdom of God is already diverse. It is already full of people from "every tongue, tribe, and nation." If

---

63. Palmer, "Imagining Space in Revelation," 41.
64. Moss and Feldman, "New Jerusalem," 351–57.

we are blessed enough to live in a community that has significant diversity, we must embrace that diversity.

In many parts of the country, the church remains the most segregated institution. Historically black denominations and congregations were invaluable during the Civil Rights Era. They still have their place of vital import for black spirituality and culture, so I am not arguing that this segregation is entirely a bad thing. White churches, however (which might include congregants from Asian and Latino backgrounds, but still get labeled "white churches" because of the general lack of a black population), need to make efforts to integrate with black churches. I do not mean that I want black churches to cease to exist. Rather, I encourage white churches to take part in activities at black churches, to enter their communities, and share in the work of partnering with God.

On the *eschatological* side of this passage, we must walk in hope for a renewed earth. When we know that our priorities and sacrifices in life please God and will be rewarded eventually, we gain an eternal perspective. From that perspective, we no longer need to seek financial wellbeing or earthly comforts, because we know God is providing all we need for us. We recognize the idolatry in pursuing riches, and we naturally want to avoid any kind of idolatry, because we love God. The vision of the New Jerusalem should cement within our minds and our hearts the certainty of God's promises. For that reason, we will close out this section with a liturgy that praises God for being our chief provider and for faithfully keeping all his promises.

Liturgy 6: God Is Provider

1. Sing the hymn, "Standing on the Promises of God." Russell Kelso Carter, "Standing on the Promises of God" (1886).

2.4 The Living Waters, Tree of Life, and Endless Day of New Creation

The three *eschatological* symbols of Revelation 22:1–5 all have long histories. In his conversation with the Samaritan woman at the well, Jesus promises "streams of living water" to all who "worship the Father in spirit and truth" (John 4:1–26). Ezekiel 47 prophetically speaks of a river whose waters flow out of the temple (the waters in Revelation's river flow from the throne). Isaiah 30:26 prophecies of a perpetual brightness coming from the heavenly bodies. The promise of the "tree of life" points most directly to the story of the garden of Eden. All three symbols, nevertheless, have their roots in the creation story. God created living waters, the tree of life, the sun, and the moon. All were present in Eden.

Since new creation is a restoration of God's original intent for humanity, we should not be surprised to see it described so similarly to the way Genesis depicts the first creation. Ezekiel's vision describes water that has grown stale and kills fish; the leaves of the trees, however, heal those waters and make them fresh again. Revelation 22:1–5 repeats the imagery of Ezekiel 47, Isaiah 30 and Genesis 1–2, but it does not use that imagery in exactly the same way. The new created order that the text promises is a restoration of the old and the worn, but it also promises completion that does away with what is no longer necessary. The reason no sun or moon is necessary in the new creation is that Jesus's return manifests God's presence physically. Revelation fills in the gaps of what earlier prophetic tradition could only hint at before Jesus's resurrection. Because of Jesus's resurrection, though, John could receive a fuller vision of *eschatological* hope.

3. JOHN'S APOCALYPTIC CONCLUSION (REV 22:6-21)

3.1 Overview of the Passage

In Revelation 22:6–8, John repeats the messianic titles and quotes that we first encountered in Revelation 1. John reintroduces himself in Revelation 22:9a. When he first introduced himself as the author of the book, he did so in the form of a letter to the seven congregations in Revelation 1:4. The reintroduction, then, begins to close that letter, helping remind us that all of Revelation is a letter to the seven congregations. The remainder of the text (Rev 22:9b–21) summarizes the main themes of the book and alludes to the genre indicators that Revelation 1 used to prepare audiences to hear the words. It includes only one bit of new material; its vice list includes one previously unstated group of people, "the dogs." Revelation 22:9b–11 encapsulates the motif that God alone is worthy of humanity's worship. The passage reminds all audiences that Revelation is a prophetic work that we must recognize as containing words that originated from God himself as spoken to John.

3.2 The Dogs

Commonly translated "dogs," the same Greek word in this vice list is used for the animal in Luke 16:21 and 2 Peter 2:22. Matthew 7:6 uses it as part of a proverb pointing to people who refuse sound advice and correction. Because 1) dogs were unclean animals according to Jewish law and 2) Matthew wrote his Gospel for a predominantly Jewish audience, that proverb likely implies that such people are ceremonially unclean. Matthew may suggest that believers who refused the rites of the New Covenant (especially baptism) are "dogs."[65]

Neither of these renderings of the Greek word can work in Revelation 22:15's context. John unquestionably refers to humans. These people might be obstinate like those targeted in Matthew 7:6, but the NT consistently clarifies that no neglect of a ritual, such as baptism, excludes anyone from the eternal kingdom. Only one NT passage uses the word in a context similar to the one in Revelation 22:15. "Beware of the dogs. Beware of the evildoers. Beware of the mutilation [a reference to circumcision with a negative bent]" (Phil 3:2). Although Paul's statement about those who inappropriately command believers to be circumcised may sound specific, the rest of Philippians 3:3–4 expounds on both "the circumcision" and "the mutilation." It refers to the former as true worship and the latter as misplaced security in one's relationship with God via the Mosaic covenant. As such, Paul is making very broad statements with each of the three warnings. To "beware of the mutilation" is to watch out for any type of teaching implying that a specific action or abstinence from a given activity is necessary to receive God's salvation. There are many types of legalism, just as there are many kinds of "evildoers," concerning whom Paul warns his audience to be on guard. Therefore, we should conclude that Paul uses "the mutilation" in the same open-ended manner as he uses the term "evildoers." Many ancient Greek authors as far back as Homer used the word "dogs" in a similar way. Although its attestation in Scripture is limited, we can find the word referring to infamous people. Paul likely used the construction he did to point out three broad categories: people known prominently for a single malicious deed ("the dogs"), those practicing wicked lifestyles ("the evildoers"), and the use of doctrines that pervert something intended for spiritual edification, using them to yield spiritual destruction ("the mutilation").[66]

John uses the word "dogs" in a manner close to Paul's in Philippians 3:2, but without the emphasis on a single deed making "dogs" infamous. John could have just as easily used the word "evildoers" here but probably chose "dogs" for a more dramatic effect. John also follows a different logical pattern than Paul's. While Paul keeps all his groupings general, John moves from general to specific and then back to general. The first group of excluded

---

65. Bauer et al., *Greek-English Lexicon*, 579.
66. Bauer et al., 579, 528.

people—"the dogs"—includes a wide variety of people full of wickedness. The next four explain certain types of wickedness that can make people "dogs." Then, the final group, "those who love and practice a lie" points to devotees of dangerous worldviews that cause the specific deeds in between the two bookends.

3.3 John's Final Statements

Revelation 22:12–17 recalls the theme of God's justice in judgment. Because this passage highlights *eschatological* judgment and includes a reference to John's *heavenly ascent* and angelic guide, it reminds all audiences that the book is a divine revelation (an apocalypse). Since the text quotes Jesus and credits him as the source of the revelation, it further reminds audiences that it is an apocalypse like no other as a "revelation of Jesus the Messiah." Those apocalyptic and messianic designations convey that John expects us to believe that his divine encounter via visionary experience was a real event orchestrated to reveal Jesus. The warnings and curses of Revelation 22:18–19 can be found elsewhere in antiquity. Authors or those put in charge of circulating a writing could give stark counsel to persuade the audiences to accept the words as having divine origins, thus displaying a form of ancient rhetoric.

Finally, Revelation 22:20–21 includes the last quote that John reports hearing from Jesus. After presenting that quote, John gives one final epistolary conclusion. His phrase "the grace of the Lord be with all" follows a similar pattern to the way Paul closed his letters. We should pay attention, however, to one significant difference. Paul's *epistles* generally addressed the same audience(s) at the beginning and at the end. John's letter, on the other hand, opens in Revelation 1 addressed to the seven congregations. His closing universalizes the whole book. Although it was initially sent to a limited group of people, John probably envisioned the scope of his letter to be wider than Paul's stated scope ever was. As such, the finality of Revelation communicates once and for all that the book is both timely and timeless. The same is true about all Scripture, but as an apocalypse, Revelation has a transcendent quality that is not easy for us in the twenty-first century to grasp. That quality, however, suggests that although it might take much work to apply these messages of John to our own situations in life, it can be done. I hope that I have presented a cogent and convincing way of accomplishing that task.

Appendix 1

Biases vs. Lies

I wrote this book at a time when the United States was constantly bombarded with illegitimate cries of "fake news" alongside the very real spread of "alternative facts." Dangerous conspiracy theories and religious cults formed around the perceived need to rebel against mainstream media and anyone who challenged the words and actions of President Trump. At the time of writing, only a small minority was deeply involved in the most threatening deceptions. The tendency, nevertheless, harmed the whole nation. In the body of the book, I suggested that Trump's presidency declared war against the hearts and minds of all people. A loyal Trump supporter is not allowed to believe anyone who contradicts Trump or makes Trump look bad. The administration has conducted a far more devious form of brainwashing than the natural cultural brainwashing we discuss throughout the book. In the final chapter, I described Trump's form of brainwashing as witchcraft. If we make room for the thoughts and beliefs that Trump wants us to have, we risk making him our god. That risk develops when we view the world through the lenses Trump provides via Twitter and alt-right news networks instead of those given to us by the word of God and the Holy Spirit.

We can ensure that we never allow political officials to lead us astray through this manner of witchcraft by thoroughly and prayerfully assessing the media we expose ourselves to. Trump has been highly effective at brainwashing large numbers of Americans, because he has trained them to listen to him and not to their own eyes and ears. Trump has made many live appearances that could not be manipulated by media entities until after the events were over. Every time he makes such an appearance, he demonstrates beyond a shadow of a doubt that most of his statements are lies. He often claims he did not say things that we all heard him say in earlier live speeches or clearly unmanipulated footage. Through this behavior, Trump has declared himself the source of truth and morality, thereby bestowing on himself a characteristic unique to God. As Richard Nixon said, "If the president does it, it isn't illegal," so Trump's mentality seems to be, "if the president says it, it isn't a lie." By defining truth on his own terms, Trump created confusion regarding who to trust.

Previous presidents have always had adversarial relationships with the news media; such a relationship helps both entities hold each other accountable. Trump, however, used the people he hired to create facts. The media needed to adjust its roles to become fact checkers instead of fact reporters and interpreters. Trump encouraged people to believe that if any report about him was negative, it must be false. He encouraged a misunderstanding of the word "bias," equating it with disinformation. Bias is nothing more than an outflow of one's worldview. Everyone is biased. When news outlets report based on bias, they interpret the facts they report based on their perceptions. The facts are undeniable, but room for debate exists in their interpretation. The way to avoid actual disinformation is to make sure that we engage with news sources that offer a variety of viewpoints. Those outlets that Trump expresses the most anger against happen to be the same ones that have the most diversity of biases. They are not "liberal media" as Trump declares.

CNN has remained the administration's most fervent target of slander and lies. If you watch CNN, however, you know that almost every panel for political issues includes both Democrats and Republicans. Their website, likewise, accommodates all points of view. The organization makes certain that its viewers and readers hear all sides and ideologies and can form their own opinions. As a general rule of thumb, written sources that combine basic reports of fact with analyses surrounding those facts are more comprehensive than cable news outlets. I highlight CNN, nevertheless, because Trump has maligned it so often. I recommend it above any other TV news media but suggest it only as a supplement to written sources.

The website https://faculty.lsu.edu/fakenews/ provides an excellent introduction on how to spot genuinely fake news as opposed to biased assessment. The site offers quizzes to help us determine how likely an individual is to believe intentional deceptions online, on TV, or in print. Its features include tips to recognize videos that have been doctored and to tell the difference between a lie and a mistake.

Occasionally, Trump's tirades against mainstream media have even extended to the TV network that he made his home at the beginning of his presidency. Fox News consists of a variety of programs and anchors with varying levels of trustworthiness. A few like Chris Wallace commit themselves to presenting and interpreting facts, as their jobs demand. Over the years of the channel's prominence, the number of anchors faithfully completing that task has diminished greatly. Strangely, Trump's lowered opinion of the network actually coincides with the network becoming more willing to invent facts that favor him.

As part of a CNN *Reliable Sources* panel for January 15, 2020, former Fox News analyst Julie Roginsky insightfully discussed this paradox by comparing Fox News in the Trump era to crack cocaine. She suggested that both Trump and his followers got fed up with Fox News because of the likes of Chris Wallace. They do not want truth, according to Roginsky; they want what makes them feel good. When viewers do not obtain the high they once got from the disinformation that existed from some Fox News hosts—especially those of evening opinion programs—they seek a new high. They achieve those highs through far-right conspiratorial commentators that invent even more facts than Fox News opinion hosts. I would argue slightly with Roginsky's analogy. Fox News continues to have some programs that report facts and interpret them. The shows that invent facts, then, are not real news; they are entertainment. Roginsky is right to say that viewers feel good about the lies, which is why they continue to watch them. She is also correct that they seek a better high when Fox News no longer gives them what they want. I fear that to connect the Fox News hosts with crack, however, risks downplaying the genuine journalism that still occurs on that channel, albeit rarely. Instead, I would describe Fox News's prime-time entertainers as the gateway drug to more nefarious influences. Agencies like Brietbart, then, would be the crack.

As Christians, we know that the truth does not always make us feel good. The biblical principle that the truth sets us free applies to all areas of life. When we interact only with news media that makes us feel good about what we think, what we believe, and who we are, we risk becoming bound to chains of other peoples' witchcraft. Seeking truth in the news media, then, means that we must stop pursuing what we want to hear but look for what is actually happening in the world around us. When we find journalists clearly backing up their data with sources (including pictures and videos that have not been manipulated or manufactured), we know we can trust that they are presenting facts. Then, we can listen to their takes on those facts alongside the other points of view represented. Once we have contemplated varying angles of the situation, then we can assess whether or not a journalist or journalistic agency is trustworthy. The critical thinking skills I sought to teach regarding the Bible are the same tools to use in this secular context.

Appendix 2

Submission to Authority

In the Gospels, Jesus answers his opponents' question by saying, "Render to the emperor what belongs to the emperor, and render to God what belongs to God" (Matt 22:21/Mark 12:17/Luke 20:25). In 2009, DePaul University professor William T. Cavanaugh wrote an insightful article on this command with the particularly perceptive title, "If You Render unto God what Is God's, What Is Left for Caesar?"[1] This title suggests that everything in life belongs to God. Since the context of the passage appears to be about taxes, most readers assume that Jesus commands the Jewish religious leaders to pay taxes. Certainly, Jesus does not tell them to avoid paying taxes. Rather, he refuses to answer their question at all, a normal technique in Jesus' interactions with religious leaders.

Jesus changes the topic from taxes to worship. Jesus used a *denarius* for his object lesson. That coin included a picture of the emperor with the inscription "lord and god" used to describe the emperor. The *denarius* was the coin used for the temple tax that Jewish leaders were required to pay.[2] Thus, Jesus might have been equating use of that coin for the temple tax to a compromise of their faithfulness to *YHWH*, but such a connection would relate only to one specific tax. No matter what he communicated about relationship with the government, however, Jesus by no means implied that people of a Judeo-Christian persuasion should not pay any taxes. But neither did Jesus suggest that God's people should unflinchingly follow governmental leaders' orders, respect their decisions, or give anything specific to them.

First Peter 2:11–17 answers the question that Cavanaugh's title asks. This passage prescribes no specific course of action regarding how to act

---

1. Cavanaugh, "If You Render to God What Is God's."
2. Keener, *Matthew*, 524.

toward authorities. It merely instructs hearers to respect at least some people in positions of authority. According to Peter, earthly systems of authority reflect God's own justice when they act justly. The text of 1 Peter 2:13–14 assumes that all governmental leaders commend people when they do good and punish people when they commit evil. Peter could not have expected anyone to accept this assumption as a reality. He made the assumption merely for the sake of argument. Like Revelation, 1 Peter was written during the reign of Emperor Domitian. Though no evidence demonstrates any widespread persecution under Domitian, not many Jews or gentile believers would have likely considered him to be an honorable leader. Because of the assumption, the text only demands honor to an individual leader when that leader acts honorably. It alludes to the general sense of order and righteousness for which all governments strive. Peter's hearers should have responded to this text with a strong regard for the system of authority, not necessarily for the authority figure himself. The same holds true for our relationships with governing authorities. As we discussed in the body of this book, Revelation called audiences to a holy resistance against the ways of the empire. In the same way, both Revelation and this passage in 1 Peter expect believers today to stand opposed to individual governmental authorities who blatantly oppose God's own order marked by truth, love, and justice.

Romans 13:1–7, if taken outside of the context just provided, would suggest that God directly appoints all governmental leaders. In a modern American context, it would equate resisting the US president with fighting against God. Paul, nevertheless, made the same type of assumption for the sake of argument that Peter did. Paul grounded the argument of the surrounding text in the ideal that demands submission to some authority figures. That ideal is only realized when an authority figure acts in a manner worthy of his/her office. When such is not the case, however, the correct response is holy resistance. Holy resistance calls for a nonviolent, sacrificial unconformity to the demands of the culture, a call undeniably present in all of Scripture.

Appendix 3

Simplistic Responses to Complex Problems

In the body of the book, I took us through detailed analyses of systemic racism and abortion to show how many American Christians react in simplistic, politically motivated ways. We looked at angles of both issues that you are probably not used to considering, without minimizing the evil of either sin. Cultural brainwashing often trains us to respond simplistically to complex issues, as do more malicious forms of brainwashing. I hope that the details provided for these two issues help you to begin analyzing your responses to other complex problems in like manner. The lists that follow offer no assessment. Some points overlap with topics we already discussed. For those that do not, you now have the tools to analyze these matters for yourself.

For the first list, I mention common dichotomies that wrongly turn multifaceted societal problems into simplistic black-and-white matters. Thus, no view on this list has any basis in reality or any significant support on either side of the political aisle. Nevertheless, President Trump often demands these simplistic dichotomies, as do illegitimate news media outlets both on the right and the left. The truth is always somewhere in the middle but too complex to arrive at through the means Americans so often employ. I provide this list of questions to help us seek debates, through which we can come closer to the truth than the dichotomies can ever provide.

Should the US government:

- Abolish the second amendment or grant unlimited access to firearms?
- Open borders or build a wall?
- Perpetually shut down the country or sacrifice lives to save the economy?

- Give preferential treatment to black people or intentionally oppress them?
- Promote anti-Semitism to protect Palestinian Muslims or condone corruption and oppression from Israel's national leaders?

In the second related list, I present false dichotomies of entities or concepts often pitted against each other in many churches in the United States, especially when intertwining politics and religion. We should never view these items as inherently opposed to each other but rather as complementary to one other when understood appropriately.

- Intellect vs. the Holy Spirit's empowerment
- Science vs. religion
- Humanity as a reflection of God's image vs. environmentalism
- Health vs. freedom

Appendix 4

Dictators, Cult Leaders, and American Politics

At the risk of oversimplifying matters, as I warned against on the last page, this final appendix consists of a single concise table. Detailed analyses would be outside the scope of this book. So, at the outset, I must point out that similarities with dictators and cult leaders do not automatically make Trump a dictator or cult leader. The purpose of this table is to show a small sample of the overwhelming number of connections that exist to show that Trump possesses tendencies of a dictatorial cult leader.

Trump's action:	Parallel dictator/cult leader action:
Promise to "make America great again" with context that requires the humiliation of those who supposedly diminished the nation.	Hitler built his campaign on a rallying cry about Germany's greatness. It demanded vengeance against all opposition.[1]
Courted evangelical votes by anti-abortion rhetoric, while simultaneously dehumanizing Mexicans, Muslims, and others.	Hitler either incited or capitalized on hypocrisy amongst Christians who supported him because of his traditional moral stances.[2]
Consistent references to mainstream media as "the enemy of the people."	Mussolini habitually intimidated the media to control how his constituents viewed him.[3]
Cries of "fake news" intended to convince people not to believe the reports of legitimate journalism in order to turn supporters against the truth and to protect Trump's image.	Jim Jones repeatedly told followers not to listen to news that covered the Peoples Temple movement unfavorably. He decried the "lies" of the media even while dying of a bullet wound as nine hundred devotees were also dying of the cyanide-laced Kool-Aid he told them to drink.[4]
Label of COVID-19 as "the China virus," wrongly blaming the Chinese government for the spread of the disease, not merely recognizing its origins in Wuhan, China.	Autocrats associated with the Ottoman Empire referred to the fourteenth-century CE black plague as "the Oriental plague," blaming Jews for the pandemic.[5]
Promotion of spurious treatments for COVID-19, including hydroxychloroquine, that originated from Trump loyalists, not doctors.	Joseph Stalin promoted the debunked medical claims of Trofim Lysenko, a loyalist whose biology was political, not scientific.[6]

1. McCreary, "Trump: America's Hitler?," para. 4.
2. McCreary, "Trump: America's Hitler?," para. 7.
3. Bosworth, *Mussolini*, 174.
4. Hassan, "Former Moonie," para. 1.
5. Schoichet, "What Historians Hear,'" para. 11.
6. Chait, "Trump Overruling Scientists," para. 1.

Glossary

Ascension/heavenly ascent: The process by which an ancient person received a revelatory vision from God.

Beatitude: A spoken blessing.

Benediction: A formal blessing often attached to the end of a letter.

Canon: The whole body of transcendent God-breathed biblical literature, understood either as what was collected by early church fathers (the Roman Catholic canon of seventy-three books) or condensed by reformers (Protestant canon of sixty-six books).

Charismatic: Pertaining to the gifts of the Holy Spirit as outlined most explicitly in 1 Cor 12.

Chiliasm: The earliest pattern for interpreting Revelation, tending to view Rev 20 as the key to understanding the whole book. It began to develop about a century after Revelation was written, demonstrating a significant temporal distance between the first followers of Jesus and the interpretation of Rev 20. That distance helps suggest that we should not use Rev 20 (but rather Rev 1) as an interpretive key for Revelation.

Ecclesiology: The study and practice of communal worship.

Ecstatic: Pertaining to the spiritual state in which an ancient person received a vision or other charismatic message from God. See "charismatic" above.

Epistle: Technically, there are small differences between "epistle" and "letter," but I do not interact with those nuances in this book. For our purposes, an epistle is a letter.

Eschatological tension: The nature of the kingdom of God as a reality that has already been established and as a reality that has yet to be established.

Eschatology: The study of the end times.

Eschaton: The moment in which Jesus will return to the earth.

Etymology: The history of any word's development, meaning, and evolution.

Extrabiblical: Referring to any document written at the same time as any of the OT or NT.

Hermeneutics: The discipline of interpreting literature.

Masoretic Text: The collection of Hebrew texts from the ninth and tenth centuries CE used alongside the Septuagint to translate what eventually became known as the Old Testament. See "Septuagint" below.

Oracle: A prophetic utterance that uses the very words that a prophet claims to have heard from the Lord rather than a paraphrase, explanation, or interpretation. It is usually accompanied by the phrase, "Thus says the Lord."

Pentateuch: The first five books of the Bible, also called the Torah, of which Moses is the central character (not the author).

Pluralism: Religious diversity that can tempt people toward compromise of their beliefs.

Recapitulation: Each section of Revelation that repeats its material from a different point of view.

Sacrament: Based on the Latin word from which it is derived, the word literally refers to anything that assists one's worship to God; most churches, however, use the word for specific rites. I use the word in both senses throughout the book; context should clarify the way in which I use it each time.

Second Temple Judaism: The period of time between the reconstruction of the Jerusalem Temple (about 515 BCE) and its destruction in 70 CE.

Schema: A pattern of organizing literary material.

Seer: An ancient person who received an apocalyptic vision.

Septet: Each of Revelation's three sets of seven judgments (seals, trumpets, and bowls).

Septuagint: A collection of Greek translations of the Hebrew Scriptures from the third century CE used to translate what eventually became known as the OT. The Septuagint is valuable to modern translators because it represents the oldest full collection available in any language, while the Masoretic Text, despite being centuries later than the Septuagint, is valuable as the oldest complete edition in the original Hebrew and Aramaic languages. See "Masoretic Text" above.

Syncretism: The mixing of religious worldviews, leading to idolatry and paganism.

Synoptic Gospels: Matthew, Mark, and Luke.

YHWH: The divine name revealed to Moses at the burning bush; Hebrew manuscripts provided four consonants without any vowels, so we have no idea how to pronounce it, making attempts like *Yahweh* and *Jehovah* of questionable appropriateness; most English translations capitalize all four letters of LORD to indicate when this word appears in the OT, but because of the completely unique character of this name, I transliterate the four Hebrew letters instead.

Bibliography

Anderson, Stuart. "H-1B Visas and Trump's Next 'Merit-Based' Immigration Plan." *Forbes*, August 6, 2020. https://www.forbes.com/sites/stuartanderson/2020/08/06/h-1b-visas-and-trumps-next-merit-based-immigration-plan/?sh=4df77bdd79bd.

Andrews, Roger. "Death and Climate Change." *Energy Matters*, Nov. 9, 2019. http://euanmearns.com/death-and-climate-change/.

Archer, Melissa L. *"I Was in the Spirit on the Lord's Day": A Pentecostal Engagement with Worship in the Apocalypse*. Cleveland, TN: CPT, 2015.

Argen, David. "If Our Countries Were Safe, We Wouldn't Leave: The Harsh Reality of Mexico's Migrant Caravan." *The Guardian*, April 6, 2018. https://www.theguardian.com/world/2018/apr/05/view-inside-mexico-migrant-caravan-trump-border-wall.

Ascough, Richard S. "A Question of Death: Paul's Community-Building Language in 1 Corinthians 4:13–18." *Journal of Biblical Literature* 123 (2004) 509–30.

———. "The Thessalonian Christian Community as a Professional Voluntary Association." *Journal of Biblical Literature* 119 (2000) 311–28.

Aune, David E. "The Apocalypse of John and the Problem of Genre." *Semeia* 36 (1986) 65–98.

———. "The Influence of Roman Imperial Court Ceremonial on the Apocalypse of John." *Biblical Research* 28 (1983) 5–26.

———. *Revelation*. Dallas: Word, 1997.

Backus, Irena. *Reformation Readings in the Apocalypse: Geneva, Zurich, and Wittenberg*. New York: Oxford University Press, 2000.

Barclay, William. *The Revelation of John*. Rev. ed. Philadelphia: Westminster, 1976.

Barr, David L. "Beyond Genre: The Expectations of Apocalypse." In *The Reality of Apocalypse: Rhetoric and Politics in the Book of Revelation*, edited by David L. Barr, 71–89. Leiden: Brill, 2006.

Barrett, Delvin, and Matt Zapotosky. "Just Dept. Investigation Winds Down Clinton-Related Inquiry once Championed by Trump; It Found Nothing of Consequence." *The Washington Post*, January 9, 2020. https://www.washingtonpost.com/national-security/justice-dept-winds-down-clinton-related-inquiry-once-championed-by-trump-it-found-nothing-of-consequence/2020/01/09/ca83932e-32f9-11ea-a053-dc6d944ba776_story.html.

Bauckham, Richard. *Jesus and the Eyewitnesses: The Gospels as Eyewitness Testimony.* Grand Rapids: Eerdmans, 2006.

———. *The Theology of the Book of Revelation.* Cambridge: Cambridge University Press, 1993.

Bauer, Walter, et al. *A Greek-English Lexicon of the New Testament and Other Early Christian Literature.* 3rd ed. Chicago: University of Chicago Press, 2000.

Bazzle, Steph. "20 Times Donald Trump Praised Dictators and Controversial Leaders." *HillReporter*, Apr. 18, 2019. https://hillreporter.com/times-donald-trump-praised-dictators-and-controversial-leaders-31009.

Beale, G. K. *The Book of Revelation.* Grand Rapids: Eerdmans, 1999.

———. *John's Use of the Old Testament in Revelation.* Sheffield: Sheffield Academic Press, 1998.

Beale, G. K., and David H. Campbell. *Revelation: A Shorter Commentary.* Grand Rapids: Eerdmans, 2015.

Beasley-Murray, G. R. *The Book of Revelation.* London: Marshall, Morgan, & Scott, 1974.

Benen, Steve. "Driven by Vengeance, Trump Is Eager to 'Punish His Enemies.'" *MSNBC*, November 7, 2016. http://www.msnbc.com/rachel-maddow-show/driven-vengeance-trump-eager-punish-his-enemies.

Berry, C. Everett. "Highlighting the Link between the Millennium and Replacement Thought: Augustinian Nonchiliasm as a Test Case." *Criswell Theological Review* 3 (2005) 71–91.

"Black Lives Matter: What We Believe." https://uca.edu/training/files/2020/09/black-Lives-Matter-Handout.pdf.

Boring, M. Eugene. *Revelation.* Louisville: John Knox, 1989.

Bosworth. R. J. B. *Mussolini.* 2nd ed. London: Bloomsbury Academic, 2011.

Bredin, Mark R. "Hate Never Dispelled Hate: No Place for *Pharmakos* (Revelation 22:15)." *Biblical Theology Bulletin: Journal of Bible and Culture* 34 (2003) 105–13.

Brighton, Louis A. *Revelation.* St. Louis: Concordia, 1999.

Buisch, Pauline P. "The Rest of Her Offspring: The Relationship between Revelation 12 and the Targumic Expression of Genesis 3:15." *Novum Testamentum* 60 (2018) 386–401.

Caird, G. B. *A Commentary on the Revelation of St. John the Divine.* New York: Harper & Row, 1966.

Campbell, Brian. *Rivers and the Power of Ancient Rome.* Chapel Hill: University of North Carolina Press, 2012.

Castelli, Elizabeth A. "Persecution Complexes: Identity Politics and the 'War on Christians.'" *A Journal of Feminist Cultural Studies* 18 (2007) 152–80.

Cavanaugh, William T. "If You Render to God What Is God's, What Is Left for Caesar?" *The Review of Politics* 71 (2009) 609–19.

Cervantes, Wendy, and Christina Walker. "Five Reasons Trump's Immigration Orders Harm Children." https://www.clasp.org/sites/default/files/public/resources-and-publications/publication-1/Five-Reasons-Immigration-Enforcement-Orders-Harm-Children.pdf.

Chait, Jonathan. "Trump Overruling Scientists to Pursue Pet Coronavirus Drug." *New York Intelligencer*, April 6, 2020. https://nymag.com/intelligencer/2020/04/trump-fauci-navarro-giuliani-scientists-coronavirus-hydroxchloroquine.html.

Charles, R. H. *A Critical and Exegetical Commentary on the Revelation of St. John*. 2 vols. Edinburgh: T. & T. Clark, 1920.

Chinni, Dante. "Data: Republican Party ID Drops after Trump Election." *NBC News*, December 10, 2017. https://www.nbcnews.com/storyline/trumps-victory-1-year-later/data-republican-party-id-drops-after-trump-election-n828141.

Clark, Andrew. "The Illegalization of Undocumented Immigrants." *Race, Politics Justice*, September 18, 2017. https://www.ssc.wisc.edu/soc/racepoliticsjustice/2017/09/18/the-illegalization-of-undocumented-immigrants/.

Cohan, John Allen. "The Problem of Witchcraft Violence in Africa." *Suffolk University Law Review* (2011) 803–72.

Collins, Adela Yarbro. *The Combat Myth in the Book of Revelation*. Missoula: Scholars, 1976.

———. *Crisis and Catharsis: The Power of the Apocalypse*. Philadelphia: Westminster, 1984.

Collins, John J. *The Apocalyptic Imagination: An Introduction to Jewish Apocalyptic*. 2nd ed. Grand Rapids: Eerdmans, 1998.

Concha, Joe. "Carl Bernstein: Woodward's Trump Tapes 'Smoking Gun' of 'Homicidal Negligence.'" *The Hill*, September 9, 2020. https://thehill.com/homenews/media/515745-carl-bernstein-woodwards-trump-tapes-smoking-gun-of-homicidal-negligence.

Corasaniti, Nick, and Maggie Haberman. "Donald Trump Suggests '2nd Amendment People' Could Act against Hilary Clinton." *New York Times*, August 9, 2016. https://www.nytimes.com/2016/08/10/us/politics/donald-trump-hillary-clinton.html.

Corbett, John H. "Paganism and Christianity." In *Encyclopedia of Early Christianity*, edited by Everett Ferguson et al., 848–51. 2nd ed. New York: Routledge, 1999.

Coulter, Leah. *Rediscovering the Power of Repentance and Forgiveness*. Atlanta: Ampelon, 2006.

Craffert, Pieter F. "Altered States of Consciousness: Visions, Spirit Possession, Sky Journeys." In *Understanding the Social World of the New Testament*, edited by Dietmar Neufeld and Richard E. DeMaris, 126–47. London: Routledge, 2010.

Croy, Clayton N. "A God by Any Other Name: Polyonymy in Greco-Roman Antiquity and Early Christianity." *Bulletin for Biblical Research* 24 (2014) 27–43.

D'Amato, Gennaro, et al. "Climate Change and Respiratory Disease." *European Respiratory Review* 23 (2014) 161–69.

Daprile, Lucas. "From Amazing Grace to Burning Cop Cars: How Columbia Spiraled Out of Control." *The State*, June 2, 2020. https://www.thestate.com/news/local/article243124356.html.

Davey, Tucker. "Developing Countries Can't Afford Climate Change." *Future of Life*, August 5, 2016. https://futureoflife.org/2016/08/05/developing-countries-cant-afford-climate-change/?cn-reloaded=1.

Dennis, Brady. "Trump Makes It Official: U.S. Will Withdraw from the Paris Climate Accord." *The Washington Post*, November 4, 2019. https://www.washingtonpost.com/climate-environment/2019/11/04/trump-makes-it-official-us-will-withdraw-paris-climate-accord/.

deSilva, David. *Seeing Things John's Way: The Rhetoric of Revelation*. Louisville: Westminster John Knox, 2009.

de Villiers, Pieter G. R. "Die kerk en sy mag in Openbaring 11." *HTS Teologiese Studies* 68 (2002) 1–10.

Diehl, Judith A. "Anti-Imperial Rhetoric in the New Testament." In *Jesus Is Lord, Caesar Is Not: Evaluating Empire in New Testament Studies*, edited by Scot McKnight and Joseph B. Modica, 38–81. Downers Grove: IVP Academic, 2013.

Dowd, Maureen, et al. "Donald Trump: The Great Disrupter." *The Hill*, October 17, 2018. https://thehill.com/opinion/white-house/411535-donald-trump-the-great-disruptor.

Drescher, Jack. "Out of DSM: Depathologizing Homosexuality." *Behavioral Sciences* 5 (2015) 565–75.

Evangelical Lutheran Church in America. *Lutheran Book of Worship*. Minneapolis: Augsburg, 1978.

Fahrenthold, David A. "Trump Recorded Having Extremly Lewd Conversation about Women in 2005." *The Washington Post*, October 7, 2016. https://www.washingtonpost.com/politics/trump-recorded-having-extremely-lewd-conversation-about-women-in-2005/2016/10/07/3b9ce776-8cb4-11e6-bf8a-3d26847eeed4_story.html.

Falaye. "Polygamy and Christianity in Africa." *Global Journal of Arts Humanities and Social Sciences* (2016) 18–28.

Farrer, Austin M. *The Revelation of St. John the Divine*. Oxford: Clarendon, 1964.

Fee, Gordon D. *Revelation*. Eugene, OR: Wipf & Stock, 2010.

Feuillet, André. "The Twenty-Four Elders of the Apocalypse." In *Johannine Studies*, edited by André Feuillet and translated by Thomas E. Craine, 183–214. Bloomington: Alba, 1966.

Fontaine, Mike. "Straight Talk about Gay Marriage in Ancient Rome: The Perils of Precedent." https://web.archive.org/web/20180717143801/https://eidolon.pub/straight-talk-about-gay-marriage-in-ancient-rome-9fd466672152?gi=846670f877e5.

Frazee, Gretchen. "A Look Inside the Facilities Where Migrant Families Are Detained." *PBS NewsHour*, Aug. 27, 2019. https://www.pbs.org/newshour/nation/new-trump-rules-would-detain-families-longer-this-is-where-they-would-stay.

Frend, W. H. C. *The Rise of Christianity*. Philadelphia: Fortress, 1984.

Friesen, Stephen J. *Imperial Cults and the Apocalypse of John: Reading Revelation in the Ruins*. Oxford: Oxford University Press.

Galambush, Julie. "Necessary Enemies: Nebuchadnezzar, YHWH, and Gog in Ezekiel 38–39." In *Israel's Prophets and Israel's Past: Essays on the Relationship of Prophetic Texts and Israelite History in Honor of John H. Hayes*, edited by Meghan Bishop Moore et al., 254–65. New York: T. & T. Clark, 2006.

"Gallup Historical Trends: Guns." https://news.gallup.com/poll/1645/guns.aspx.

Garcia, Arturo. "Did a US Veteran Influence Kaepernicks' 'Take a Knee' Protest of Police Brutality?" https://www.snopes.com/fact-check/veteran-kaepernick-take-a-knee-anthem/.

Gentry, Kenneth L., Jr. "Definition." https://postmillennialworldview.com/postmillennialism-defined/.

Gerson, Lloyd P. "A Platonic Reading of Plato's *Symposium*." In *Plato's Symposium: Issues in Interpretation and Reception*, edited by James Lesher et al., 47–70. Washington, DC: Center for Hellenic Studies, 2007.

Gibson, Caitlyn. "What Is 'Gaslighting'? And How Does It Relate to Donald Trump?" *The Washington Post*, January 27, 2017. https://www.newsobserver.com/news/politics-government/article129199504.html.

Girard, René. "'The Ancient Trail Trodden by the Wicked': Job as Scapegoat." *Semeia* 33 (1985) 14–41.

Gnuse, Robert K. "Seven Gay Texts: Biblical Passages Used to Condemn Homosexuality." *Biblical Theology Bulletin* 42 (2015) 68–87.

Gomez, Allen. "Migrant Children Report Sexual Assaults while Detained by U.S." *USA Today*, February 26, 2019. https://www.usatoday.com/story/news/politics/2019/02/26/thousands-migrant-children-report-sexual-assaults-us-custody-border-detain/2988884002/.

Gourley, Bruce T. "Religious Liberty, Sexuality and the Bible." *Baptist Studies Bulletin*, April 2015. http://www.brucegourley.com/baptist-studies-bulletin-archives-articles-bruce-gourley/religious-liberty-sexuality-bible/.

Greenwood, Lee. "God Bless the U.S.A." *You've Got a Good Love Comin'*. MCA Music, 1984, track no. 10.

Halper, Evan, et al. "What if Trump Loses but Won't Concede? How a National Crisis Could Play Out." *Los Angeles Times*, September 20, 2020. https://www.latimes.com/politics/story/2020-09-24/if-trump-lost-and-tried-to-hold-onto-power-what-could-he-do.

Hoekema, Anthony. *The Bible and the Future*. Grand Rapids: Eerdmans, 1979.

Hope, Valerie Margaret. "Dulce et decorum est pro patria mori': The Practical and Symbolic Treatment of the Roman War Dead." *Mortality* 23 (2018) 35–49.

Garrison, Greg. "What Clergy Said When Influenza Closed Churches in 1918." *Advanced Local Alabama*, April 17, 2020. https://www.al.com/coronavirus/2020/04/what-clergy-said-when-influenza-closed-churches-in-1918.html.

Goodkind, Nicole. "Trump's Tax Cuts Benefit Rich Americans, Not Middle-Class Families, Voters Say by 2–1 Margin in Republican Poll." *Newsweek*, September 21, 2018. https://www.newsweek.com/trump-tax-cuts-rich-americans-republicans-1133372.

Gorman, Michael J. *Reading Revelation Responsibly: Uncivil Worship and Worship: Following the Lamb into the New Creation*. Eugene, OR: Cascade, 2011.

Gryboski, Michael. "Evangelical Leaders Reject Trump's Demonization of Migrants." *The Christian Post*, November 11, 2018. https://www.christianpost.com/news/evangelical-leaders-reject-trump-demonization-migrants.html.

Guggenheim, David, dir. *An Inconvenient Truth*. Los Angeles: Lawrence Bender Productions, 2006.

Haddad, Tareq. "Hilary Clinton Cleared of Mishandling Classified Information after 3-Year Email Probe, Trump So Far Silent." *Newsweek*, October 19, 2019. https://www.newsweek.com/hillary-clinton-cleared-wrongdoing-private-email-probe-1466426.

Harwood, John. "How the Republican Party Opened Itself up to the Trump Takeover." *CNN*, July, 26, 2020. https://www.cnn.com/2020/07/26/politics/republican-party-trump-stuart-stevens/index.html.

Hassan, Steven. "Take It from a Former Moonie: Trump Is a Cult Leader." *Daily Beast*, October 13, 2019. https://www.thedailybeast.com/take-it-from-a-former-moonie-trump-is-a-cult-leader/.

Hemer, Colin J. *Letters to the Seven Churches of Asia in Their Local Setting*. Sheffield: Sheffield Academic Press.

Hicks, John Mark. "How Churches of Christ Responded When the 'Spanish Flu' Killed Millions." *The Christian Chronicle: An International Newspaper for Churches of Christ*, March 17, 2020. https://christianchronicle.org/how-churches-of-christ-responded-when-the-1918-spanish-flu-killed-millions/.

Hoskier, H. O., ed. *The Complete Commentary of Oecumenius on the Apocalypse*. Ann Arbor: University of Michigan Press, 1929.

"How to Protect Yourself & Others." https://www.cdc.gov/coronavirus/2019-ncov/prevent-getting-sick/prevention.html.

Humphrey, Edith McEwan. *And I Turned to See the Voice: The Rhetoric of the New Testament*. Grand Rapids: Baker, 2007.

———. *Grand Entrance: Worship on Earth as It Is in Heaven*. Grand Rapids: Brazos, 2011.

"Inside President Donald J. Trump's First Year of Restoring Law and Order." https://web.archive.org/web/20171221124905/https://www.whitehouse.gov/briefings-statements/president-donald-j-trumps-first-year-restoring-law-order/.

Isgrigg, Daniel D. "How Pentecostals Responded to the 1918 'Spanish Influenza' Pandemic: Lessons from Assemblies of God History." *Influence: The Shape of Leadership*, March 23, 2020. https://influencemagazine.com/en/Theory/How-Pentecostals-Responded-to-the-1918-Spanish-Influenza-Pandemic.

Jauhiainen, Marko. "The Measuring of the Sanctuary Reconsidered (Rev 11,1–2)." *Biblica* 83 (2002) 507–26.

Jeffers, James S. *The Greco-Roman World of the New Testament Era: Exploring the Background of Early Christianity*. Downers Grove: IVP Academic, 1999.

Jervis, Rick. "Zero Tolerance: New Immigration Policy Separates Parents, Kids." *USA Today*, June 10, 2018. https://www.usatoday.com/story/news/2018/06/10/immigrants-zero-tolerance-mcallen-separate-families-trump/687348002/.

Jobes, Karen. "Distinguishing the Meaning of Greek Verbs in the Semantic Domain for Worship." In *Biblical Words and Their Meaning: An Introduction to Lexical Semantics*, by Moisés Silva, 201–11. Rev. ed. Grand Rapids: Zondervan, 1994.

Johnson, Alan F. *Revelation*. Rev. ed. Grand Rapids: Zondervan, 1996.

Johnson, Darrell W. "Always on the Brink: Revelation 3:1–6." *Crux* 1 (2004) 2–8.

Jones, Robert P. "Racism among White Christians Is Higher than among the Nonreligious. That's No Coincidence." *Think*, July 27, 2020. https://www.nbcnews.com/think/opinion/racism-among-white-christians-higher-among-nonreligious-s-no-coincidence-ncna1235045.

Judge, Edwin A. "The Mark of the Beast, Revelation 13:16." *Tyndale Bulletin* 42 (1991) 158–60.

Kaleem, Jaweed. "Megachurch Pastors Defy Coronavirus Pandemic, Insisting on Right to Worship." *Los Angeles Times*, March 31, 2020. https://www.latimes.com/world-nation/story/2020-03-31/coronavirus-megachurches-meeting-pastors.

Kapperler, Victor E. "A Brief History of Slavery and the Origins of American Policing." https://plsonline.eku.edu/insidelook/brief-history-slavery-and-origins-american-policing.

Keener, Craig S. *A Commentary on the Gospel of Matthew*. Grand Rapids: Eerdmans, 1999.

———. *IVP Bible Background Commentary: New Testament*. 2nd ed. Downers Grove: IVP Academic, 2001.

———. *Revelation*. Grand Rapids: Zondervan, 2000.

Keith, Tamara. "Trump Outlines 'Merit-Based Immigration Plan.'" *NPR Morning Edition*, May 16, 2019. https://www.npr.org/2019/05/16/723677591/trumps-new-immigration-plan-doesn-t-address-undocumented-immigrants.

Kiddle, Martin. *The Revelation of St. John*. New York: Harper, 1940.

Klauck, Hans-Josef. *Ancient Letters and the New Testament: A Guide to Context and Exegesis*. Waco: Baylor University Press, 2006.

Kochhar, Rakesh. "How Americans Compare with the Global Middle Class." https://www.pewresearch.org/fact-tank/2015/07/09/how-americans-compare-with-the-global-middle-class/.

Koester, Craig R. *Revelation: A New Translation with Introduction and Commentary*. New Haven: Yale University Press, 2014.

Korte, Gregory, and Alan Gomez. "Trump Ramps up Rhetoric on Undocumented Immigrants: 'These Aren't People. They Are Animals.'" *USA Today*, May 16, 2018. https://www.usatoday.com/story/news/politics/2018/05/16/trump-immigrants-animals-mexico-democrats-sanctuary-cities/617252002/.

Kovacs, Judith, and Christopher Rowland. *Revelation: The Apocalypse of Jesus Christ*. Malden: Blackwell, 2004.

Krodel, Gerhard. *Revelation*. Minneapolis: Augsburg, 1989.

Ladd, George Eldon. *The Blessed Hope: A Biblical Study of the Second Advent and the Rapture*. Grand Rapids: Eerdmans, 1956.

———. *A Commentary on the Revelation of John*. Grand Rapids: Eerdmans, 1972.

Lasine, Stuart. "Guest and Host in Judges 19: Lot's Hospitality in an Inverted World." *Journal for the Studies of the Old Testament* 29 (1984) 37–59.

Lau, Maya, and Laura Nelson. "Empty Trucks, Falsified Records, Late Mail: How Louis DeJoy's Changes at Postal Service Brought Chaos." *Los Angeles Times*, September 17, 2020. https://www.msn.com/en-us/news/us/empty-trucks-falsified-records-late-mail-how-louis-dejoys-changes-at-the-postal-service-brought-chaos/ar-BB198OxM.

Lee, Chie-Chiew. "Rest and Victory in Revelation 14:13." *Journal for the Studies of the New Testament* 41 (2019) 344–62.

Lee, Lydia. "The Enemies Within: Gog of Magog in Ezekiel 38–39." *Hervormde Teologiese Studies Theological Studies* 73 (2017) 10–17.

Lenski, R. C. H. *The Interpretation of St. John's Revelation*. Columbus: Lutheran Book Concern, 1935.

Levine, Amy-Jill. "What Goes Wrong with the Third Quest?" Lecture at Asbury Theological Seminary, Wilmore, KY, October 13, 2017.

Levy, Gabrielle. "Abortion Rates: Where and Why They're Falling." *US News & World Report*, March 21, 2018. https://www.usnews.com/news/data-mine/articles/2018-03-21/abortion-rates-where-and-why-theyre-falling.

Lind, Dara. "People Are Dying Because of the Trump Administration's Immigration Policy: Family Separations and Deportations Have a Body Count." *Vox News*, June 12, 2018. https://www.vox.com/2018/6/12/17448778/separated-family-father-suicide-killed-deported.

Lizorkin-Eyzenberg, Eli. "Does God Hate Divorce?" *Israel Bible Weekly* (2019) 1.

López, René. "A Study of Pauline Passages with Vice Lists." *Bibliotheca Sacra* 168 (2011) 301–16.

MacLeod, David J. "The Seventh 'Last Thing': The New Heaven and the New Earth." *Bibliotheca Sacra* 157 (2000) 439–51.

Macumber, Heather. "The Threat of Empire: Monstrous Hybridity in Revelation 13." *Biblical Interpretation* 27 (2019) 107–29.
Mann, Pamela S. "Toward a Biblical Understanding of Polygamy." *Missiology: An International Review* (1989) 11–26.
Mantayla, Kyle. "Pat Robertson Is Now Deeply Concerned about the Murder of Jamal Khashoggi." *Right Wing Watch*, June 11, 2019. https://www.rightwingwatch.org/post/pat-robertson-is-now-deeply-concerned-about-the-murder-of-jamal-khashoggi/.
Marcieca, Jennifer. "A Field Guide to Trump's Dangerous Rhetoric." *The Conversation*, June 19, 2020. https://theconversation.com/a-field-guide-to-trumps-dangerous-rhetoric-139531.
Matthews, Chris. "U.S. Airstrike Kills Top Iranian General." *MSNBC*, January 3, 2020. https://www.msnbc.com/transcripts/hardball/2020-01-03-msna1319301.
Mazza, Ed. "Trump Is Fighting the 'War on Christmas' in July and Twitter Is Fighting Back" *HuffPost*, August 1, 2018. https://www.huffpost.com/entry/donald-trump-war-on-christmas-july_n_5b6124dae4b0fd5c73d43c01.
McCreary, Jerry. "Trump: America's Hitler?" *The Berkshire Edge*, October 31, 2020. https://theberkshireedge.com/trump-americas-hitler/.
McEleney, Neil J. "Vice Lists of the Pastoral Epistles." *CBQ* 36 (1974) 203–19.
McIntire, Mike, et al. "The President's Tax Records: Tax Records Reveal How Fame Gave Trump a $427 Million Lifeline." *New York Times*, September 8, 2020. https://www.nytimes.com/interactive/2020/09/28/us/donald-trump-taxes-apprentice.html?action=click&module=Top%20Stories&pgtype=Homepage.
Morris, Leon. *The Revelation of St. John*. Grand Rapids: Eerdmans, 1984.
Moses, Robert E. "Love Overflowing in Complete Knowledge at Corinth: Paul's Message Concerning Idol Food." *Interpretation: A Journal of Bible and Theology* 72 (2018) 17–28.
Moss, Candida R., and Liane M. Feldman. "The New Jerusalem: Wealth, Ancient Building Projects, and Revelation 21–22." *New Testament Studies* 66 (2020) 351–66.
Mote, Edward (text) and William B. Bradbury (melody). "My Hope Is Built on Nothing Less." 1834.
Mounce, Robert H. *The Book of Revelation*. Rev. ed. Grand Rapids: Eerdmans, 1998.
Murphy, Frederick J. *Apocalypticism in the Bible and Its World: A Comprehensive Introduction*. Grand Rapids: Baker, 2012.
Murray, Michele. *Playing a Jewish Game: Gentile Christians Judaizing in the First and Second Centuries CE*. Waterloo, Ontario: Wilfred Laurier University Press, 2004.
Musopole, Augustine C. "Witchcraft Terminology, the Bible, and African Christian Theology: An Exercise in Hermeneutics." *Journal of Religion in Africa* 23 (1993) 347–54.
Nelson, Louis. "From 'Locker Room Talk' On, Trump Fends off Misconduct Claims." *Politico*, December 12, 2017. https://www.politico.com/story/2017/12/12/trump-timeline-sexual-misconduct-allegations-defense-292146.
Newport, Frank. "Democrats Racially Diverse; Republicans Mostly White." *Gallup*, February 8, 2013. https://news.gallup.com/poll/160373/democrats-racially-diverse-republicans-mostly-white.aspx.
Nixon, R. E. "Boanerges." In *The New Bible Dictionary*, edited by J. D. Douglas, 1354. London: InterVarsity, 1963.

Nothstine, Ray. "Trump: 'Why Do I Have to Repent or Ask Forgiveness if I Am Not Making Mistakes?'" *The Christian Post*, July 23, 2015. https://www.christianpost.com/news/trump-why-do-i-have-to-repent-or-ask-for-forgiveness-if-i-am-not-making-mistakes-video-141856/#7LDIoCqtXH4dGxWz.99.

Nunberg, Geoff. "Is Trump's Call for 'Law and Order' a Coded Racial Message?" *NPR*, July 28, 2016. https://www.npr.org/2016/07/28/487560886/is-trumps-call-for-law-and-order-a-coded-racial-message.

Olson, Daniel C. "'Those Who Have Not Defiled Themselves with Women': Revelation 14:4 and the Book of Enoch." *The Catholic Bible Quarterly* 59 (1997) 492–510.

Osuna, Manuel Garcia. "Cordova." In *Catholic Encyclopedia: An Internal Book of Reference on the Constitution, Doctrine, Discipline, and History of the Catholic Church*. New York: Appleton, 1910. https://www.newadvent.org/cathen/04359b.htm.

Palladino, Martina. "Cult of Fire: Honoring Nature's Purifier, Transformer, and Destroyer." *Natural History* (2019) 41–43.

Palmer, Erin. "Imagining Space in Revelation: The Heavenly Throne Room and New Jerusalem." *Journal of Theta Alpha Kappa* (2015) 35–47.

Pentecost, J. Dwight. *Things to Come: A Study in Biblical Eschatology*. Grand Rapids: Zondervan, 1958.

Peterson, Robert A. "Does the Bible Teach Annihilationism?" *Bibliotheca Sacra* 156 (1999) 13–27.

Philbrick, Nathaniel. *Mayflower: A Story of Courage, Community, and War*. New York: Penguin, 2006.

Pinnock, Clark H. "The Destruction of the Finally Impenitent." *Criswell Theological Review* 4 (1990) 243–59.

Porter, Tom. "Trump's Refusal to Commit to a Peaceful Transfer of Power Comes from Three Crucial Aspects of His Character: His Hatred of Losing, His Willingness to Cheat, and His Nonchalance about Violence." *Business Insider*, September 24, 2020. https://www.msn.com/en-us/news/politics/trumps-refusal-to-commit-to-a-peaceful-transfer-of-power-comes-from-three-crucial-aspects-of-his-character-his-hatred-of-losing-his-willingness-to-cheat-and-his-nonchalance-about-violence/ar-BB19nBug.

Portier-Young, Anathea E. *Apocalypse against Empire: Theologies of Resistance in Early Judaism*. Grand Rapids: Eerdmans, 2011.

Quinn, Annalisa. "Everyone Wants to 'Influence' You." *The New York Times Magazine*, November 20, 2018. https://www.nytimes.com/2018/11/20/magazine/everyone-wants-to-influence-you.html.

Rappleye, Hannah, and Lisa Riordan Seville. "24 Immigrants Have Died in ICE Custody during the Trump Administration." *NBC News*, June 9, 2019. https://www.nbcnews.com/politics/immigration/24-immigrants-have-died-ice-custody-during-trump-administration-n1015291/.

Rayome, Alison DeNisco, and Katie Conner. "Mail-in Voting versus Absentee Voting: Differences to Know before Election Day." *CNET*, September 3, 2020. https://www.cnet.com/how-to/mail-in-voting-vs-absentee-voting-every-difference-to-know-before-election-day/.

Reddish, Mitchell G. *Revelation*. Macon: Smyth & Helwys, 2001.

Rissi, Mathias. *Time and History: A Study on the Revelation*. Richmond: John Knox, 1966.

Rowland, Christopher. *The Open Heaven: A Study of Apocalyptic in Judaism and Early Christianity*. New York: Crossroads, 1982.

Russell, D. S. *The Method and Message of Jewish Apocalyptic: 200 BC–AD 100*. Philadelphia: Westminster, 1964.

Salmon, Barrington M. "Trump Has Done Irreversible Damage." *The Final Call*, October 29, 2019. https://www.finalcall.com/artman/publish/National_News_2/Trump-has-done-irreversible-damage.shtml.

Sampathkumar, Mythili. "Last Surviving Prosecutor at Nuremberg Trials Says Trump's Family Separation Policy Is 'Crime Against Humanity.'" *The Independent*, October 16, 2018. https://www.independent.co.uk/news/world/americas/trump-border-crisis-nazis-nuremberg-trial-ben-ferencz-family-separation-migrants-un-a8485606.html.

Saunders, Martin. "If Necessary, Use Words . . . What Did Francis of Assisi Really Say?" *Christian Today*, August 28, 2017. https://www.christiantoday.com/article/if.necessary.use.words.what.did.francis.of.assisi.really.say/112365.htm.

Schenck, Rob. "Should Christians Own Guns? Why This Conservative Evangelical Is Skeptical." *Sojourners* 45 (May 2016) 14–18.

———. "Trump's Rhetoric Is Inciting Violence, just like Mine Did." *TIME*, August 6, 2019. https://time.com/5645371/trump-rhetoric-violence/.

Schloss, Eva. "Anne Frank's Stepsister: Donald Trump Is Acting like Hitler." *Newsweek*, January 27, 2016. https://www.newsweek.com/holocaust-memorial-day-anne-frank-refugee-crisis-donald-trump-420312.

Schochet, Leila. "Trump's Immigration Policies Are Harming American Children." *Berkley Law School Center for American Progress*, July 31, 2017. https://www.law.berkeley.edu/wp-content/uploads/2017/09/ImmigrationPolicyChildren-brief1.pdf.

Schoichet, Catherine E. "What Historians Hear as Trump Describes Coronavirus 'Chinese' and 'Foreign.'" *CNN*, March 17, 2020. https://www.cnn.com/2020/03/12/us/disease-outbreaks-xenophobia-history/index.html.

Scott, Walter. *Exposition of the Revelation of Jesus Christ*. New York: Loizaux, 1990.

Silwa, Jim. "Immigrant Family Separations Must End: Firsthand Observations of Mental Health Impact on Children." *American Psychological Association*, February 7, 2019. https://www.apa.org/news/press/releases/2019/02/immigrant-family-separations.

Smalley, Steven. *The Revelation to John: A Commentary on the Greek Text of the Apocalypse*. Downers Grove: InterVarsity, 2005.

———. *Thunder and Love: John's Revelation and John's Community*. Milton Keynes: Word, 1994.

Smith, Saphora, and Charlene Gubash. "Saudi Arabia Sentences 5 to Death for Jamal Khashoggi Murder." *NBC News*, December 23, 2019. https://www.nbcnews.com/news/world/saudi-sentences-5-death-jamal-khashoggi-s-killing-n1106396.

Steinmann, Andrew E. "The Tripartite Structure of the Sixth Seal, the Seventh Trumpet, and the Sixth Bowl of John's Apocalypse (Rev 6:12–7:17; 9:13–11:14; 17:12–16)." *Journal of the Evangelical Theological Society* 35 (1992) 69–79.

Stevens, Stuart. "2020 Election: If Republicans Care about America, They Should Vote for Joe Biden." *USA Today*, June 26, 2020. https://www.usatoday.com/story/opinion/2020/06/26/republican-party-has-lost-its-way-republicans-should-vote-for-joe-biden-2020-column/3254053001/.

———. *It Was All a Lie: How the Republican Party Became the Party of Trump*. New York: Knopf, 2020.

———. "Wake Up, Republicans: Your Party Stands for All The Wrong Things Now." *The Washington Post*, January 1, 2020. https://www.washingtonpost.com/opinions/wake-up-republicans-your-party-stands-for-all-the-wrong-things-now/2019/12/31/.c8347b32-2be8-11ea-9b60-817cc18cf173_story.html.

Stevenson, Gregory M. "Conceptual Background to Golden Crown Imagery in the Apocalypse of John (4:4, 10; 14:14)." *Journal of Biblical Literature* 114 (1995) 257–72.

———. *Power and Place: Temple and Identity in the Book of Revelation*. Berlin: de Gruyter, 2001.

Strelan, Rick. "Outside Are the Dogs and the Sorcerers . . . (Revelation 22:15)." *Biblical Theology Bulletin: Journal of Bible and Culture* 33 (2003) 148–57.

Stroud, James Edward. *The Knights Templar and the Protestant Reformation and the Case for the Modern Day Monk*. Grand Rapids: Zondervan, 2011.

Swain, Simon. *Economy, Family, and Society from Rome to Islam: A Critical Edition, English Translation, and Study of Bryson's 'Management of the Estate.'* Cambridge: Cambridge University Press, 2013.

Swete, Henry Barclay. *The Apocalypse of St. John*. 3rd ed. London: MacMillan, 1918.

Tadmor, Hayim. *The Inscriptions of Tiglath-Pileser III King of Assyria: Critical Edition with Introduction, Translations, and Commentary*. Jerusalem: Israel Academy of Sciences and Humanities, 1994.

Thompson, Leonard L. *The Book of Revelation: Apocalypse and Empire*. Oxford: Oxford University Press, 1990.

"Trump Words Linked to More Hate Crime? Some Experts Think So." https://www.snopes.com/ap/2019/08/07/trump-words-linked-to-more-hate-crime-some-experts-think-so/.

Tukker, Marilize E. "Where Sexuality and Spirituality Meet: An Assessment on Christian Teaching on Sexuality and Marriage in Relation to the Reality of 21st Century Moral Norms." *HTS Theological Studies* 69 (2013) 1–8.

Turner, Tom. *City as Landscape: A Post Post-Modern View of Design and Planning*. London: Taylor & Francis, 1995.

Várhelyi, Zsuzsanna. *The Religion of Senators in the Roman Empire: Power and the Beyond*. Cambridge: Cambridge University Press, 2010.

Viljoen, F. P. "Die betekenis en funksie van die himnes in Openbaring 4–11." *Acta Theologica* 23 (2003) 213–37.

Waldron, Samuel E. *The End Times Made Simple: How Could Everyone Be So Wrong about Biblical Prophecy?* Amityville: Calvary, 2003.

Wall, Robert W. *Revelation*. Peabody: Hendrickson, 1991.

Wallace, Daniel B. *Greek Grammar beyond the Basics: An Exegetical Syntax of the New Testament*. Grand Rapids: Zondervan, 1996.

Walther, James Arthur. "The Address in Revelation 1:4,5a." *HBT* 17 (1995) 165–80.

Walvoord, John F. *The Revelation of Jesus Christ*. Chicago: Moody, 1996.

Watson, Kathryn. "Trump on Charlottesville: 'I Think There's Blame on Both Sides.'" *CBS*, August 15, 2017. https://www.cbsnews.com/news/trump-on-charlottesville-i-think-theres-blame-on-both-sides/.

Wesley, John. *Notes on the Bible*. Grand Rapids: Asbury, 1987.

Westenholz, Joan Goodnick. *Legends of the Kings of Akkade*. Winona Lake: Eisenbrauns, 1997.

Wick, Peter. "There Was Silence in Heaven (Revelation 8:1): An Annotation to Israel Knohl's 'Between Voice and Silence.'" *Journal of Biblical Literature* 117 (1998) 512–14.
Williams, Daniel K. "Regan's Religious Right: The Unlikely Alliance between Southern Evangelicals and a California Conservative." In *Ronald Regan and the 1980s*, edited by Cheryl Hudson and Gareth Davies, 135–49. New York: Macmillan, 2008.
Williams, S. N. "Deism." In *New Dictionary of Theology*, edited by Sinclair B. Ferguson and David F. Wright, 190. Downers Grove: Intervarsity, 1998.
Witherington, Ben, III. *New Testament Rhetoric: An Introductory Guide to the Art of Persuasion in and of the New Testament.* Eugene, OR: Cascade, 2009.
———. *Revelation.* Cambridge: Cambridge University Press, 2003.
Witherington, Ben, III, and Darlene Hyatt. *Paul's Letter to the Romans: A Socio-Rhetorical Commentary.* Grand Rapids: Eerdmans, 2004.
Wong, Daniel K. "The Two Witnesses in Revelation 11." *Bibliotheca Sacra* 154 (1997) 344–54.
Woods, Henry. "Blessed John de Britto." In *Catholic Encyclopedia: An Internal Book of Reference on the Constitution, Doctrine, Discipline, and History of the Catholic Church.* New York: Appleton, 1910. https://www.newadvent.org/cathen/08461a.htm.
Wright, N. T. "Abandon the Study of the Historical Jesus? No, We Need History: A Response to 'The Jesus We'll Never Know.'" *Christianity Today*, April 9, 2010. https://www.christianitytoday.com/ct/2010/april/16.27.html.
———. *The Resurrection of the Son of God.* London: SPCK, 2003.
———. *Surprised by Hope: Rethinking Heaven, the Resurrection, and the Mission of the Church.* San Francisco: HarperOne, 2008.
Yardley, Jim. "Pope Francis Suggests Donald Trump Is 'Not Christian.'" *The New York Times*, February 18, 2016. https://www.nytimes.com/2016/02/19/world/americas/pope-francis-donald-trump-christian.html.
Yount, Steve. "Churches Closed in 1918 Too: Here's What Christians Can Learn Today." *The Christian Post*, April 9, 2020. https://www.christianpost.com/voices/churches-closed-in-1918-too-heres-what-christians-can-learn-today.html.
Zoll, Rachel. "White Christians Are Now a Minority of the U.S. Population." *PBS NewsHour*, September 6, 2017. https://www.pbs.org/newshour/nation/white-christians-now-minority-u-s-population-survey-says.

www.ingramcontent.com/pod-product-compliance
Lightning Source LLC
Chambersburg PA
CBHW071244230426
43668CB00011B/1583